THE LORDSHIP OF IRELAND IN THE MIDDLE AGES presents a totally new approach to medieval Irish history. Thematic rather than narrative in its treatment, it succeeds in examining the feudal lordship of Ireland as a whole, and in tracing the origins of the conflicting Gaelic and Anglo-Irish traditions which were to determine the whole pattern of Irish history in succeeding centuries.

In the opening chapters the author provides essential background information which sets the Anglo-Norman invasion, the grant of Ireland to Henry II and his son John's achievements as Lord of Ireland in perspective. The central section of the book covers the thirteenth century—the high point in the history of the lordship. The increased stability and prosperity resulting from the newly adopted feudal system made Ireland a valuable asset to England; but the strain placed on the English exchequer by the French wars, and general apathy and lack of organisation on the part of the English king gradually set in motion a process of decline from which the lordship was never to recover. Relative peace gave way to lawlessness and an endless struggle for power among the most influential Gaelic and Anglo-Irish families: determined not to accept defeat and English domination, the Gaelic Irish fought relentlessl. to preserve their culture, and the so-called 'Gaelic revival' was in fact a major factor in the collapse of the lordship. The final section of the book examines this collapse, stressing the Irish government's desperate lack of military and financial resources, and its failure to find any solution until the idea of controlling a limited area, the Pale, was put into practice in the fifteenth century. In the last chapter the author indicates the relevance of his subject to the present day by discussing the immense heritage of the middle ages.

THE LORDSHIP OF IRELAND fills an obvious gap in studies on Irish history. Not only is it a coherent, comprehensive and up-to-date study of a fascinating and important period; it is at the same time refreshing and highly readable.

THE LORDSHIP OF IRELAND
IN THE MIDDLE AGES

The Lordship of Ireland in the Middle Ages

J. F. LYDON

UNIVERSITY OF TORONTO PRESS

First published in Canada and the United States
by University of Toronto Press, Toronto and Buffalo

© James F. Lydon 1972

ISBN 0—8020—1883—1

ISBN microfiche 0—8020—0224—2

Printed and bound in the Republic of Ireland

Do mo mhuintir

Contents

Foreword

FIFTEEN years teaching the history of medieval Ireland have shaped this book. Since there is no lack of narrative accounts I have tried to be more analytical in my approach and to interpret rather than merely describe events wherever possible. This has necessitated a dangerous amount of generalisation and even a degree of involvement which may be repugnant to some. But I have tried to write a history of the medieval lordship of Ireland in a meaningful way, so as to make coherent an often confused pattern of events. This could only be done through drastic selection; and that, of course, always carried the risk of a too subjective approach. But as Eoin MacNeill, the great historian who has always been an inspiration, once wrote: 'Neither apathy nor antipathy can ever bring out the truth in history'. I shall be well content if I succeed in provoking some positive response in the reader, so that he, too, becomes involved in our medieval past.

I wish to thank Miss Felicity Thompson, Mrs Shelia Comiskey, Miss Heather Hanan and Miss Nancy O'Sullivan of Trinity College who typed the manuscript, and Mary Dowey of Gill and Macmillan who guided the book into print.

Those who are stimulated to further enquiry will find a very easy guide to the literature in P. W. A. Asplin *Medieval Ireland c. 1170-1495*. The relevant volumes in the *Gill History of Ireland* (ed. James Lydon and Margaret MacCurtain) contain critical bibliographies: Donncha Ó Corráin *Ireland before the Normans*, Michael Dolley *Anglo-Norman Ireland*, James Lydon *Ireland in the Middle Ages*, Kenneth Nicholls *Gaelic and Gaelicised Ireland in the Middle Ages*, John Watt *The Church in Medieval Ireland*.

James F. Lydon

I The Prelude to Invasion

THE death of Brian Boru at the battle of Clontarf in 1014 marked the end of the most successful attempt to establish a kingdom of Ireland. King Brian, obscure in origin and without the kind of respectable ancestry admired by the conservative Irish, had forced his way through a succession of usurpations to the kingship of Ireland. As high king (he called himself *Imperator Scottorum*) he attempted to establish for his dynasty an unassailable position. But the revolt of the kingdom of Leinster put an end to his aspirations and left the high kingship as a prize to be fought over by the strongest dynasties in Ireland. Thus was created the political condition which allowed the Angevin king, Henry II of England, to intervene in Ireland and to exercise his claim to feudal lordship there. Out of the dynastic struggle for the high kingship in the twelfth century came the expulsion of the king of Leinster in 1166, his appeal for help to Henry II, the licensing of expeditionary forces from south Wales, and finally the arrival of Henry with a great army. This was followed by the submission of the Irish kings and the Welsh-Norman feudatories. The lordship of Ireland became a reality and the treaty of Windsor in 1175, concluded between the Angevin king and the high king of Ireland, established in legal form the relationship between feudal monarchy and Gaelic kingship for the future.

There is another strand which must be taken into account. Henry II became lord of Ireland not merely by right of conquest, submission and the treaty of Windsor, but by right of a papal grant of 1154. The famous privilege of Adrian IV, usually referred to as the Bull *Laudabiliter*, conferred the lordship of Ireland on the Angevin. There was, of course, a price—the reformation of the Irish Church. The quickening of the human spirit in the twelfth century had not left Ireland untouched, and not least among its results was the great reform movement which sought to bring the Irish Church into full conformity with the Latin Church of the west. The papacy, anxious for the successful completion of this movement in Ireland and sceptical of the ability of the Irish reformers to do this without the backing of a powerful centralised monarchy, was easily induced to grant the island as a dependant lordship to Henry II, the most powerful monarch in western Europe.

These two strands in the story, political and ecclesiastical, are intertwined. Political change had an important bearing on the development of the movement for church reform in Ireland. And the Church, as always in the middle ages, exercised a powerful and unifying force on Irish political life. In the person of Henry II the two are closely bound up with each other, for when he arrives in Ireland at the head of his army he comes not only to put the coping stone on the great reform movement of the twelfth century, but also as a feudal monarch determined to settle the political problem which was derived from the power vacuum created by the death of King Brian. Henry is to the ecclesiastics the secular reformer they longed for, and to the warring Gaelic leaders and the Anglo-Norman feudatories the powerful, titular lord to whom allegiance is due. It is well, then, to remember that both the ecclesiastical and political antecedents of the Anglo-Norman invasion are intertwined. To treat them separately, as we shall do, can only be excused on the ground that it makes them easier to understand.

One of the great battles of Irish history was fought at Clontarf, near Dublin, on Good Friday 1014. In Irish and Scandinavian traditions the battle put an end to Norse attempts to gain supremacy in Ireland. Strange portents were recorded before the battle, such as showers of scalding blood and other awful happenings, which were taken to presage an event of momentous importance. And in truth the battle which followed was momentous for the future of Ireland. It was unusual in many ways: it lasted the day long, from morning to evening; the forces engaged were enormous by contemporary Irish standards; the slaughter was great. Most of the leaders on both sides fell, the greatest of them being Brian Boru, high king of Ireland. 'Brian fell but saved his kingdom', says the Norse saga of Burnt Njal after describing the battle. But in fact he lost his kingdom, for his death marked the end of everything he had achieved. The real issue at Clontarf was not, as tradition insists, the simple one of renewed Norse ambitions to rule Ireland, but rather the sovereignty of King Brian which had been challenged by the Kingdom of Leinster. And the real result of the battle was the success of that challenge and the end of the hegemony created by Brian. For although the Leinstermen and their foreign allies were decisively defeated at Clontarf, Brian's successors were unable to maintain what he had created and Ireland was once again subjected to the ambitions of powerful, warring dynasties struggling to exercise suzerainty over the whole country as Brian had once done. It is this result which makes the battle important in the future history of the island. To understand why this was so, we must know something of the legacy which Brian Boru left after him.

In Irish legal tradition, stretching as far back as the memory of men could reach, the high kingship of Ireland—the supreme kingship which gave its holder titular rights over all the other monarchs in the country, so that in title at least the high king was king of Ireland—was confined to the dynasties of the Uí Néill in the northern half of the island. Modern scholarship has shown that this tradition was really a fiction created to suit the ambitions of powerful Uí Néill kings who, in their reaction to the Scandinavian settlements of the ninth century, had begun to extend the area of their sovereignty. But in the early eleventh century the fiction was generally accepted as historical reality and in seizing the high kingship, as indeed in his seizure of lesser kingships in the south, Brian Boru was regarded as a usurper who had broken the custom of the ages. His usurpation defied Irish customary law and was based on the new principle that might is right. The high kingship was therefore thrown open as a prize for the man who could take it by force. And so in the generations which followed Brian's death the strong men of Ireland entered the arena and fought for the greatest prize of all.

One can understand how easily this tremendous break with the past was accomplished. Irish Society had been excessively conservative, held back by the dead hand of the past which imposed a complex of conventions (what one modern scholar has called 'taboos') which made political development impossible. But the Scandinavian invasions and settlements changed all this. These fierce northmen knew nothing of the immemorial customs which made Irish society so hidebound and in a short space of time they demonstrated the weaknesses which made the different Irish territories so easy to attack. It was not long before the Irish kings realised the fatal defects in the system which had sustained them for so long and in reacting against the invaders they found themselves, almost despite themselves, throwing off the shackles of conventions which threatened their existence. One can see this most clearly perhaps in the conduct of war, which now became more total as customs limiting the scale of war and the areas in which it might be fought were swept away. The traditional structure of society, with its familiar and rural nature, began to change. Customary law remained essentially unchanged, but it ceased to mirror the society of the time and slowly began to lose touch with reality. This is why D. A. Binchy, the greatest living expert on early Irish law, can say that before the end of the ninth century the traditional custodians of the law in Ireland found that 'under the stress of the Norse invasions, the traditional structure of society was already collapsing about their ears'. Such was the shattering effect of the northmen on Ireland. For Binchy, their coming marked 'the passing of the old order'.[1]

In this climate of change Brian Boru's break with custom was made all the easier. He may have been regarded by the diehard traditionalists as a usurper, but he did not shock society to the same extent as he undoubtedly would have done two centuries earlier. And he justified his appeal to force by neutralising the danger which the northmen presented and by extending throughout Ireland a rule of law which the island had not known since first the Viking terror began. He also had precedents for his actions in the growth of Uí Néill sovereignty in the north, though like many another Irishman he paid lipservice to the laws of his ancestors by concocting a fictitious claim to the supreme monarchy based on a spurious historical right. The important point is, however, that he in turn passed on to the future a precedent which the great rivals of his house did not hesitate to invoke by striving to seize this supreme prize of the high kingship for themselves and their heirs.

In another way the impact of the Scandinavians was important in introducing a new element into Irish political life. The typical Irish petty kingdom, the tuath, or confederacy of tuaths of the kind over which the great dynastic rulers presided, was organised in such a way that it was virtually impossible under the customary

[1]D. A. Binchy, 'The Passing of the Old Order', in B. Ó Cuív, ed. *Proceedings of the International Congress of Celtic Studies*, Dublin, 1962, 132.

law for the ruler to extend the area of his territorial dominion. Kingship itself, although elective, was hereditary and confined to the family (up to and including second cousins) of the ruler. It was impossible for a powerful king to become the king of a neighbouring tuath, to become what was later called 'a stranger in sovereignty'. Nor could he conquer land, because again the land belonged to the family and could not be alienated. The ruler was never, in the feudal sense, *dominus terrae* ('lord of the land') and so his power, such as it was, had to rest on another basis. The most powerful monarch, no matter how ambitious, was therefore severely restricted and though he might succeed to the higher degrees of kingship which the law recognised and inherit the vague financial and other customary rights which his more exalted position conferred on him, there was little scope for him to exercise those rights and none at all for him to become in any effective sense the real ruler of the territories which accepted his greater title. He could not depose kings, set up puppet rulers subject to himself or impose his will on territories outside his ancestral tuath. Like everyone else in Ireland he was subject to a law which was immutable and which he in no sense administered. He could not, therefore, legislate. Under these circumstances, so long as respect for conservative tradition remained unchanged, it was impossible for anyone to weld the large number of petty kingdoms in Ireland into larger political units, much less to establish a real and united kingdom of Ireland. The sort of progression which had occurred in Anglo-Saxon England from small, tribal kingdoms to a kingdom of England was impossible here.

But here again the impact of the northmen was of enormous importance. It is not possible now to be precise in assessing the full degree of change they ushered in, but it can hardly be doubted that under their influence ambitious Irish kings, of whom Brian Boru is the supreme example, began to break with tradition in their quest for power. In the period after Clontarf one dynasty after the other demonstrates the change which had occurred. Expansion on a territorial basis can be seen in the careers of many rulers, perhaps most of all in the activities of Turloch O Connor of Connacht who went closest of all to emulating the achievement of Brian Boru. Turloch not only deposed kings; he divided kingdoms and created new ones and in many other ways demonstrated the new powers and greater resources which the new-style rulers commanded. It could be argued, too, that the concept of lordship was creeping in as kings gained control of more land and as the native system of clientship, with its close resemblance to the contractual relationship of lord and vassal in the feudal system, became the norm in the free classes of society. This is what one might expect, apart from anything else, from the renewed contacts with feudal Europe which the movement for ecclesiastical reform established, and in particular from the arrival of foreign religious orders which were accustomed to dealing with feudal lords on a contractual basis. One must not make too much of the slight evidence which exists or seek to find an incipient native feudalism in Ireland which was strangled by the Anglo-Norman invaders. Conservative traditions were long in dying and basically the organisation of the tuath remained unchanged. But clearly the new rulers now had greater resources at their command which they could employ in the wars they fought. A rising population, for which there is no real evidence beyond analogy with the rest of western Europe, might have increased the resources on which they could draw; but one must also postulate a growing control over land, the real basis of wealth, to explain the growing power of the important Irish kings.

It would be impossible to do more than outline here the story of the struggle for power which followed the death of Brian Boru, and to tell the truth such a story would not have much relevance to the invasion of the Anglo-Normans in the 1160s. The main events which led up to the invasion belong to the years immediately before 1166, the year in which the king of Leinster sought the help of Henry II. But in order to make that crucial event comprehensible, it is necessary to relate briefly the history of the struggle for the high kingship which led to the expulsion of the Leinsterman. In this struggle the main protagonists were the three great dynasties of Ireland: in the south the O Briens, in the north the Mac Lochlainns and in the west the O Connors. Lesser rulers appear on the stage from time to time, but only in a supporting role almost to the end. At various times during the century and a half after Clontarf three O Brien kings of Munster, two of the Mac Lochlainns of Ulster and two of the O Connors of Connacht won their way through to the possession of the coveted title, though they nearly all held it, as the annalists describe it, 'with opposition'. Of none of them could it be said that he was in truth the king of Ireland, though some came close enough to this.

Munster produced two outstanding O Brien kings during this period, Turloch and his son Muirchertach, who between them ruled from 1064 to 1119. Both were called king of Ireland in the Irish annals and both received letters from abroad in which they were given the same style. Turloch was a grandson of Brian Boru and he was not slow in asserting his claims to the supreme monarchy. So successful was he that Pope Gregory VII gave him the title of 'noble king of Ireland' and when Lanfranc, the new Norman archbishop of Canterbury, was seeking to promote a reformation of the Irish Church and wished to contact the most powerful secular ruler so as to entice him to lend support to the reform movement, he wrote to Turloch whom he addressed as 'magnificent king of Ireland' and whom he clearly recognised as the man possessing supreme authority. Indeed the archbishop commented that God had been merciful in raising up someone who loved peace and justice to the government of souls and bodies and in conferring 'this gift on the people of Ireland when He gave Your Excellency the authority of kingly power'. Turloch, it must be confessed, fell short of the praise lavished on him by Lanfranc; but if he did, his son Muirchertach came closer to realising his ambition of ruling Ireland. Like his father, he too engaged in correspondence with an archbishop of Canterbury, in which he styled himself *Rex Hiberniae* and in which he was called by Anselm 'by the grace of God most glorious king of Ireland'. He was powerful enough to ally himself with a king of Norway, Magnus Barelegs, who seems to have earned his nickname because he wore some sort of kilt, a habit he picked up in Ireland. Magnus had an Irish sweetheart, to whom he addressed poetry, and he procured an Irish bride for his son: this was the daughter of Muirchertach. An alliance between the two kings was a natural consequence and though it is impossible to be sure of the extent to which the Norse king's help was instrumental in enabling Muirchertach to extend his sovereignty, there can be no doubt that it was not negligible. Indeed Magnus died in Ireland, in 1103, when he was killed fighting in Ulster, almost certainly as an ally of O Brien.

An attempt was also made to involve King Magnus in a conspiracy against Henry I of England. Nothing came of this, but it is a measure of the reputation which Muirchertach O Brien held outside Ireland that he too was courted for his support. One of the key figures in the plot was Arnulf Montgomery, lord of Pembroke, and it was he who was responsible for the overtures made to the Irish king. He sent the steward of his castle of Pembroke, Gerald of Windsor, to Ireland to seek O Brien's promise of help. The result of Gerald's mission was to procure the daughter of Muirchertach as a bride for Arnulf, and with her a fleet of ships. Indeed if we are to believe the contemporary Norman chronicler, Ordericus Vitalis, the Normans of Wales hoped eventually to be able to gain a kingdom in Ireland through this marriage—a curious anticipation of the similar ambition of a later lord of Pembroke, Richard fitz Gilbert, or Strongbow as he is better known in Ireland. This whole episode, in fact, is interesting because it involves an area in Wales from which the later Anglo-Norman invaders of Ireland came and the ancestor of the leaders of these first invaders. For the Gerald of Windsor who came to Ireland was the father of Maurice fitz Gerald and grandfather of the other Geraldines who participated in the first conquest of Ireland later on in the twelfth century.

It may be that it was as a result of all this that Henry I broke off relations with Muirchertach O Brien. According to a contemporary writer, William of Malmsbury, the king of England decided to place an embargo on trade with Ireland and this had the effect of quickly forcing the Irishman to come to terms. 'For of what value could Ireland be, if deprived of the merchandise of England', writes William, a sentiment which might find an echo even today. On the whole, however, relations between the two kings seem to have been good, in itself a testimony to Muirchertach's prestige abroad. We are even told that on one occasion representatives of the Norse kingdom of the Hebrides and Man requested Muirchertach to send them a regent until their own young ruler came of age.

But within Ireland itself O Brien never succeeded in asserting his authority through the whole island. His main opponent was the Mac Lochlainn king in Ulster, who consistently refused to acknowledge the overlordship of O Brien. So Muirchertach was occupied for much of his reign in attempting to force his authority on the north. It was during the later stages of this struggle that a new dynasty came to the forefront in Ireland, in the person of

Turloch O Connor, king of Connacht. Occupying a position of strategic importance between the southern and northern kings and making judicious use of alliances, now with one side and now with the other, O Connor was able slowly to work his way to supremacy in the west. He was under twenty when he became king in 1106, but he had a long reign ahead of him until he died in 1156. During that time he successfully entered the contest for the high kingship and in the end it was he who came closest to emulating Brian Boru in realising his ambition to rule Ireland. Already before the death of Muirchertach O Brien in 1119 O Connor had begun to expand southwards into Munster. But O Brien's death, followed by that of his great northern rival Mac Lochlainn in 1121, gave Turloch an opportunity which he was quick to seize. From now on he was to demonstrate the traits which were to make him great. His military exploits illustrate very well the power and resources of these new-style Irish kings. He employed fleets on the inland waterways of western Ireland, built and garrisoned castles (some of which seem to have been of stone) at strategic points, fortified bridges of which the one at Athlone across the Shannon was the most important, and generally showed an ability in the art of war which was to bring him the high kingship in the end. He was ruthless in dealing with his enemies, and brutal when he thought it expedient, as when he blinded his own son in 1136 because he threatened to become a rival. He employed the old Roman tactic of *divide et impera* ('divide and rule') with telling effect, dividing the kingdom of Meath into three in 1125. Munster was partitioned in 1118, with an O Brien allowed to retain Thomond, the northern half, and a Mac Carthy given Desmond, the southern half. Here Turloch's policy was clear: the division of the ancient provincial kingdoms would prevent powerful rivals from appearing to challenge his position as high king. In dealing with Leinster he resorted to another device which shows how far the ancient Irish concept of kingship had been left behind: he installed his son Conor as king in place of the dynasty with traditional right to rule. As a 'stranger in sovereignty' Conor did not last long, for within a year a Leinster revolt forced his father to remove him.

Turloch's restless drive to secure suzerainty over Ireland was not calculated to win him friends. His intervention in Leinster was in the long run to be instrumental in bringing the Anglo-

Norman invaders to Ireland, for it made of Dermot Mac Murrough an implacable enemy who when all else failed him in the end did not hesitate to look abroad for help against his hated O Connor rival. It was natural for Mac Murrough to ally himself in Ireland with any king who opposed the hegemony created by O Connor, and in Muirchertach Mac Lochlainn of Ulster he found the man he sought. Just as the northern kings resisted all O Brien attempts to force submission on them, so too they consistently refused to accept the high kingship of O Connor. The full story of the long struggle between Connacht and the north, and the complicated diplomacy which accompanied it, as each side found and discarded allies, is much too complicated to be briefly related. The constant factors which are relevant to us are the continuous rivalry between Connacht and Ulster and the alliance between Mac Murrough and Mac Lochlainn. O Connor, too, had one ally who was constant and who played an important role in the events which led up to the Anglo-Norman invasion. He was Tiernan O Ruairc, king of the midland kingdom of Breifne. So that before the death of Turloch O Connor in 1156 the chief Irish protagonists of the invasion had appeared on the scene.

Tiernan O Ruairc was involved in a famous episode which also played its part in the story of Mac Murrough's exile from Ireland. In Irish popular history the episode is always referred to as 'the rape of Dervorgilla' and is given the tragic consequences of the well known Helen of Troy story played out in an Irish setting. It was not the first time, or the last, that an Irish woman played a fatal part in the working out of Ireland's destiny, and down the years Dervorgilla has continued to haunt the imagination of the Irish people. She was the wife of O Ruairc and in 1152 she was abducted by Mac Murrough during the course of a campaign. The story relates that years before Mac Murrough had been her suitor, but political expediency forced her into marriage with O Ruairc. She brought a famous marriage dowry with her, a great herd of cattle; when she was snatched away by Mac Murrough the cattle went too. The infatuation did not last long, and within a year Dervorgilla, with her dowry, was restored to her husband. But the injury to O Ruairc's pride was unforgiveable and from this time onwards he was bent on revenge. Long afterwards, in 1167, Mac Murrough finally paid him the com-

pensation which the law demanded, one hundred ounces of gold.
In the meantime O Ruairc had shown that nothing less than the
complete destruction of Mac Murrough would satisfy him,
which led him in the end to be the instrument which forced the
Leinsterman to look abroad for help. One can sympathise with
O Ruairc. He had lost face, which to the cynical and vicious
gossip-mongers of the time was enough to destroy him. It was
not so much the loss of Dervorgilla which angered him as the
shame of it—a point which was emphasised by Gerald of Wales
in his account of the incident: 'King O Ruairc was heart-struck
by his shame and by his loss, though he felt the former more than
the latter'.

In the seesaw struggle between the west and the north O Ruairc
and Mac Murrough had important parts to play on opposite
sides, and their power largely depended on which side had the
ascendency. Even before he died Turloch O Connor had found
that old age was blunting his appetite for power, and gradually
the upper hand passed to Muirchertach Mac Lochlainn. It was he
who in 1157 presided as high king over the great assembly of
ecclesiastical and secular rulers which met on the occasion of the
consecration of the church of Mellifont, the first Cistercian abbey
in Ireland. In 1159 he decisively defeated Connacht, now led by
Turloch's son Rory. And in 1161 he seems to have accepted some
form of submission from Connacht, Leinster and Meath which
established his rights as overlord without question and which
seems to indicate a further development of the high kingship
from a tribal monarchy to something approaching a feudal
monarchy. But in 1166 he fell from power, less as a result of any
opposition he encountered from Rory O Connor or his allies
than from his own stupid action in violating the church law of
sanctuary and thereby outraging his own people who turned
against him. His fall, of course, gave Connacht the chance to gain
the ascendency again. It also meant the end for Mac Murrough,
who had pinned everything on the continued success of Mac
Lochlainn. For O Connor could no longer tolerate the existence
of an unfriendly ruler in Leinster and would either have to cut
Mac Murrough down to size or, better still, get rid of him
altogether. He might, perhaps, have been content to deal fairly
leniently with the Leinsterman, as he was to do later on during
the course of the Anglo-Norman invasion; but Tiernan O

Ruairc was there to see that the complete destruction of Mac Murrough was accomplished and his wishes could not be entirely ignored. Indeed it was O Ruairc who led the invasion of Leinster and accomplished the destruction of Mac Murrough's capital at Ferns. So in August, 1166, Mac Murrough decided that there was no hope of retrieving his position without foreign help and he therefore sailed to Bristol in order to find it. As we shall see, he eventually succeeded in recruiting help in Wales and returned to Leinster in August 1167 with the first band of invaders. With their help he not only eventually managed to regain control of Leinster, but was also enabled to begin a policy of expansion which would lead, as he hoped, to the high kingship itself.

This long attempt to establish a kingdom of Ireland had often brought war and destruction to many parts of the country. Life in those days was harsh and society possessed few of the safeguards which the modern state provides for the wellbeing of its citizens. Only the fittest were able to survive and cruelty was common-place. To maim a rival so as to make him unfit to rule was tolerated, as indeed it was throughout the known world. Blinding, in particular, is frequently mentioned in the annals of the time. But it would be wrong to suppose, as many have done, that the period after 1014 was one of anarchy and destruction, of cruelty and horror, unrelieved by any spark of humanity or the civilising force of literature and the arts.[2] If war, as we have already said, became more total, it remained on the whole a local matter and never was the whole island affected by a single war. There is evidence, too, that as kings became more powerful attempts were made to impose the equivalent of a Truce of God on their dominions. And there is another side to the picture, showing a society which valued learning and cherished beauty, a society which prized values and patronised the arts of peace that a cruel and war-mongering aristocracy, of the kind supposedly pre-dominant in Ireland, would never have upheld.

Ireland had once, and with good reason, been famous for her schools and artists, her saints and scholars. But the Viking invaders had destroyed many of the centres of art and scholarship

---

[2]A. L. Poole writes of this period as one of 'bewildering anarchy' and says that 'we need not dwell on this sordid chapter of Irish history in which battles and raids, murder and mutilitation were of daily occurrence' (*From Domesday Book to Magna Carta*, 2nd ed., Oxford, 1955, 302).

when they plundered the monasteries and forced the most gifted monks to seek asylum in the heart of continental Europe. Despite everything, however, the artistic traditions survived the destructive impulse of the Scandinavians and in the end even benefitted by borrowing skills and motifs from these foreign invaders. Brian Boru, who was once described by Robin Flower as a typical 'culture-king in a Europe emerging from the Dark Ages', used his new power and prestige to promote learning and the arts in much the same way as King Alfred before him had done in England. And in the period after the battle of Clontarf the revival of the old skills can clearly be seen. The art of the bronzesmith and metalworker finds impressive testimony in many shrines and crosses from the eleventh and twelfth centuries, of which the Cross of Cong (1123) and St Manchan's Shrine (c. 1130) are the greatest examples. In the High Crosses of the eleventh century and in the decorations of the new Romanesque churches of the twelfth century (the masterpiece being Cormac's Chapel on the Rock of Cashel) the art of the stone-mason can still be seen. Nor was the art of illumination, in which the Irish genius had found some of its greatest expression in the past, completely sterile. Here the native tradition remained strongest and despite the contact with Canterbury and elsewhere in England the Irish illuminator remained fiercely independent. It is clear, too, that the Irish schools had not only recovered from the shock of the Vikings, but that some of them were once again sufficiently famous to attract scholars from outside who were eager to study in Ireland. The textbooks used at Glendalough around 1100 compare favourably with those of continental schools of the time and the rapidity with which the teaching of Peter Lombard in Paris reached Ireland is a testimony to the contact of these schools with the exciting world of scholarship abroad. There was a tendency for much of this new learning to be concentrated in a few monasteries, which may be a sign of the new prestige of the great rulers who patronised these monasteries. Even so it was available to all and the schools themselves, like that at Glendalough, were cosmopolitan rather than parochial in their populations.

The continued interest in history and literature is well attested by the surviving manuscripts of the period. Not only were the old tales rewritten, but new ones were composed. There were, too, important changes which demonstrate that this was far from being an age of intellectual stagnation. For one thing the tradition which was preserved and enlarged was no longer solely in the custody of monastic scribes but slowly passed into the care of a special order of lay scribes and was later to be disseminated by the hereditary bards attached to the noble families. It is noticeable, too, that by the beginning of this period the centre of gravity, as it were, of this tradition shifts to the area around the lower reaches of the Shannon and it was from this same area that the most important of the lay families who later became the chief custodians of the tradition were to be drawn. It is no coincidence that this was the area where Brian Boru and his O Brien successors were strongest and is doubtless the result of the intellectual revival which they promoted. Such patronage was important in the success of this Irish renaissance and it is a striking feature of the period that lay patrons supported the artists, scholars and ecclesiastics who were shaping the new Ireland. The stimulus which these lay patrons provided, kings and aristocracy alike, is in sharp contrast to the old Ireland where the monasteries seem to have been almost the sole patrons of the arts. It is as if the new rulers desired to assert their new status by exercising a royal patronage in commissioning works of art. The O Briens, the O Connors and lesser kings like Cormac Mac Carthy almost vied with each other in patronising the artists and scribes of their time. Even Dermot Mac Murrough of Leinster, who has left a particularly evil reputation behind him in the annals of the period, was not to be outdone. He founded the first convent of nuns in Dublin and granted land to the new priory of All Hallows near the city. And the infamous Dervorgilla has a permanent monument to her munificence and good taste in the 'Nun's Church' at Clonmacnois, one of the glories of Irish Romanesque for which she was responsible.

All of this activity of revival and development in the arts, in literature and in learning was so widespread that we can truly speak of a renaissance in Ireland, which was part and parcel of that great renewal in Europe which is commonly known as the renaissance of the twelfth century. And just as one manifestation of this renaissance in Europe was the renewal within the Church, so too in Ireland ecclesiastical reform was a major preoccupation with the churchmen of the time. They were concerned not only with the abuses which were common throughout western Europe, such as simony, secularisation and moral laxity, but more especially with reorganising the Irish Church so as to bring it into line with the Church outside. For through a peculiar metamorphosis, which can be largely explained by the rural and tribal nature of early Irish society, the Church in Ireland had become monastic and abbatial in its organisation, rather than diocesan and episcopal as was the case elsewhere in the post-Roman world. There were, of course, bishops in Ireland, but they were not the rulers of the Church and were retained almost exclusively to discharge a sacramental function which no one else was competent to do. It was the abbots who ruled and the monasteries which were the centres of rule. Peculiar as this set-up may have been, it had in the past proved its worth not only within Ireland itself, but in the great expansion of Irish Christianity to Britain and Europe. The decline of monasticism, however, largely as a result of the Viking upheaval, meant that the Church in its institutional aspect was deeply affected and by the eleventh century it was becoming clear that a great reformation was needed. Even before then reforms had been instituted, of which the *Céli Dé* movement, associated in particular with the monastery of Tallaght, was probably the most important. But the real problem remained and had to be tackled. The laicisation of abbacies was an abuse which required urgent attention and the general slackness in the observation of the regular life was hardly less urgent. The laity, too, dependent as they were on the monasteries for their spiritual life—in the absence of any real parochial organisation it was the monasteries which were entrusted with the care of souls— naturally felt the effects of all this and began to backslide rapidly. In particular the law of the Church governing marriage was gravely abused and many old pagan practices, tolerated under the customary Brehon law, reappeared.

Such abuses among the clergy and the laity were roundly condemned by the reformers when they became active. St Malachy could speak of his flock being 'Christian in name but pagan in fact', and the strictures of churchmen such as Anselm, and later even the Pope, demonstrate only too well the view of outsiders that the Irish Church was in a degraded state. We must be cautious, however, in accepting such condemnations at their face value. The abuses existed, but as we have seen the monasteries after 1014 enjoyed a remarkable revival which argues strongly against the exaggerations of some of the more zealous reformers of the twelfth century. But more important evidence of this is the growth of new Irish monasteries in Germany, especially the group of Benedictine abbies associated with Ratisbon. A constant stream of monks from Ireland maintained this family of *Schottenklöster* in which asceticism flourished—though not to the exclusion of the Irish love of scholarship, as the career of the great Irish *inclusus*, Marianus of Ratisbon, illustrates so well. The flourishing condition of these monasteries, supplied from Ireland, shows more than does anything else how exaggerated were the reports of the Irish church.

It is noticeable, too, that the early reformers were not so much concerned with the moral laxity of the time or the increased secularisation of the Church as with problems of organization. It seems clear that for them the transformation of the Irish Church from a monastic into a diocesan one was the most urgent and important problem to be faced. Yet abroad, and particularly in Rome, the 'bad press' which the Irish Church received was to play its part in deciding the fate of the country. For it was this which was responsible for the Bull *Laudabiliter* in which Adrian IV granted Ireland to Henry II of England, on condition that he took in hand the work of reformation there.

The real beginnings of reform go back to the reign of Brian Boru. It was he who gave the first real impulse to reform and thereafter the movement was to find its strongest adherents and real innovators in the southern half of Ireland. This needs to be emphasised, since it is still widely believed that the real driving force was supplied only in the twelfth century by St Malachy of Armagh. But he inherited from the south a programme of reform which was already well established and it was from the south that he continued to derive his greatest inspiration, at least until he met St Bernard of Clairvaux. Malachy undoubtedly was the greatest figure among the reformers, but he was by no means unique and still less was he an innovator of particular significance.

The interest of King Brian is important for another reason: it illustrates the close connection there was between the ambitions of powerful rulers and the reform movement within the Church. Brian, and those who came after him, were anxious to win the respect of churchmen. They were willing to lend their assistance to any reform which did not conflict with their own interests. It could be argued that they saw in a reformed and strong, unified Church an ally which could be used in implementing the political unity for which they strove. And so they presided at synods, supported the decrees of reform, and generally were prominent on occasions of great ecclesiastical importance. The reformers, too, needed the backing of secular authority. Without it they could never achieve the reorganisation of the Church on diocesan lines. The creation of territorial dioceses was bound to conflict with local secular interests and could never have been achieved without the kind of powerful backing which only the great kings could supply. This is well illustrated by the story of the struggle to establish a proper diocese based on the old monastery of Armagh. The family of Uí Shinaigh had for generations past been hereditary abbots of the monastery there and in this period lay abbots had been appointed, a scandal which was remedied when the reformer Cellach, himself a member of the family, had taken orders and finally had himself consecrated bishop. In his own person, therefore, he joined the two offices of abbot and bishop and thus was able to introduce the new reforms which would leave the bishop at the head of the ecclesiastical hierarchy. Before his death he nominated Malachy as his successor to the bishopric. But the Uí Shinaigh reasserted their rights as hereditary abbots and it was only after a long struggle, backed by the armed force of O Brien and Mac Carthy, that Malachy was able to take possession of his see.

Conflicts of this kind were bound to arise when the reformers tried to end the laicisation of abbacies. Nor could territorial dioceses be established without secular backing, in a land where the only reasonable unit on which to base the diocese was the petty kingdom, the tuath. The difficulties encountered by St Malachy in his attempt to transform the ecclesiastical area which had the monastery of Bangor as its capital into the new diocese of Connor show how easy it was to run foul of the local ruler, and indeed Malachy was forced to flee for his life from the locality when a Mac Lochlainn king took exception to what he was doing.

The support of the great kings was necessary, therefore, if the reformers were to be able to carry through the programme they had adopted. As we have seen, both Lanfranc and Anselm realised this and each of them wrote to the high king of Ireland urging upon him the work of reform. But no Irish king during this period ever became a true high king, with the whole island under his suzerainty. And failing that, the full programme of reform could never be satisfactorily completed. It may be that this was realised in Rome and that this was why Henry II, who had made the offer anyway, was called in to put the coping-stone on the reformation. At any rate it seems certain that this was the bitter realisation forced on the reformers themselves: failing to find the strong ruler they needed in Ireland, they were willing to accept a foreign king who would supply the authority, and more important the machinery for enforcing that authority, which was essential for a successful conclusion to a hundred and fifty years of reform.

This does not mean that little had been achieved. On paper, through the great reforming synods, all problems had been solved. In particular during the period which followed the first synod of Cashel in 1101—when, symbolically, the great Rock of Cashel, for centuries the seat of the kingship of Munster, was handed over to the Church and was soon graced by that complex of ecclesiastical buildings which still survives—a succession of great men led the Irish Church through a programme of rejuvenation and reorganisation. The new sees in the Scandinavian towns, especially that of Dublin, with their close links with England and the continent, provided a model for the rest of Ireland to follow. Bishop Gilbert of Limerick in 1100 supplied a blueprint of reform in his tract *De Statu Ecclesiae*. Old centres of scholarship, such as Lismore, disseminated the new usages associated with the Gregorian reform; and the great schools, like that at Glendalough, introduced the new learning which was the handmaiden of reform abroad. For the first time the papacy provided legates to Ireland and under them a series of reforming synods was held which gradually refashioned the fabric of the Church and condemned the abuses which were practiced by clergy and laity alike. In the new dioceses the new-style bishops set to work to carry out the decrees of these synods. Most important, too, was the introduction of foreign religious orders into Ireland for the first time. The Cistercians, who has been in the forefront of reform on the continent, were brought to Ireland by St Malachy about 1142 and from their first abbey of Mellifont no less than seven other foundations were made by 1153. It would be difficult to exaggerate the contribution which the Cistercians made to Irish life in the years which followed: agriculture, architecture, and above all the religious life benefitted enormously. But the Cistercians were not the only, or even the first, foreign order to appear in Ireland. A Benedictine monastery of the Congregation of Savigny was founded in Dublin in 1139 and was known as St Mary's Abbey; about the same time the Augustinian Canons Regular appear also. There can be no doubt that the new orders were intended to supply the sort of support to reform which some of the old, independently minded native monasteries were unwilling to provide. But time had begun to run out for the reformers. The grant of Ireland to Henry II may not have become immediately effective, but it was to provide a convenient excuse in 1171 when the king wished to invade Ireland. Before then, however, the exiled king of Leinster was to return with the first band of Anglo-Normans and the disturbances which followed finished any hope the reformers had of completing their work under a native high king.

II The Founding of the Lordship of Ireland

DERMOT Mac Murrough was nearly sixty when he left Leinster in 1169, an old man who in twelfth-century conditions was well past his prime. It is an indication of his extraordinary vigour and ambition that old as he was he undertook a difficult journey abroad in search of help. But Dermot was no ordinary person. All his life he had been driven by ambition and he was endowed with abilities which enabled him to pursue his destiny relentlessly. As a youth he had been tutored by men steeped in the glories of Leinster's heroic past and he had been reared to revive the greatness of his kingdom. One of his tutors was the abbot of Terryglass for whom the *Book of Leinster* had been compiled, that great compendium of Irish history and literature. We can hardly doubt that Dermot was deeply imbued with the spirit of that book, which had as part of its purpose the exaltation of Leinster and the belittling of Connacht and Munster. One of its poems exclaims: 'If I had seven heads I could not tell all the prowess of the Leinstermen even in a month, without seven tongues in each separate head'. The same spirit which had forced the Leinstermen to resist the upstart (as they regarded him) Brian Boru was to drive Mac Murrough to the assertion of Leinster's claims to independence and even in the end to the high kingship itself. From the moment he began to rule in 1134 he never ceased to assert the greatness of his dynasty. One of his first acts as king was to invade Ossory and re-establish the dependence of that kingdom on Leinster. Meath, too, felt his aggression and in 1137 he attacked the old Norse state of Waterford which he forced to submit. All the time his ambition was to make Leinster great once more. When the time was propitious he even reasserted Leinster's rights, based on the historical literature on which he was reared, to the high kingship of Ireland. As we shall see he did this when his foreign allies enabled him to extend successfully the boundaries of his rule; when he died he passed on this ambition and the spurious right which went with it to his son-in-law and heir

Strongbow. The latter's success in following the programme initiated by Mac Murrough was enough to make Henry II take fright and come to Ireland to prevent the emergence of a rival Norman kingdom there.

Dermot's relations with Dublin in particular are also important in dictating the road he was to follow in the year of his exile. The battle of Clontarf may have meant the end of Norse pretensions to power in Ireland, but the cities and kingdoms they had founded remained, never wholly absorbed by the Irish kingdoms. Of these Dublin and Waterford were the most important. Here the Ostmen, as the Norse settled in Ireland were now called, carried on their trade with the world overseas and occasionally embroiled themselves in the Irish wars of the time. Dublin could muster a fleet of two hundred ships and was therefore an important power which different Irish kings from time to time tried to control. It is noticeable, for instance, that each of the great contestants for the high kingship made a point of asserting their supremacy over the Norse kingdom of Dublin, while at the same time they were content to leave it in a semi-autonomous position. But Leinster enjoyed a special relationship with these Norse states and Dermot Mac Murrough in particular was careful to ensure that his rights in both states were respected. He was frequently in Dublin, where he had a house, and it was through these visits that he came to know a number of Bristol merchants who traded with Ireland. It was perfectly natural, therefore, when he left to seek help abroad that he should travel first to Bristol where he had useful contacts.

One of the people whom Dermot knew best was the wealthy Bristol merchant and civic official, Robert fitz Harding, a man of great influence. His father and grandfather before him had many connections with the family of Dermot and there may even have been a marriage connection with a relative of Dermot's. At any rate it was to fitz Harding's house in Bristol that Dermot came and there he found a welcome and financial support. There was another way, too, in which the connection with fitz Harding was useful because it was almost certainly he who provided Dermot with an introduction to Henry II. Years before during the civil war in England fitz Harding had supported the young Henry and for this he was subsequently rewarded with a grant of the fief of Berkeley. His influence with the king was now to be of crucial importance to Dermot for it enabled him to procure an audience with the most powerful king in western Europe. There is evidence that Henry II had employed a fleet from Dublin in his campaign against the Welsh in 1165 and in this way may have established some connection with the king of Leinster. But that is unlikely and it seems certain that it was the fitz Harding connection which led Dermot to Henry.

Mac Murrough did not stay long in Bristol before he went in search of King Henry. He had to travel across England and all the way to the southwest of France before he found him. We do not know what was said or done at the meeting between the two kings, but according to Giraldus Cambrensis, who was related to the Geraldines who played such an important part in the subsequent invasion of Ireland and who himself was a witness to some of the events he describes in his history of that invasion (*Expugnatio Hibernica*), Dermot was received with great kindness by Henry and was 'loaded with gifts by the royal munificence'. There seems to be some confirmation of this in the English pipe roll of this year which records gifts made by the king to various Irishmen who are not, unfortunately, named, though one of them is referred to as the chancellor of the Irish king, undoubtedly Mac Murrough. Henry was engaged in troubles of his own at that time and would certainly have been unable to give direct help to Mac Murrough. But he did give him a letter, sealed with his great seal, which was more or less a licence enabling him to recruit help wherever he could find it in the dominions of the English king. This letter is quoted in full by Giraldus and because of its great importance it is worth reproducing it here:

Henry, king of England, duke of Normandy and Aquitaine, and count of Anjou, to all his liegemen, English, Normans, Welsh and Scots, and to all nations subject to his sway sends greetings. Whensoever these our letters shall come unto you, know you that we have taken Dermot, prince of the men of Leinster, into the bosom of our grace and goodwill. Wherefore, too, whosoever within the bounds of our dominions shall be willing to lend aid to him, as being our vassal and liegeman, in the recovery of his own, let him know that he has our favour and permission to that end.

The really significant feature of this letter patent is that Mac Murrough is referred to as the 'vassal and liegeman' of Henry II, and indeed Giraldus tells us that Henry had received his 'bond of allegiance and oath of fealty' before he issued the letter. Dermot, then, became Henry's man, his vassal, accepting the overlordship of the English king, holding his kingdom of Leinster from him and rendering certain services for it. But thereby too he became entitled to the protection of his lord, which was the primary obligation any feudal lord had to render to his vassal, and undoubtedly the letter was Henry's way of fulfilling that obligation to long as he was preoccupied in France—though, as we have seen, he may have given him money as well. At any rate Henry had for the first time established his rights as feudal lord, which were his since the grant of Pope Adrian in 1155, over one Irish king. It may well be, too, that the vague address to 'all nations subject to his sway' was deliberately meant to refer to the Irish, whose lord he was *de jure*, so as to help Dermot when he returned to Ireland to fight for the restoration of his kingdom.

With the letter in his possession Dermot returned to Bristol where once again he lodged with fitz Harding. From Bristol, with its close trading connections with Leinster, he was able to keep an eye on the situation at home while he sought the help he needed. He often had the letter read in public and made liberal offers of land and money to anyone who would help, but without effect. At last he succeeded in establishing contact with Richard fitz Gilbert, earl of Pembroke, nicknamed Strongbow, the name by which he was to be known in Irish tradition. Unlike fitz Harding, Strongbow had been on the wrong side in the civil war in England and had supported Stephen to the end. He was now in straitened circumstances and out of favour with the king. For him the future was black. He was exactly the sort of disaffected man who might listen to the Irish king's proposition and with his powerful connections and the help of Jewish money lenders, for all that he was now down on his luck, he would be able to raise enough support to bring a powerful force to Ireland if he ever gave his mind to it. Dermot held out a tempting bait: his daughter Eva in marriage, and the kingdom of Leinster after his own death. It was too tempting for Strongbow to resist and he accepted the offer and promised to help Dermot to regain Leinster, though he was prudent enough to insist that he must first get permission from Henry II. With this Dermot had to be satisfied, and so he pressed on for home.

He travelled along the coast through south Wales, a district

3

which had long and intimate connections with Leinster. On the way he found ready recruits among the Flemish mercenaries who had been settled there and seems to have enlisted some Welshmen as well. He visited Rhys ap Gruffudd, the local Welsh prince, and while he was his guest succeeded in engaging the services of a hostage he held, Robert fitz Stephen, the first of the 'race of Nesta' to be recruited. Nesta was the daughter of Rhys ap Tewdwr and aunt of Dermot's host. Her sons and grandsons, illegitimate as well as legitimate, were to figure prominently in the subsequent invasion of Ireland. Chief among these were the Geraldines, the fruit of her marriage with Gerald of Windsor, who were prominent in the politics of Pembroke and Cardigan and were well fitted by their experience in wars against the Welsh to participate in the enterprise of Mac Murrough in Ireland. The first of them to be enlisted was Maurice fitz Gerald, who with fitz Stephen was promised the town of Wexford and two adjoining cantreds. In return, they agreed to come to Ireland the following spring, as soon as they were able to raise a sufficient force of men among their numerous kinsmen and retainers. And with this firm promise Dermot left for home.

He arrived back in Leinster in August 1167, almost a year to the day after he had left. With him came Richard fitz Godebert, a Fleming, and a small force of Welsh and Flemish mercenaries. In a short time Dermot had re-established himself at Ferns, his old capital, and was soon recovering his ancestral territory of Uí Cennselaigh. It is clear that the high king was at first alarmed by all this, for he took the unprecedented step of mounting a winter campaign against Dermot, whom he defeated. What followed was so extraordinary that it requires explanation: a peace was concluded which allowed Dermot to retain Uí Cennselaigh, though its terms prevented him from attempting to regain Leinster. Remembering what had happened just over a year previously, when Mac Murrough had been forced to quit Ireland, it is astounding that he should now be allowed to retain what he had retaken. The only explanation seems to be that O Connor had just before this been forced to face a resurgent O Brien in Munster and was in no position to wage an all-out war against Mac Murrough through the winter. It seems, too, that Dermot had agreed to recognise O Connor as high king and had probably appeared to be a much chastened man.

It was now that Dermot showed his real mettle. Instead of embarking on a foolhardy attempt to win more of Leinster, and at the same time assuage his injured pride, he was content to wait until the promised help from Wales arrived. All through 1168 he waited, when it must have been difficult to curb his natural instincts to fight, while O Connor was preoccupied with his problems in Munster. It wasn't until May 1169 that the first contingent arrived from Wales, under Robert fitz Stephen. With him were between three and four hundred men, including knights and other men at arms, mounted and unmounted archers. The hard core of this, and of the subsequent armies which landed in the south-east, were the knights; but it was the Welsh archers who were to prove the most useful in Ireland, with their great mobility and the tremendous range of their revolutionary weapon, the longbow. It seems a tiny force to us, but it was sufficient to provide Dermot Mac Murrough with a professional nucleus for his army. And this small nucleus with its new weapons and techniques was able to cause havoc among the Irish levies until it was opposed by an overwhelmingly superior force. It enabled Dermot now to take the town of Wexford which, true to the promise he had made earlier, he gave in fee to fitz Stephen and Maurice fitz Gerald. Then he set out to reduce Leinster to his obedience once more, with such effect that the high king was thoroughly alarmed at his success. So once again O Connor invaded Leinster and once again, because of his vast superiority in numbers, he defeated Dermot. This was in the autumn of 1169. What followed is difficult to understand. Just as he had done in 1167, the high king now concluded another treaty with Mac Murrough by which Dermot agreed to recognise the high king, gave a son as a hostage for his good behaviour, and promised to send his foreign allies back to Wales. In return, he was to be allowed to retain the kingdom of Leinster. The only explanation for this, and that is not very satisfactory, is that O Connor was still too worried about the situation in Munster to take any sort of firm action against Leinster; and so he had to be content with promises from Dermot and the hope that the handing over of a hostage would keep the Leinster king in hand.

But Dermot had no intention of curbing his ambition or of ridding himself of his mercenaries, now his trump card. He despatched fitz Stephen to Munster to help O Brien against

O Connor, a move which produced unhoped for results in the defeat of the high king. This unexpected success inflamed Dermot's ambition, as did the fortuitous arrival of Maurice fitz Gerald with re-inforcements from Wales—he brought about ten knights, thirty mounted archers, and a hundred foot. Giraldus Cambrensis tells us that Dermot now 'began to look for higher things'. As he had done long ago, he questioned O Connor's right to the high kingship and reasserted the claims of his own ancestors: 'Does he lay claim to Leinster, because some of its princes have been occasionally subject to the kings of Connacht? By the same reason, I may challenge a right to Connacht, because it has been sometimes held under my ancestors when they were monarchs of Ireland'. He tried to persuade the Geraldines to enter on a campaign to win Ireland, but they insisted that more help must first be procured. And so Dermot wrote to Strongbow, reminded him of the promise he had made two years before, and asked him to come as soon as possible. 'All Leinster is now ours again,' he wrote. 'If you are timely with us, and in force, the other four parts of the kingdom will be easily united to the fifth.' This inducement to take the whole of Ireland was calculated to rouse Strongbow to action and it did not fail. He had seen how successful the Geraldines had been and decided that the risk could not be very great, while the rewards were spectacular. So he began his preparations to bring the largest force possible to Ireland. He sent Raymond le Gros ahead with a small force in May 1170, and in August he landed himself near Waterford with something over a thousand men. This episode is described in the Annals of Ulster as 'the beginning of the woes of Ireland', which in the event was to prove accurate enough. For the arrival of Strongbow changed the whole character of the war. Up to 1170 it had still been primarily a local affair between two Irish kings, one of whom was helped by foreign mercenaries. It was still within O Connor's power to control the situation. But the arrival of Strongbow was tantamount to an invasion. From now on the foreigners were to take control and gradually occupy more and more of Ireland.

First Waterford was taken, where Strongbow married Eva Mac Murrough and became Dermot's heir. Then the army moved up through Leinster to Dublin, whose importance Strongbow fully appreciated. Under cover of an armistace and while the Ostmen was negotiating terms with the besiegers, the city was taken. From now on the capital of the settlement which was to be carved out in Ireland was to remain in foreign hands. From Dublin, under Dermot's direction, the programme of seizing Ireland was initiated with an invasion of Meath. But now the high king and some of the other kings at last became fully aware of the danger in their midst and took belated action. A huge army was collected in the summer of 1171 and Dublin was placed under siege. With dramatic suddenness the whole situation had changed and Strongbow found himself faced with the prospect of complete ruin. He was the victim of a number of circumstances which he could not possibly have foreseen and a shrewd high king, such as O Connor could never be, would have seized the advantages given to him and driven the invaders from Ireland.

The invaders had managed so well in the early stages of the conquest that not even the temporary defection of one of the leaders, Maurice de Prendergast, who deserted to the king of Ossory, could embarrass them. It was the death of Mac Murrough in May 1171 which first caused trouble to Strongbow. For the men of Leinster refused to accept him as their king and Wexford was attacked. This was all the more serious because the previous year Henry II had become alarmed at the success of his subjects in Ireland, ordered them to return and surrender what they had won to him before Easter 1171, and placed an embargo on the sending of reinforcements or supplies to Ireland. The king had every reason to be worried, for he was now faced with the distinct possibility of a rival feudal monarchy emerging in Ireland under Strongbow. After the capture of Dublin O Connor had sent a message to Mac Murrough reminding him of the treaty he had accepted in 1169 and insisting that he abide by its terms. He received what Giraldus calls an 'arrogant reply' from Mac Murrough in which Dermot stated that he would not desist from the enterprise he had undertaken until he had reduced Connacht, which he now claimed as part of his inheritance, to subjection and obtained the high kingship of all Ireland. His offensive in Meath, which was outside his own territory, was a clear indication of the nature of his enterprise. But more than that an advance was made southwards into Munster and the northern state of Uriel felt it expedient to recognise the claims of Mac Murrough and avoid invasion by giving him hostages. All this must have been known to Henry II and he saw clearly that

Strongbow was not only willing but powerful enough to carry on where Mac Murrough left off. So some action was called for and the best he could do immediately was to issue his warning and proclaim the embargo.

The trouble in Leinster and the failure of supplies from home placed Strongbow and his followers in a serious predicament. It was necessary to conciliate Henry and messengers were immediately despatched to surrender all the conquered lands to the king. But meantime the situation in Leinster deteriorated and supplies were running short. In the summer O Connor and his army arrived and Dublin was placed under siege, cut off from communication with the other two strongholds in Wexford and Waterford. Dublin was invested not merely by land but by sea as well, for a fleet of thirty ships, mainly from the Isle of Man, arrived to help the Irish. There is no doubt that O Connor had nothing to do but hold his position and starve the besieged into surrender. So desperate was Strongbow that he negotiated with O Connor offering to recognise him as high king and do homage to him for Leinster—in effect, to cut himself off from England and his liege lord Henry II. But O Connor, naturally enough, was unwilling to see Leinster go to a 'stranger in sovereignty' and offered him only the Ostman towns of Dublin, Wexford and Waterford which had always been in foreign hands. This was not enough for Strongbow and so the siege went on. Finally it was decided to risk everything on one desperate sortie from the city and through the military incapacity of O Connor the plan was allowed to work. He split his army into two, sent one half to cut the harvest in the vicinity of Dublin and the other on a raid into the territories won by Strongbow in Leinster. As a result a successful raid was made from Dublin on the Irish camp and enough food supplies captured to last for months. At this O Connor lost heart and decided to raise the siege. It must have been difficult for him to keep his army together now that the harvest was ripe; and, besides, the siege of itself was now no longer a sufficient guarantee of victory with so much food gone into the city. An assault might still have won him the day, but the Irish had little experience of this kind of warfare and their effort would most likely have been repulsed by Strongbow.

This was a great victory for the Anglo-Normans and left the way clear for a further endorsement by Strongbow of Mac

Murrough's programme of expansion. But he had more than the Irish and their high king to contend with now, for Henry II had already made up his mind to come to Ireland and look after his own interests personally. Even while the siege of Dublin was in progress preparations were being made in England for his journey to Ireland and by October he was on his way, landing at Waterford on the seventeenth of that month. With his arrival the first phase of the conquest came to an end and a new one was inaugurated which was to see the real beginnings of the medieval lordship of Ireland.

Henry had long before this been interested in Ireland, which too often had provided a safe refuge for enemies and traitors from England and Wales. Shortly after he became king he put a proposal before his council for a conquest of Ireland which he suggested should be given to his youngest brother, William of Anjou. It was in preparation for this that the grant of Ireland was procured from Pope Adrian IV. But the plan came to nothing and Henry afterwards lost all interest in Ireland until the circumstances of the Anglo-Norman invasion forced his hand. The papal grant was still valid, however, and could always be invoked should the need arise. There is no evidence that Henry in fact did make use of the Bull while he was in Ireland: it would have been embarrassing for him to have to do so, with the murder of St Thomas of Canterbury on his hands and papal legates seeking him out to force him to do penance for the crime. But there is no doubt that the Irish knew about the Bull or that it played its part in encouraging them, especially the bishops, to submit to Henry. It is probably true also that by coming to Ireland and fulfilling the terms of the Bull—which, remember, placed on the king the responsibility for reforming the Irish Church—the king felt that he would be doing something to placate the pope and make reconciliation easier to achieve. But what was uppermost in Henry's mind in deciding to come to Ireland was undoubtedly fear. The success of Strongbow alarmed him, as did the failure of his order that the leaders of the invasion were to return to do homage to him for their conquests before Easter 1171. Even his mandate that no one was to leave England to join Strongbow in Ireland was not entirely successful: the English pipe rolls refer to a number of people who defied the king and left for Ireland. There was no assurance that matters would not get further out of hand unless he intervened personally and took control as soon as possible. And there is the evidence of one contemporary English chronicler that 'the king and inhabitants of that land . . . sent ambassadors to the king of England to pray him to come into Ireland and by taking over the lordship of the country himself to relieve them from the insolence and tyranny of earl Richard (Strongbow)'. So Henry set in motion the bureaucratic machine which would make the necessary preparations for an expedition to Ireland.

What is most astonishing about these preparations is their widespread and comprehensive character. No part of England seems to have been spared in seeing that the king came as well prepared as possible. It is obvious that Henry came ready for a tough campaign and did not expect to be able to live off the land while in Ireland. Enormous quantities of wheat and oats were shipped across the Irish sea, with a supply of handmills for milling flour while on the move. Beans, salt, cheese and a vast amount of bacon were brought over, the bacon being shipped in such quantity that it was clearly intended to form part of the regular diet of the soldiers during the campaign. No other kind of meat was supplied. Henry himself, of course, was not content with the staple diet of the soldiers and one of the most interesting cargoes which accompanied him was the 569 lb. of almonds which the bishop of Winchester supplied at a cost of £5. 18s 7d. Cloth in large quantities was supplied for the troops: the city of Winchester, for instance, sent two thousand ells of burel, a coarse grey woollen cloth which was suitable for the dampness of an Irish winter. But again the king was expected to dress in better finery, so he was supplied with 25 ells of scarlet cloth, 26 ells of green, 12 pieces of silk cloth, 2 skins of mountain cats and 5 otter skins, as well as 10 pairs of boots. His swords were specially refurbished, the scabbards decorated with gold and the blades and hilts with sterling silver. And finally, as an indication that Henry, who was a great huntsman, intended to take time off to enjoy himself while he was in Ireland, we find that Lincolnshire supplied him with five gerfalcons.

Getting all these supplies, not to mention the men, horses, grooms, equipment of all kinds and attendants to look after it, to the ports was an enormous task. Then shipping had to be found and prepared to carry the stores and the horses and miscellaneous cargoes of all kinds, which meant that many ships had to be completely overhauled. For example, special stalls had to be constructed to house the horses, bridges had to be built to take the animals on board and decking and side walls had to be reinforced and protected against the powerful and huge destrier, the horses which carried the knights. It may well be that part of the enormous quantity of timber and nails supplied was used for this purpose; but most of it was intended for use in Ireland, as were the axes, spades and pickaxes which were provided in great numbers: the city of Gloucester, for example, sent 1,000 shovels, 60,000 nails, and iron for 2,000 spades; and the county of Gloucester sent 2,000 pickaxes and 1,000 spades. Gloucester also shipped 5 carts and 4 waggons to Ireland, possibly for carrying the king's treasure and valuables while he moved around the country, and the unusual cargo of 5 wooden towers (2 from Lancaster and 3 from Carlisle) was also carried to Ireland—these were almost certainly intended for siege warfare or the construction of castles. Finally we should mention the 1,000 lb. of wax which was provided by Winchester, which is a sure indication that the king expected to seal a great many charters and letters while he was in Ireland, and the spices and cordials which were supplied by Joseph the doctor for medicinal use.

Just how large a fleet was finally assembled to carry the army and all the supplies to Ireland it is impossible to say. Roger of Hoveden, a contemporary, writes of 'four hundred great ships with warriors, horses, arms and food'. The army itself must have been large, to judge by the quantities of provisions brought to Ireland and the amount of money which went to raise paid levies. The general opinion of the chroniclers is that about 500 knights and 1,000 others came to Ireland with the king, which is just the sort of large army we would expect Henry to assemble to meet the threat of an independent Norman Ireland. This was his main purpose and to achieve it he needed a comfortable superiority in numbers. But before he left England a much chastened Strongbow, who undoubtedly knew of the preparations for a royal expedition to Ireland, came to Gloucestershire and there did homage to Henry for Leinster, renewed his oath of fealty, and handed over the cities of Dublin, Wexford and Waterford and the adjacent lands along the coast. Notwithstanding this, the king and his army pressed on for Ireland, so we must assume that the submission of Strongbow of itself did not wholly avert the danger from Ireland: the Geraldines had still to be dealt with and indeed fitz Stephen was now a prisoner of the Ostmen of Wexford, who were to hand him over to the king after his arrival in Ireland, with the condemnation, according to Giraldus Cambrensis, that 'he had been the first to invade Ireland without the royal licence and had set others a bad example'. But it is most unlikely that the possible danger from the Geraldines, largely neutralised by the submission of Strongbow, was enough to justify Henry in pressing on with his large-scale expedition and we can only conclude that the great army which he brought to Ireland was now also intended to be employed against any Irish opposition to his lordship.

As it happened, the only opposition he seems to have en-countered was from the Ostmen of Waterford who attempted to block the passage of his fleet to the city by throwing three iron chains across the estuary. The ringleaders were soon caught and hanged for their trouble, a salutary lesson which probably inhibited those who may have thought of opposing Henry in the future. The Geraldines caused no trouble and in Wexford the first of the Irish kings made his submission to Henry. This was Dermot Mac Carthy, king of Desmond who, according to Giraldus Cambrensis, 'came of his own free will and made his submission to the king of England, doing homage and swearing fealty to him as lord, and giving hostages for the regular payment of a yearly tribute'. He was followed by others, so that by the time Henry left Ireland in 1172 all the Irish kings, with the exception of the high king and the kings of the north-west, had submitted to him and given him hostages, some of which were brought back to England. His great army was therefore never used, but we can be sure that its presence was largely instrumental in bringing the Irish and the Anglo-Normans to submission. It provided a show of strength calculated to impress the foolhardy who might other-wise have been tempted to resist the king. There is evidence that even the high king had thoughts of submission, though they did not materialise, by which time it was too late to use the army against him, even if Henry wished to do this which is doubtful, for the campaigning season was long since past. So on this score Henry had every reason to be satisfied with himself. While he was in Dublin during the winter he went out of his way to impress the Irish with the magnificence of his court, entertaining them to a lavish feast at Christmas in the course of which they were introduced to many strange and exotic dishes.

Henry was also anxious to pose as a patron of ecclesiastical reform in Ireland and impress the pope with his concern for the wellbeing of the Church. So his first journey from Waterford was made with this in mind. He went to Lismore, whose bishop was papal legate in Ireland, and from there to Cashel, the seat of the metropolitan see of Munster. There can be no doubt that during both visits he explained his plans for a council of Irish bishops to meet at Cashel in the near future, and shortly afterwards summonses to the council were sent out. It met early in 1172 and passed a number of decrees which are important in the history of the reform movement within the Church. Organisational reform had already been dealt with in earlier synods; the bishops assembled at Cashel therefore concentrated on canon law and liturgical matters. More important, however, was the acceptance by the bishops of Henry as lord of Ireland. They knew of the submission of the Irish kings and they undoubtedly saw in Henry the embodiment of the centralised authority they had long sought for the full implementation of their reforming decrees. Furthermore they were aware of the grant of Adrian IV and while it was true that Henry was held responsible for the murder of St Thomas of Canterbury, it must have been known that already legates were on their way from Rome to arrage for the pardon of the king and impose a suitable penance. The bishops seem to have drawn up letters in which they informed the pope, Alexander III, that 'instigated by divine inspiration' Henry had conquered Ireland and procured the submission of the Irish, and that under his influence illicit practices within the Church were beginning to disappear. These letters were probably carried to Rome by messengers sent by the king, for Henry lost no time in turning to good account with the pope the achievements of a Church council held under his auspices. Much later, in September, the response of the pope showed how favourable an impression had been made. He sent three sets of letters, one to the Irish bishops, another to the Irish kings, and finally one to the king himself, in which he praised the achievement of Henry in Ireland and spoke of his 'delight' over the king's 'triumph' in Ireland. He told the Irish kings of his 'joy that they have taken

Henry for their king' and exhorted them to persevere in their fealty. The bishops were admonished to 'smite with ecclesiastical censure any of the kings, princes or people who shall dare to violate the oath and fealty they have sworn'. And more important, he issued a privilege in which he confirmed the earlier Bull of Adrian:

> We ratify and confirm the concession of the said pope made to you concerning the lordship of the kingdom of Ireland . . . to the end that the foul customs of that country may be abolished, and the barbarous nation, reckoned Christian in name, may through your care assume the beauty of good morals, and that the Church of those regions, hitherto disordered, may be set in order, and the people may henceforth through you attain the reality as well as the name of the Christian profession.

We need not take too seriously the grave charges levied against the Irish Church in this privilege, the result of misinformation in the past and of highly coloured reports sent by Henry after the council of Cashel. But the privilege and the letters show vividly the impression which Henry had succeeded in making in Rome. He had made good use of the opportunity given him to pose as a reformer and gained prestige in Rome and the willing support of the Irish hierarchy in asserting his rights to the lordship of Ireland.

He was not slow in utilising those rights. While he was in Dublin he issued a charter in which he granted the city to be inhabited by his men of Bristol, with all the liberties and free customs which they had in Bristol and throughout his dominions. It was the first grant of the kind made in Ireland and was to be one source of municipal institutions in the lordship. It is not clear if many Bristol men availed of the opportunity and settled in Dublin. Some certainly did, as the roll of Dublin citizens from the end of the twelfth century shows. But the great majority of the names enrolled there come from other towns in England and Wales, with a few from Scotland and France. The Ostmen seem to have been pushed aside to form a separate community apart, on the north side of the river Liffey, where the modern Oxmantown still preserves in its name the trace of their new settlement. Grants of land, or confirmations of earlier grants, were also made by the king. By far the most important of these was the grant of the whole of the ancient kingdom of Meath to Hugh de Lacy for the service of fifty knights. There can be no doubt that this was intended as a means of keeping Strongbow in check. As we have seen, he had designs on Meath and had earlier invaded and occupied part of it. Henry was content to leave him Leinster, which he held by inheritance from Mac Murrough and by conquest, and he confirmed him in its possession in return for the service of one hundred knights. But he was determined that Strongbow would be confined to Leinster and the grant of Meath to de Lacy went part way towards achieving this. Before he left Ireland from Wexford in April 1172, Henry made other arrangements for the safeguarding of his interests in Ireland. He appointed constables with garrisons in the towns which had been handed over to him—Dublin, Wexford and Waterford; he had earlier installed constables and garrisons in Cork and Limerick, which had been ceded to him by Mac Carthy and O Brien when they made their submissions. Finally he appointed Hugh de Lacy as his justiciar, or chief governor, in Ireland, another indication of his lack of trust in Strongbow who was the obvious man for the post of king's representative in Ireland.

The grant of Meath to de Lacy raises one problem which must be examined if we are to understand what Henry achieved in Ireland. It is significant that the charter making the grant speaks of 'the land of Meath . . . as Murcardus Ua Mulachlyn best held it'. This was Muirchertach Ua Maelsechlainn, father of Dervorgill, the last king to hold Meath intact. Henry was therefore ignoring the dismemberment of Meath, which had occurred during the wars for the high kingship, and restoring the boundaries of the ancient kingdom. But he was also ignoring the rights of the pre-Norman proprietors and of those who had submitted to him. The problem is: what did these submissions mean? There is no simple answer to this, for despite the large quantity of wax which was brought to Ireland, Henry does not seem to have issued any charters to the Irish kings; if he did none have survived. So we cannot be certain of the precise nature of the relationship which was established between him and them. It seems clear that they were his vassals, holding their kingdoms of him, and that their sovereignty under him was guaranteed. They gave him hostages and paid an annual tribute, or rent, for their kingdoms. In return they could expect Henry to protect them and their kingdoms. Indeed, there seems little doubt that while many factors may have influenced individual Irish kings in accepting the overlordship of the king of England, for most of them it was primarily a matter of self-protection: this great foreign king, with his enormous army and obvious wealth and power, would be able to safeguard them from the avaricious invaders who threatened to despoil them of their lands. How, then, was Henry able to grant away Meath to de Lacy? The case of Leinster is different, because it had been conquered by Strongbow who was in any case in feudal law the heir of Dermot Mac Murrough. Meath had been dismembered on a number of occasions, and despite the repeated attempts of the Maelsechlainns to regain the complete kingdom, there were only three people who had what might be regarded as serious claims by the time Henry II arrived in Ireland: Rory O Connor, the high king; Tiernan O Ruairc, king of Breifne; and Strongbow, the heir of Mac Murrough. It was only to be expected that Henry would not tolerate the claims of Strongbow, who in any case did not press them. O Connor's claims were not very strong, even if his failure to accept the overlordship of Henry had not debarred him from consideration; and O Ruairc, who had submitted, had really forfeited his claims when the last Maelsechlainn king to succeed in gaining temporary hold of the kingship submitted to Dermot Mac Murrough in 1170. There was no question, then, of Henry breaking faith with the Irish when he made this grant. His whole aim at this time was to contain the Anglo-Normans and it suited his purpose very well, apart altogether from any question of his obligation to protect the Irish kings in their lands, to restrict the area under the control of the invaders.

After he left Ireland in 1172 he seems to have held to this policy, so long as circumstances permitted him to do so. Strongbow in Leinster and de Lacy in Meath set about establishing control over their vast lordships, through incastellation and subinfeudation. In this they were unhampered by the king, but as might be expected they encountered stiff resistence from many of the Irish. De Lacy in Meath found that Tiernan O Ruairc was his greatest obstacle and decided to try to reach a settlement by negotiation after the failure of the use of force. During the discussion between the two parties, O Ruairc was killed—by treachery, according to the Irish sources—and de Lacy was able to press on with his feudalisation of Meath. In Leinster Strongbow had his own troubles which kept him busy. Then in 1173 his lieutenant, Raymond le Gros, led a raid on Lismore, thirty miles outside the boundaries of Leinster. It produced a quick reaction from Dermot Mac Carthy, within whose territory Lismore lay, and in the ensuing encounter the Irish were beaten. Thirteen shiploads of booty, we are told, were carried off by Raymond. Here was a clear infringement of the settlement made by Henry II, at the expense of one of the Irish kings who had submitted to him. Reprisals quickly followed. O Brien penetrated into Leinster and sacked Kilkenny and a punitive expedition led against him by Strongbow was heavily defeated by the Irish at Thurles. The high king had been the ally of O Brien in this success and he now turned his attention to Meath which was invaded. In 1175 a counterattack under Raymond le Gros drove the invaders out and restored a measure of peace, though a great part of the land had been laid waste and the two famous monasteries of Durrow and Clonard were plundered.

This renewal of strife in Ireland and the threatened expansion of the Anglo-Normans outside the area to which they had been confined by Henry II was alarming and seems to have persuaded the high king that the time had come to try to make some definitive arrangement with Henry which could maintain an equilibrium between Anglo-Norman and Gaelic Ireland. So O Connor opened negotiations with Henry, with the archbishop of Dublin, St Laurence O Toole, as his ambassador. The result was the so-called Treaty of Windsor of 6 October 1175. This arrangement created a definite frontier between the two parts of Ireland which comprised the lordship of Henry II: Meath, Leinster, and those parts around Dublin, Wexford and Waterford which the king had retained in his own hands were excluded from the authority of the high king; but elsewhere the high king was to 'have all the land and its inhabitants under him and shall bring them to account so that they shall pay their tribute to the king of England through him, and he shall maintain their rights'. O Connor is recognised as high king, though he is a liege king of Henry II and shall therefore like the other kings pay tribute for his kingdom. The tribute is specified: one hide of each ten animals slain. It was also agreed that if the high king were unable to collect the tribute or to maintain control over those who rebelled against him, he was to have the help of the king's constables in Ireland. O Connor's high kingship is clearly recognised: but it was in future to be restricted to the area outside the Anglo-Norman settlement. He was to take hostages from the other kings and he was in turn to give hostages of his own to the king of England. Finally he was to see to it, if requested, that those Irish who had fled from 'the lands of the king of England's barons' would return. This probably referred in the main to the servile class of Irish, the *betagii* (or betaghs), who would provide the serf population on the manors of Anglo-Norman Ireland.

This was an arrangement which suited both of the principals in the negotiations perfectly. On the one hand it secured for O Connor his position as high king, and even strengthened it, for he now had the additional support of the king's forces in Ireland; and on the other hand it procured for Henry a satis-factory system whereby the tribute and hostages owing to him would be collected, while at the same time it prevented (in so far as this could be prevented) what he feared most—the develop-ment of an independent Norman kingdom in Ireland. Dividing the island into two, one part feudal and the other Gaelic, may not have been an entirely satisfactory solution; but under the cir-cumstances it was the best that could be hoped for. Where the whole thing broke down was in the intermediaries, the feudatories who in the end proved impossible to control from England, and the Irish kings who had never accepted the high kingship of O Connor and were not prepared to do so now. It is true that immediately after the treaty was concluded it was invoked by O Connor against O Brien of Thomond, so that a combined Irish and Anglo-Norman army marched on Limerick to assert the rights of the high king, deposed O Brien and set up another as king of Thomond in his place. But there can be no doubt that this was a flash in the pan and that in the long run O Connor would prove quite incapable of asserting his rights fully or collecting the tribute for Henry II. The more serious weakness, however, was Henry II's inability to control his Anglo-Norman subjects in Ireland. This was particularly the case after the death of Strongbow in May 1176. Raymond le Gros, who had married the earl's sister, now grew ambitious and had to be checked. This was the task of William fitz Audelin, who was sent to Ireland in 1176 as the king's chief governor. But if fitz Audelin succeeded in keeping Raymond in check, he was unable to prevent other Anglo-Normans from violating the Windsor settlement by striking out on their own into Gaelic Ireland. One of these was

John de Courcy who in January 1177 led an invasion of Ulster with spectacular success and succeeded in carving out a principality for himself there. Another was Miles de Cogan who attempted to do the same thing a little later in Connacht, though without success in the end. It was clear that Henry's attempt to maintain a balance in Ireland between the two peoples was not going to work. And so within two years of accepting the treaty of Windsor he departed from its principles. In May 1177 he held a meeting of his council at Oxford and there a new arrangement was made for Ireland. The rights of the kings who had submitted to Henry were ignored and the kingdoms of Thomond and Desmond (or Limerick and Cork as they are called in the accounts of the council) were granted away over the heads of O Brien and Mac Carthy—Desmond to Robert fitz Stephen and Miles de Cogan, Thomond to three others who later renounced the grant, on the interesting pretext that the land had not yet been conquered, so that a new grant was made to Philip de Braose. Most important of all was the grant of the lordship of Ireland to the king's youngest son John and the new grantees were made to do homage to him for their Irish lands, as well as doing homage to the king.

There does not seem to be any reason to doubt that Henry now realised that there was no effective way of keeping the Anglo-Normans in check in Ireland and that therefore the restrictions imposed by the treaty of Windsor should be removed. The safest thing to do, so that there would be no repetition of the Strongbow attitude of independence, was to make what have been called speculative grants of land in Ireland, which ignored the rights of the Irish kings who had accepted the lordship of Henry. Such speculative grants would procure homage in advance for lands which were to be conquered and define the service which was to be rendered for those lands. In this way the rights of the lord of Ireland would be safeguarded. It was a coldblooded way of dealing with the Irish problem and was, of course, highly inequitable as far as the native Irish were concerned. Through speculative grants many Irish kings, whose sovereignty had been guaranteed by Henry, soon found themselves made the tenants of mesne lords who were intruded between them and the king. But Henry had no time to solve the problem in any other way and took the easy way out.

4

In the event this was to prove disastrous for, apart from the very tenuous link supplied by the homage and fealty rendered, it left even less control in the hands of the absent lord of Ireland. The new grantees had to be allowed the means of making good their grants and this helped to increase their spirit of independence. From now on the government of Ireland as it developed was to find itself faced by this spirit, which all too often led to defiance. Had the whole of Ireland been conquered and feudalised it might have settled down in the course of time. But the Irish reacted strongly to this betrayal of Henry II and now began to resist the extension of the feudal area. Relations between the two races were soured and prevented the one from being fully assimilated to the other. Feudalism had been violently intruded into Ireland and was to remain a foreign body in the Gaelic world until the end of the middle ages, something to be resisted by the Irish. The result of this was endemic war which made it all the more impossible for the lord of Ireland to control either race. It is an oversimplification to say that all this was the result of Henry II's failure to cope satisfactorily with the problem of Ireland, but he must shoulder a large part of the responsibility. It was part of the legacy which he passed on to his son John when he made him lord of Ireland in 1177.

III The Lordship of John and the Founding of Anglo-Ireland

KING Henry's youngest son John was only ten years old when he was made lord of Ireland in 1177. He was not therefore expected to assume personal responsibility for the lordship immediately. But it seems clear that in making this grant Henry II had taken another step in evolving an Irish policy. Between John and the throne stood three elder brothers, so there can have been little hope of his succession. It looks, then, as if Henry envisaged the complete separation of the lordship of Ireland from England, which would certainly have meant the evolution of a feudal monarchy there under John and his successors. Eight years later, in 1185, he sent John to Ireland for the first time, with an army, a large amount of money, and a number of trained and experienced officials. The young man was expected to take charge of his responsibilities and to establish an administration which would safeguard his rights in Ireland.

The arrival of John was not premature. Events had moved rapidly in Ireland since his father had concluded the treaty of Windsor in 1175 and there was a very real danger that a lack of direct control from England might allow the lordship to fall into the hands of ambitious men. Such a man was Hugh de Lacy, lord of Meath. The English chronicler, Roger of Hoveden, tells us that in 1179 the Irish complained to Henry of 'unjust and violent' treatment by de Lacy and others. They found a sympathetic listener in Henry who was already worried about de Lacy's activities in Ireland. His worries appeared to be justified when in 1180 de Lacy married Rose O Connor, the daughter of the high king, and the spectre of Strongbow seemed to loom again. Through this marriage de Lacy might very well have seemed to be aiming at making himself high king: Giraldus tells us that 'a deep suspicion arose that his policy was to usurp all power and dominion, and throwing off his allegiance, to be crowned king of Ireland'. The *Annals of Loch Cé* refer to de Lacy as 'king of Erinn', though this is clearly not intended to be taken literally. Nevertheless, such suspicions die hard and it was to ensure that they were not realised that the young Lord John was sent to Ireland.

Among the people who accompanied John was Gerald de Barry, better known as Giraldus Cambrensis (Gerald the Welshman), who was intimately related to the Geraldines of the first conquest. He had already been in Ireland a short time before tihs and had therefore a first hand knowledge of the county and its people. He has left us an account of this expedition as he saw it and a brilliant analysis of its failure. Giraldus was naturally prejudiced in favour of his relatives in Ireland and in his opinion they were the people who best knew how to deal with the problems of the conquest and who should have been left alone to get on with the job. He was also a supreme egoist. But for all his egoism Giraldus was a shrewd observer and couldn't help but pinpoint the causes of John's failure in Ireland. In his autobiography he lists three. 'The first,' he says, 'was that when he ought rather to have been sent against the Saracens for the succour of the Holy Land, he was sent against Christians.' This was the churchman in Giraldus speaking and is not to be taken seriously. He is much closer to the mark in the second cause listed: 'The second that, being himself young and little more than a boy, he followed the counsel of the young men whom he took with him, who were utterly unknown in Ireland and themselves knew nought, whereas he rebuffed the honest and discreet men whom he found there who knew the customs and habits of the country, treating them as though they had been foreigners and of little worth.' Finally the churchman comes to the fore again in listing the third cause: 'The third was that he was not disposed to render any honour to God and to His Church in those parts,'—a failing which was all the worse because John's father had first obtained Ireland from the pope 'that he might exalt and uplift the Church of Ireland and cause Peter's Pence to be paid in that country as in England'. The second of these causes was obviously the one which Giraldus considered the most important and in his autobiography he refers the reader to his *Expugnatio Hibernica* for a fuller exposition of this.

In that earlier work Giraldus does not mince words in condemning John and those who accompanied him to Ireland. It is clear from the surviving records that John was furnished with a large army, plenty of money and supplies, and a number of advisers who might have been able to prompt him on the best course of action in Ireland. But John's youth and inexperience, his interest in pleasure rather than work, and his foolish disdain for the Irish and their strange ways, were all to lead him to disaster. One of the accounts of an English pipe roll records the hire of a ship 'to carry into Ireland Roger Rastel and other sportsmen, with their horses and dogs', a strange cargo for what was intended to be a serious military expedition. But it indicates the frivolity with which the young John approached his responsibilities in Ireland and forecasts the attitude he was to adopt during his sojourn there.

Straight away he showed his lack of judgment, indeed his bad manners. Shortly after he landed a group of Irish kings approached his court to do homage to him as lord of Ireland. Instead of receiving them with the dignity which was their due, John and his foppish companions made a mockery of the Irishmen, jeering at their strange dress and pulling their beards which, in the Irish fashion, were worn long. According to Giraldus the outraged Irishmen quickly made their escape and spread the word of the insults which they had suffered, describing all they had observed in John's court. 'They said they had found him to be a mere boy, surrounded by others almost as young as himself; and that the young prince abandoned himself to juvenile pursuits; and they further declared that what they saw promised no mature or stable counsels, no security for the peace of Ireland.' As a result other Irish kings who were preparing to attend on John now decided to have nothing to do with him. More than that, they agreed that they should form a league to 'defend with their lives their ancient liberties', a decision which Giraldus saw as a major disaster. For, as he points out, Irishmen who had formerly been at each others' throats now became friends, united to resist the foreigner. 'We speak of what we know,' he writes, 'and testify what we have seen. And forasmuch as we insulted and drove from us those who came first to pay their respects, as God humbles the proud, by this example we deterred all the chief men of the country from making their submission.'

No one could accuse Giraldus of a bias in favour of the Irish, so when he is roused to protest over the treatment meted out to them by John and his companions we must give heed. Worse was to follow. Having deprived them of their dignity, about which the Irish were naturally sensitive, the newcomers then proceeded to deprive them of their lands. This alienated those whom Giraldus calls 'our own Irishmen' still further. These 'had faithfully stood by us from the first coming over of fitz Stephen and the earl (Strongbow) . . . betaking themselves to our enemies, became spies upon us and guides to show them the way to us, having the more power to do us injury from their former familiarity with us.'

On top of all this, John made the situation worse by handing over to his inexperienced followers the care of the castles and towns on the coast, and for these Giraldus reserves his most bitter recriminations: 'Keeping themselves carefully within the town walls, they spent their time and all that they had in drunkenness and surfeiting, to the loss and danger of the good citizens, instead of the annoyance of the enemy.' Having been pushed to one side, the earlier settlers held themselves aloof. They manifested the first signs of an antagonism which was to persist throughout the middle ages and beyond, the mutual distrust of the Anglo-Irish and newcomers from England, or the 'English by blood' and the 'English by birth' as they were subsequently called. They saw, according to Giraldus, the hard work of the first conquerors being frittered away by the incompetence and injustices of these new arrivals.

As an eyewitness to the events which he describes, Giraldus cannot be dismissed out of hand as prejudiced in favour of the first conquerors who included so many of his relations. And so his evidence has always stood in condemnation of John. But there is no other evidence to support the view that John's expedition was in fact a military disaster. It seems clear that he made little effective use of the troops who accompanied him. But the months which he spent in Ireland were not completely wasted, for they mark the beginning of a new expansion of the colony under men who were to found some of the greatest families in medieval Ireland. When John built castles at Lismore in county Waterford and Ardfinnan in county Tipperary they were to serve not only as strong points for holding down territories already conquered, but also as bases for an expansion into parts of Munster which were still in Irish occupation. His grants of land, which are evidence in support of the accusation of Giraldus that John ignored the rights of Irish kings who had accepted the overlordship of Henry II, were clearly designed to augment systematically the area of feudal Ireland, while at the same time rewarding some of the friends who were with the young John at the time. More than that, it is likely that some of these grants were intended to link up some of the great fiefs created during the earlier period of settlement, so as to bind the colony into a coherent whole.

Before John came to Ireland, conquest and subinfeudation had already feudalised a considerable part of the island. The whole coast from Drogheda to Cork was occupied. Before he died in 1176 Strongbow had successfully asserted his claims to Leinster and had subinfeudated most of it, although he did leave some parts, especially the highlands, in Irish hands. Most of Dublin and Waterford, which had been retained by the king, had also been parcelled out in fiefs. Across from Dublin a solid wedge of settlement had been driven westwards by Hugh de Lacy who occupied his lordship of Meath as far as the Shannon. To the north of Drogheda the old Irish kingdom of Uriel was still unoccupied. But further north yet, John de Courcy had conquered that part of Ulster which stretched eastwards of the Bann, comprising most of the modern counties of Antrim and Down. In Munster, the attempt to make good the 1177 grant of the kingdom of Limerick had failed. But a good start had been made in the kingdom of Cork and a large area stretching east and west of the city was successfully occupied. The rest of Munster was still in Irish hands, as was the whole of Connacht.

The impetus behind all of this expansion lay mainly in the personalities who dominated the events of the first conquest of Ireland. Strongbow, de Lacy, the Geraldines, and the lesser men who followed them were remarkable for their initiative and vigour. They were difficult to control and, as we have seen, impossible to contain. Typical of them was John de Courcy, whose exploit in winning east Ulster with what was only a handful of men exemplifies the drive and ruthless determination which won so much of Ireland for the Normans. Like so many others who came to Ireland, he was rapacious for land and dreamed of conquest. Giraldus Cambrensis, in a splendid speech which he puts into the mouth of Robert fitz Stephen on the eve of the siege of Dublin, shows us the kind of spirit which moved these men to action:

[Since] we are not only brave, but well armed, can it be supposed that an unarmed multitude and mere rabble are able to resist us? . . . It may be the consequence of this enterprise that the five portions into which this land is divided may be reduced unto one, and the dominion of the whole kingdom devolve on our posterity. If the victory be won by our prowess, and Mac Murrough be restored, and the realm of Ireland be secured by our enterprise for us and our heirs for ever, how great will be our glory, how worthy of being achieved even by the loss of life and the contempt of death.

Early in 1177 de Courcy set out from Dublin to conquer land for himself in the far north. It is unlikely that he did this without first procuring a grant from Henry II, though an unlicensed expedition would not have been out of character. We are told in *The Song of Dermot and the Earl* (the *chanson de geste* which was composed early in the thirteenth century about the life and deeds of Strongbow) that Henry had indeed said to de Courcy that he could have Ulster 'if he could conquer it'. By 'Ulster' was meant the old Irish kingdom of Ulidia, roughly that part of the province which lay to the east of the river Bann and Lough Neagh. With a small force of about three hundred in all de Courcy succeeded in conquering the whole of that territory, despite the overwhelming superiority in numbers which he had to face. This was an achievement which was fit to rank with the exploits of the Normans anywhere. And it was entirely the result of de Courcy's enterprise, daring, and military skill,—a man who was, according to Giraldus, a 'born soldier', who 'in action was always to be found in the van taking upon himself the brunt of the battle'. Giraldus describes him further: 'A tall man, with big-boned, muscular limbs, large of frame and powerfully built, he had great personal strength and his intrepidity was remarkable.' Like someone out of the heroic past, he was a fit subject for an epic story, and though the only one to survive is a late Anglo-Irish tale in the *Book of Howth*, the man and his exploits gave rise to innumerable legends after his death. The Irish, too, seem to have been favourably impressed by his courage and military prowess, and he may even have been allowed to succeed the local king Mac Dunlevy. He certainly employed the style *Princeps Ultonie*, which appears in the dedication of the *Life of St Patrick*, written by Jocelin of Furness, one of the community of English Cistercian monks whom de Courcy translated to Down. He coined his own money, the true sign of his sovereign claims, married the daughter of the king of Man, and allied himself not only with his father-in-law, but with the kings of Scotland and Norway as well. Like so many of the other Anglo-Norman leaders, de Courcy went out of his way to make friends with those Irish whom he thought might be useful to him, so that later we find them co-operating with him in attempting to push forward across the Bann the frontiers of his great lordship. Nor did he fail to make use of the local traditions of the area in which he was campaigning. Downpatrick, which he made his capital, was reputedly the burial place of St Patrick and de Courcy therefore encouraged the monk Jocelin to write the life of the saint. The name of another great Irish saint, Colmcille, was hardly less powerful in that part of Ireland and de Courcy was reputed to have constantly carried with him a book of the prophecies of the saint, one of which foretold how a needy man, a stranger from afar, would come to Downpatrick with a small force and take possession of the place—a prophecy which seemed to point to de Courcy, who may have used it to weaken resistence to him as one fated to succeed. For good measure, we are told by Giraldus, he propagated a prophecy of Merlin which foretold that a white knight on a white horse and with the figures of birds graven on his shield would be the first to conquer Ulster, a description which fitted de Courcy in every detail.

De Courcy's exploit, then, demonstrated the qualities which many of the first conquerors of Ireland possessed. But by 1185, when John came to Ireland, the most important of these were dead. Strongbow died in 1176, Hugh de Lacy ten years later, Miles de Cogan in 1182 and Robert fitz Stephen not long afterwards. And Raymond le Gros died not long after 1190. Many of them, too, left no sons to carry on. So a new impetus to conquest was needed, a new generation of conquerors to push forward the frontiers of the feudal area. Such were the men who were favoured by John in 1185 and the years following, the Butlers, de Burghs, de Verdons and Pipards. It was they who were to spearhead the new expansion. But the initiative came from John in the new grants he made in Ireland, beginning with those of 1185. The most important of these grants related to Munster, for through them the frontiers of the colony in the southern province were pushed westwards to the Shannon. Theobald Walter, a brother of the archbishop of Canterbury and founder of the Butler family which dominated so much of the subsequent history of Ireland, was given lands in the modern counties of Clare, Offaly, Limerick and above all in the northern parts of Tipperary. The south of Tipperary went to Philip of Worcester, while still more land in the same area was granted to William de Burgh, founder of another great family in Ireland whose future, however, was to lie mainly in Ulster and Connacht. In making these grants John ignored the rights of Donal O Brien, king of Thomond, and also the earlier grant of 1177 which had made over the whole of that kingdom to Philip's nephew, William de Braose, so that all the other feudatories in the area were made his sub-tenants.

The other area in which important grants were made lay north of Drogheda. Here Peter Pipard was given lands in Louth and to a lesser extent in the modern counties of Monaghan and Armagh as well, while Bertram de Verdon was granted fiefs in the old Irish kingdom of Uriel, in Louth, and even further north in Armagh. The important thing about these grants was that they linked the conquests made by de Courcy in the north with Meath and Dublin, so that the whole coast from the north of Antrim to the west of Cork (and the greater part of the island eastwards from the line of the Shannon in the south and midlands and from the Bann in the north) soon lay in Anglo-Norman hands.

Much of this rapid expansion of feudal Ireland had taken place within about twenty years of the first invaders landing in Ireland. And while the initiative came from the remarkable personalities who dominated the history of that expansion, there were factors working in their favour which made the whole thing possible. Chief of these was the military superiority which they enjoyed over the Irish. Even a hundred years later the Irish annals show how charging knights in open country could terrify the opposition into confused flight without ever striking a blow. It is no wonder, then, that so much of the open country everywhere fell into Anglo-Norman hands. But much of Ireland consisted of terrain where the fully armoured knight on his heavy horse was virtually useless. Even here, however, the invaders had a trump card in the Welsh archers whom they brought to Ireland. Long before the longbow was to bring glory to England in the French wars, in the hands of Welshmen it had won for the Anglo-Normans in Ireland the greater part of the island. And to give them mobility in the often rough and difficult countryside through which they fought, the invaders employed light cavalry, using small, speedy ponies (*hobini*) carrying lightly-armoured men (*hobelarii*).[3]

In the type of fighting men employed, and in the weapons and armour which they used, the Anglo-Normans held a great advantage over the Irish who fought 'naked' (that is, without the protection of armour) and who relied on out of date weapons, such as the sling and the axe. They were, too, less experienced than the Anglo-Normans, who had learnt the art of war in Wales or, in some cases, on the continent. Indeed one can say that soldiering as a profession did not exist in Gaelic Ireland; the armies were, in a very real sense, amateur. With the invaders came many mercenaries, men whose profession was war, and who proved their worth in the very early days of the invasion when they were employed by Dermot Mac Murrough in Leinster.

A ready supply of fighting men was supplied by the feudal structure which the settlers imposed on Ireland. As the land was conquered it was parcelled out in fiefs which were normally held by military service. When Strongbow was granted Leinster, the service of one hundred knights was required of him, while Hugh de Lacy was required to provide fifty knights for Meath. And as these great feudatories subinfeudated their vast fiefs, they in turn demanded a service of knights from the tenants who held land from them. Where the area of land was smaller than a single knight's fee—that is the area of land which it was calculated could be held in return for the service of one knight—then the grantee was required to provide in foot soldiers the equivalent of a fraction of a knight. For example, it was calculated in some places that one foot serjeant was the equivalent of one eighth of a knight. In a way, then, we can regard the occupation as a military one, with each area as it was feudalised expected to produce a fixed quota of knights or footsoldiers. This provided a solid nucleus of knights (estimated at about 430 by the early

[3]These were the 'hobelars', first developed in Ireland, who were later to help to revolutionise the art of war when they fought in the armies of Edward I in Scotland.

thirteenth century) and a modicum of footsoldiers as well. In addition to this, the operation of other feudal customs, such as 'castle guard', provided for the needs of local defence. And on top of all that the invaders, even in the early days of the conquest, were often able to augment their armies by employing Irish forces. The *Song of Dermot and the Earl* tells how Strongbow, after he claimed the kingdom of Leinster as the heir of Dermot Mac Murrough, summoned the military service to which the king was entitled by ancient custom.

To conquer land, then, the Anglo-Normans were able to rely on their military superiority. What is most astonishing about this conquest, however, is that it was achieved by comparatively small numbers in the face of an opposition which was numerically vastly superior. But the Irish lost this advantage because not only were they unable to unite, even locally, against the foreigners, but all too often weakened themselves further by internal dissensions on which the Anglo-Normans were quick to capitalise. The civil wars among the O Connors of Connacht or later among the O Briens of Thomond are good examples of this. It was only to be expected, too, that ambitious Irish kings would make use of the disturbed conditions produced by the invasion to score off old enemies and to further their own interests. Traditional rivalry among ruling dynasties also led Gaelic kings to support the invaders and through marriage some of the greatest of them became related to leading Anglo-Normans and obliged to offer support or at least remain neutral in the wars of conquest.

For this attitude the Gaelic rulers have always been condemned by patriotic historians. Local interests should never have been allowed to prevent a successful resistance to a piecemeal conquest—so the argument goes. Local particularism was the fatal weakness in the Gaelic body politic. But it is unrealistic to regard the rulers of Ireland in this way. All attempts at building up a central monarchy had failed and left in the island a number of ambitious local rulers who were primarily concerned with defending, and if possible expanding the territorial limits of their own suzerainty. What can one expect, then, but that after the Anglo-Norman invasion their horizons would continue to be limited to their own and perhaps neighbouring localities. And as has often been pointed out, this very 'defect' proved to be an asset in the long run for it made the complete conquest of Ireland particularly difficult to achieve. No one dynasty represented the whole island, not even in the most symbolic way. So that not one, but many ruling dynasties had to be forced to accept the over-lordship of the king of England before Ireland could be con-quered. And as time was to show, this was beyond the resources of the invaders. Not only was the conquest incomplete, therefore, but even within the conquered regions there remained large areas which were still Gaelic and which were to be a source of great trouble in the future. The mountainous parts of Dublin and Wicklow, situated dangerously close to the capital of the lord-ship, are a case in point.

To consolidate their conquests the invaders built castles. At first these were simple structures of the mote-and-bailey type, huge mounds of earth surrounded by a deep fosse, with a wooden pallisade and a building of some sort on top, and usually with a large enclosed space, or bailey, alongside. These were perfectly adequate for the immediate purpose of providing shelter in time of attack and great numbers of them were built; their remains still dot the Irish countryside. But when conditions became more settled they were gradually replaced by more imposing buildings of stone, of which the great fortress of Trim is probably the most outstanding example in Ireland today.

Through incastellation the conquered land was to be held down, and so it was important that a sufficient number of castles should be built in the right places to achieve this purpose. For as Giraldus Cambrensis observes, there was nothing to be gained by erecting 'a great number at once, in a variety of places, at great distance from each other, where they would be entirely disconnected and would afford no mutual aid in time of need'. They should, therefore, be built 'by degrees' on carefully chosen sites. And so the Irish landscape was given a new physical feature in the stone castles which sprang up throughout the whole colonised area, symbols of the new feudal society which had been intruded into the Gaelic tribalism in existence for centuries.

The expedition of the Lord John in 1185, then, was not a total failure since it marked the beginning of a new phase in the colonisation of Ireland. It was probably on this occasion also that a real beginning was made in the system of government which was to last for centuries to come. With the conquest spreading so rapidly and settlers being introduced, the absent lord of Ireland was faced with the problem of how to maintain his rights in his lordship. Fundamentally it was a question of how to exercise some degree of control over feudatories protected by customary law, a problem which every ruler in feudal Europe had to face at one time or another. The solution was not simply for the ruler to be stronger, but to have at his disposal a sophisticated system of government which enabled him to exercise control from a distance. And so the lord of Ireland supplied the centralised government which the ambitious Gaelic kings had been unable to develop. Because he was an absentee, the office which was developed in England to fill the place of an absent king was transmitted to Ireland. This was the office of justiciar, the title which the chief governor normally enjoyed down to the fourteenth century when that of lieutenant of the king began gradually to supercede it. Under the justiciar, as was customary in every feudal state, was a council which consisted in the main of the tenants in chief or those who held their land directly from the king. Everywhere in the feudal world it was the duty of the tenant in chief to give advice (*consilium*) to his lord when it was requested and this was normally done at an assembly. So in Ireland such meetings, or councils, were held from the earliest days of the colony, to give the justiciar advice on problems of particular importance. This feudal council did not, of course, meet regularly nor did all the tenants in chief attend it at the one time. But it was frequently summoned and from it was to emerge the parliament which was one of the most important and distinctive contributions of the middle ages to the way of life we enjoy today.

The council was primarily an occasional and advisory body, so that the justiciar needed the help of professional administrators who would assist him in the day to day tasks of government. He had under him, therefore, a corps of trained clerks who looked after the routine work of administration. There is little doubt that in the early days, when there was no need for a developed administration, such clerks were borrowed from the household of the archbishop of Dublin or from that of the justiciar himself. But as the colony grew so did the need for a central administration with its own staff of trained clerks. One of the first requirements was to look after the financial interests of the lord of

Ireland and for this an exchequer was established in Dublin. When exactly this happened is not clear, but it seems to have been in working order well before the end of the twelfth century. It was the first great department of state in Ireland and from it was to develop the rest of the bureaucracy which would administer the medieval lordship on behalf of the king. Behind the exchequer lay the county and the sheriff, the representative of the central authority in the localities. It must be remembered that it was only gradually that Ireland was shired and a system of local government spread through the colony. In the same way, although the common law of England was introduced when John was lord of Ireland and royal justice made available to those who could pay for it, it was only slowly that the system of royal courts and justices was established in Ireland.

In all this a real beginning was made during the period before John became king of England in 1199 and it is very likely that it was on the occasion of his visit in 1185 that much of the foundations were laid for later development. His accession in England was crucial, of course, in the history of Ireland for it finished the independence of the lordship for good. It was only to be expected, then, that the early years of the thirteenth century would witness a growing uniformity in the pattern of government in both countries. The government of Ireland was naturally much less complex and less sophisticated than that of England and local custom here was to produce differences of a minor character. But on the whole the system in Ireland was assimilated as closely as was possible to that of England. This meant that a greater efficiency in the administration not only enlarged the area over which the king was able to exercise his rights, but increased the capacity of his government in Ireland for maintaining control over the feudatories.

There was no place now for the independent spirit of the first conquerors and King John reacted violently to any manifestation of it. This can be exemplified by his treatment of John de Courcy, who was brought down with the connivance of Hugh de Lacy to whom John granted the lordship of Ulster in 1205. The downfall of de Courcy came after a prolonged attack, during which he had ignored repeated summonses by the king. He retained his heroic stature to the last and a later legend tells how it was only through the treachery of his servants that he was captured on

Good Friday while he was at his devotions in the monastery of the Holy Trinity in Downpatrick. Before he was taken he grabbed a wooden cross from a grave and with it killed thirteen of de Lacy's followers! His fall has been interpreted as revenge on the part of King John and this would certainly fit in not only with what we know of the character of the king, but also with one important aspect of his earlier relations with de Courcy. For when John rebelled against his brother King Richard in 1194 (as a result of which, incidentally, he was deprived of his lordship of Ireland for a time) it is possible that de Courcy had promoted support for the king in Ireland and thus earned for himself the bitter enmity of John. This may well be one reason why de Courcy was subsequently hounded by King John. But it is not the only one, for the attack on de Courcy was part of a wider attempt to curtail feudal rights in Ireland and extend the power of the king. One aspect of this was the advancement of new and, it was hoped, more loyal men in Ireland at the expense of long-established and suspect feudatories. A good example was the grant of Limerick to William de Braose in 1201 and his subsequent promotion there over the heads of William de Burgh and others. Another aspect was the royal attack on franchises. In 1208 William Marshal and Walter de Lacy received new charters for Leinster and Meath, which curtailed the franchises by making special reservations on behalf of the crown. The first instrument used by John in his attempt to undermine the feudal power of the magnates was Meiler fitz Henry the justiciar, who was so active on the king's behalf that he overreached himself and had to be removed from office. He was succeeded late in 1208 by John de Gray, Bishop of Norwich, a man of vast experience in affairs of state, close to the king and one of his few confidants. There can be no doubt that his appointment was intended to mark the beginning of a new attack on the feudatories. But before he arrived to take up office, Ireland was disturbed by the arrival of William de Braose, fleeing for his life from the wrath of John. He was first of all given shelter and protection by William Marshal, lord of Leinster, who refused to hand him over to the justiciar. Then for greater security de Braose found asylum with his son in law Walter de Lacy, lord of Meath. Hugh de Lacy, lord of Ulster, also promised all necessary help. This was an open act of defiance which must have seriously alarmed the king. His

justiciar in Ireland was powerless against such a combination of
the three greatest magnates in the lordship. The only answer was
for the king to come in person at the head of a great army and
to force the magnates into submission. But to do that he had to be
able to leave England in security and this was not possible until
the summer of 1210. On 20 June he landed in Ireland for the
second time, again with a large army, which in contrast to what
happened in 1185 he was to use to good effect during his stay here.

His immediate purpose in mounting this expedition was to
capture de Braose and impose his will on the de Lacy brothers.
William Marshal, who defended his action in sheltering de Braose
in 1208 by saying that he was only doing his duty in giving
succour to his lord in distress, had been reconciled with the king
and joined him on this expedition. In the following weeks John
moved rapidly against the chief castles of his enemies, finally
forcing the last of them, the great fortress of Carrickfergus in
Ulster, into surrender before the end of July. By then, however,
both the de Lacys and de Braose had fled overseas. The king
moved on at a more leisurely pace now, reaching Dublin on 18
August and finally leaving Ireland six days later. His campaign,
which lasted just about nine weeks, had been a tremendous
success. The great lordships of Meath and Ulster, together with
the lordship of Limerick, were now in his hands. All the feudatories had been forced into complete acceptance of him. Of the
great magnates only William Marshal was left and if ever there
was a man whose loyalty to the king could be depended upon it
was he. For Marshal was essentially the perfect knight and despite
many annoyances suffered at the king's hands he never wavered
in his loyalty. For John there was no danger in Leinster so long
as it remained in Marshal's hands.

The king, then, had rapidly achieved his main purpose in
coming to Ireland in the summer of 1210. But he had done much
more than that. There is some evidence that King Philip of France
had reason to expect a rebellion on his behalf against John in
England and Ireland: this danger had now been forestalled, in
Ireland at least. And on this occasion, too, John was able to procure
the submission and, more important, the active support of a
number of Gaelic rulers. Indeed most of Gaelic Ireland seemed
prepared to accept him and one account describes how no less
than twenty Gaelic leaders did homage to John while he was in

5

Dublin. It was on this occasion, too, that a meeting of the magnates was held at which they were made to swear that they would observe the laws and customs of England.

Just how successful King John was in establishing his control over Ireland can be seen in the events of the troubled years after 1210. For when the English baronage became estranged from the king and a section of them plunged the kingdom into civil war, the barons of Ireland remained loyal to John and never once did any of the important ones make any attempt to use the difficulties of the king to assert his independence. On a number of occasions they showed their loyalty in a practical way. In 1211 they fought for the king in his campaign against Llywelyn of Wales. Two years later, 1213, when there was imminent danger of a French invasion of England, an army was mustered in the south of England to protect the coast. Among those present, according to the chronicler Roger of Wendover, were John de Gray and William Marshal at the head of 500 knights and many other horsemen from Ireland. The figure is, no doubt, an exaggeration; but it represents the presence of a large force of Irish tenants in chief. The most striking proof of loyalty came in January 1213, when a remarkable manifesto was issued by William Marshal and twenty-six of the magnates of Ireland, protesting that they were grieved and astonished to learn that the pope proposed to absolve the subjects of the king from their allegiance. At the end they say about the king that 'we are ready to go with him into life and into death'. Even if it is true that this declaration was procured by Marshal at the direct instigation of King John on the model of a similar, though now lost, declaration made by a number of English barons, it is still a remarkable example of the success of the king in dealing with his Irish feudatories and winning their loyalty. So important was it at the time that it, and not the English manifesto, if there ever was one, was copied into the *Red Book* of the English exchequer.

To this pledge of loyalty the Irish barons remained true, testifying to the good relations which now existed between them and the king. For however hard John had pushed his rights, at critical moments he seemed always able to conciliate the magnates of Ireland. So we find arrangements being made to restore Walter de Lacy to his lordship of Meath, though typically John insisted that he pay a huge fine of 5,000 marks. A great number of lesser tenants in Meath and Ulster were also restored, but no move was made to bring back Hugh de Lacy, the dispossessed earl of Ulster. It may be that John thought his treachery too great. But it is just as likely that plans for a Scottish colony in Ulster were given priority. For early in 1212 a huge grant of 140 knights' fees in Ulster had been made by the king to the earl of Galloway. This was intended as part of a two-pronged attack on the recalcitrant Gaelic rulers, the other part being a projected expansion from Connacht. But the plan came to nothing in the end.

During the critical months of 1215 the king took no chances in Ireland. A number of grants show him being conciliatory and an order issued in February made the Irish government buy scarlet cloth for robes to be given to the Gaelic kings and 'other faithful subjects of the king'. Who these kings were is not specified, but they could be any of a large number. For it is an extraordinary fact, when we remember the breakdown in relations with the Gaelic chieftains which resulted from John's irresponsible treatment of some of them in 1185, that in the course of his reign as king most of them were willing to accept his lordship over Ireland. In 1210 he had been supported in his campaign by some of the greatest of them, including O Connor of Connacht, O Brien of Thomond and, very surprisingly, O Neill of Tir Eoghain. This can only be because he was willing to deal fairly with them and was able to offer them some measure of protection from the Anglo-Norman magnates. Indeed it has been said that it was part of John's policy in Ireland 'to favour the Irish chiefs for policy's sake rather than justice'[4]—that is to use them as a counter balance, in favour of the royal authority, against baronial power. The full story of the king's relations with Gaelic Ireland is too complicated to be related briefly here. But an examination of his dealings with the O Connors of Connacht or with the O Briens and Mac Carthies of Munster would hardly support the claim that John 'favoured' them in any way. Indeed all the evidence shows what, in fact, we should expect, that the king was no less intent on asserting his rights over the Gaelic chieftains than over the feudal baronage and that he always drove the hardest bargain he could. John's true attitude towards Gaelic Ireland is perhaps best seen in his directive of 1216 which ordered the justiciar not

[4] E. Curtis, *A History of Medieval Ireland*, 2nd ed., London, 1938, 96.

to allow any natives to be promoted to cathedral chapters. This was a deliberate attempt to prevent the election of bishops of Gaelic origin. And it was John, too, who saw to it that if any man of Gaelic Ireland claimed a right to land, then the claim must be based on evidence of possession since the Anglo-Norman invasion. No claim based on possession before the invasion would be accepted, unless of course it were confirmed by the king. Here again there is no sign that the native race were 'favoured' in any way. Rather was the king asserting his rights as supreme *dominus terre* ('lord of the land') in Ireland.

What was uppermost in John's mind was to be in a real sense lord of Ireland. And it was urgent that his lordship should be defined and secured if it were to have any real substance. For the colony continued to grow throughout this period. There was an important expansion in Desmond, for example, so that by 1214 one Irish annalist could say that 'the Galls overran the whole of Munster in every direction, from the Shannon to the sea'. It was therefore imperative that the king's rights should be defined and safeguarded in the face of feudal autonomy. This John did. The building of Dublin castle, commenced on his instruction in 1204, is symbolic. Thereafter it remained the centre of the royal administration in Ireland. And it was through this system of administration that King John was able to protect his rights. It is some measure of his success that from early in his reign he was able to procure large sums of surplus revenue from the Irish exchequer. So stable was the government before the end of his reign that not only was he able to have ships impressed in the Irish ports for service against the French, but he had galleys specially constructed for him in Ireland.

Perhaps the most striking proof of King John's success in Ireland lies in a comparison between the state of the lordship when he acquired it and at his death. Not only had a great expansion in the area of Anglo-Norman Ireland taken place, but good government had been provided through an efficient admiinistration and a fair measure of order established. The Gaelic chieftains had nearly all been persuaded to acquiesce in the lordship of the foreign king and to accept the creation of feudal fiefs in their midst. They were, as a result, quieter than they had ever been since Dermot Mac Murrough returned to Leinster. The whole colony had been given the stability and comparative peace it needed in order to consolidate its position. A good part of Ireland had already been feudalised and, through settlers, Anglicised. Through royal charters a number of towns had been given the freedom they required to become not merely commercial centres, but centres of foreign culture as well. Even the Church was well on the way to being thoroughly feudalised and Anglicised in the more important levels of her hierarchy. The foundations of Anglo-Ireland had thus been firmly laid.

IV The Limit of Expansion

WHEN King John died he left a doubtful heritage to his nine year old son Henry. England was invaded and partly in the hands of the French. Many of the barons had been alienated from the king and were supporting the invaders. A depleted treasury left the government with insufficient resources to carry on adequately. The lordship of Ireland, on the other hand, remained loyal and comparatively peaceful and it was significant that the justiciar, Geoffrey de Marisco, offered shelter to the Queen Mother and the king's younger brother. Since the new king, Henry III, was so young, the government was placed in the hands of a regent, nominated by King John before he died. This was William Marshal, lord of Leinster and heir of Strongbow. Not only did he have vast interests in Ireland; he had a first hand knowledge of conditions in the lordship, having spent the years from 1207 to 1213 there. With disaffection so rife in England, Marshal saw that there was no point in taking chances in Ireland or in relying too optimistically on the continued loyalty of the Anglo-Irish barons. It may be, too, that he was personally well disposed towards the Anglo-Irish, with whom he had much in common since the days when together they had felt the heavy hand of the late king. At any rate he went out of his way to reassure them. The first official letter of the new government to Ireland, which announced the death of John and the coronation of his son Henry, went on to say that the king wished to forget the ill-feeling which had once existed between his father and the nobles, to 'uproot evil customs' and to 'restore the good days of their noble ancestors'. The expression of such conciliatory sentiment was intended to assuage whatever fears the Anglo-Irish might have felt at the prospect of a minority in England (always a dangerous situation) and to hint that in future baronial interests would not be forgotten. That Marshal was in control must have been reassuring and he soon showed that his heart was in the right place by continuing the work of restoring confiscated fiefs—for example, Nicholas de Verdon had the castle of Dundalk and land in Louth restored to him—and by promising the magnates all the liberties and privileges enshrined in *Magna Carta*, a promise which was soon fulfilled when the Charter was extended to Ireland in February 1217.

While conciliating the Anglo-Irish in this way, Marshal was still punctilious about maintaining the king's proper rights in Ireland. This was all the more necessary now, given the perilous situation in England. As long as the war against the French was in progress money was desperately needed, and even when peace was finally made in September 1217 and England secured for the young Henry III, the financial difficulties of the government were even further increased by the war indemnity which was owing to the French. It was essential, therefore, to procure the greatest possible assistance from Ireland, and this could only be done if a firm control were maintained over the government there. Marshal sent to the justiciar a list of debts owing to the king and ordered them to be enforced. In November 1217 he ordered a tallage[5] to be levied on the royal demesne, while at the same time an aid[6] was to be sought not only of the tenants in chief but of Gaelic kings as well. Marshal knew well that the justiciar, Geoffrey de Marisco, was inclined to take an independent, and even defiant, line and would have to be controlled if the king's rights were to be safeguarded. A powerful Anglo-Irish magnate in his own right, Geoffrey as justiciar seemed a throwback to an earlier stage in the history of the lordship. He successfully resisted all attempts to bring him down and it was not until 1221 that he was finally dismissed from office. By then Marshal was gone—he died in 1219 — and the new effective head of the government was Hubert de Burgh, justiciar of England. Unlike Marshal he had never been to Ireland and had no great landed interests here. But he did have one vital connection with the lordship through his nephew Richard de Burgh, whose career in Ireland he was actively to promote.

[5]A tallage was a tax which the king had the right to levy on his own demesne lands.

[6]A feudal aid was a financial levy which the lord had the right to impose on his tenants when he was in real need. *Magna Carta* limited the king's right to an aid to three occasions: the ransom of his own person; to make his eldest son a knight; for once marrying his eldest daughter.

In the meantime there was one man who so far had not succeeded in having his confiscated lands restored to him. This was Hugh de Lacy, the dispossessed earl of Ulster. His brother Walter had, as we saw, been given back Meath, though he remained in England and left the running of his vast lordship to his half-brother William. It is very likely that King John had been unwilling to restore both brothers to power in Ireland, fearing, perhaps, a recurrence of the troubles which gave rise to their rebellion in 1210. But William Marshal seems to have thought otherwise. With almost unseemly haste after the death of John, in November 1216, an official approach was made to de Lacy in an attempt to persuade him to return to the king's peace. This was one of the first acts of the new government, and it carried the extraordinary admission that the late king might have transgressed against Hugh, although the new king was obviously in no way responsible for this. Some powerful force must have driven Marshal to court de Lacy in this way and we can only suppose that it was the realisation that his absence had removed from Ulster the strong hand which was necessary to maintain the peace there. Certainly negotiations were now begun and de Lacy seems to have accepted a safe conduct in 1217 to come to the king and discuss the whole business. It was probably the death of Marshal which changed the official attitude and a harder line was adopted. During the later stages of the protracted negotiations the terms offered were unacceptable to de Lacy. As a result the negotiations broke down in the summer of 1223. By July de Lacy was already in Ireland, raiding in Ulster.

Even before that Hugh had already shown that nothing was going to stop him from recovering Ulster. When William Marshal's son William II sailed to Ireland in the winter of 1222, some of his castles were ravaged by Llywelyn of Wales, aided by Hugh de Lacy. The Welsh prince's daughter was married to William de Lacy, the half-brother of Hugh (she was later captured and held prisioner in Cavan), and it seems likely that Welsh help was being sought for an attack on Ulster. But other foreign aid was also sought: in a letter to her brother, Henry III of England, Queen Joanna of Scotland told him of a rumour that the king of Norway would land in Ireland in the summer of 1224 to aid Hugh de Lacy. The government was well aware that an invasion to recover Ulster was planned and orders went out that

Irish castles in general, and those in Ulster in particular, were to be well garrisonned so as to prevent them from falling into de Lacy's hands.

When Hugh landed in Ireland in the summer of 1223, he used Meath as his base, thanks to the help of his half-brother William. A protracted war followed, during which the government tried to put down Hugh, and Walter de Lacy, the absentee lord of Meath, tried to recover what was rightfully his in Ireland. For a time the government was so hardpressed that the justiciar had to borrow money from the citizens of Dublin and, so it was later reported, had to purchase a truce from de Lacy! Hugh had reason to hope that some of the Gaelic kings would help him in rebellion against the government. His step-mother, Rose O Connor, daughter of the last high king, was with him until she was captured in the O Reilly crannóg (or island fortress) in county Cavan when it fell. But most of the Gaelic rulers held aloof—which certainly argues that they were on the whole well satisfied with the existing situation in Ireland—and some of them, especially Cathal O Connor of Connacht, were active against him. A letter from the king of Connacht to Henry III leaves no doubt of his attitude, or indeed of the seriousness of the situation in Ireland: 'Wherefore, unless it is better that the peace of Ireland should be subverted by this disturber and by default of some of the king's subjects, Cathal prays the king to send a force thither to restrain Hugh's insolence'.

It was not until he went to Ulster that Hugh de Lacy found a Gaelic king who was willing to join him. This was Aedh O Neill who supported him in an attack on the lands held by the Galloway Scots. By then the great castle of Trim had fallen and Meath was being reduced to order again by Walter de Lacy, the returned lord. The crucial stage in the war was reached when the government forces were joined by O Connor of Connacht, Mac Carthy of Desmond and O Brien of Thomond, the three great provincial kings of Gaelic Ireland. Against such a combination de Lacy and his northern allies could not stand. So Hugh finally surrendered and was sent to the king.

For two years he had defied the government, created havoc in the midlands and in Ulster, and almost proved too strong to be put down successfully. It must be admitted that the government did not always show itself to be in a complete state of readiness for war at this time, despite the instructions sent to Ireland before de Lacy landed, and this is probably one reason why the war dragged on so long. For example, an inventory of stores in the important castle of Athlone in 1224 showed that this vital fortification on the Shannon, guarding the entrance to Connacht, contained the following: 'four coats of mail, two with and two without headpieces; nine iron hats; one helmet; two mangonels, with 120 strings and slings; one cable; one crossbow with a wheel; 2,000 bolts; one small brazen pot; two pairs of fetters; five broken tuns; five basins; four broken tubs; two anchors; the ironwork of two mills; one chasuble; one consecrated altar; one figured cloth to put before the altar'. This was hardly what a well-equipped castle might be expected to contain!

Nevertheless, de Lacy had shown that it was possible for a determined man, with sufficient backing, to resist the government successfully. The old attitude of independence, which had brought King John to Ireland in 1210, was still alive. It is all the more surprising, then, to find him being restored to his earldom in 1226, almost as if nothing had happened. True, he had to hand over hostages and find sureties for his future good behaviour. But it is hard to understand the reasoning behind the restoration, unless it was that the government valued his presence in Ulster and wished to detach him from alliance with O Neill, turning him into a prop of English power in the North. For there is no doubt that Hugh de Lacy proved eminently capable of succeeding where even John de Courcy failed. During the 1230s and 1240s he was able to consolidate his hold on Ulster, successfully establishing the O Neills as dependent kings, and seems to have made all the Gaelic chieftains subordinate to himself. He thus vindicated the restoration of his earldom.

Meanwhile another massive expansion of feudal Ireland had been undertaken under the aegis of the English government, which backed de Burgh claims to Connacht. Hubert de Burgh, the justiciar of England, was quick to look after the interests of his nephew in Ireland, even if this meant an injustice to a loyal Gaelic ruler. The full story of relations with the O Connors of Connacht throughout this period is much too complicated to be briefly related. The intrusion of the Anglo-Normans was facilitated by civil war among the O Connors over a disputed succession to the kingship. The man supported by the government was Aedh O Connor, son of the late King Cathal, who had been consistently loyal to the king and supported the government in Ireland. On his death the *Annals of Connacht* burst out in a great panegyric, lauding him as best in everything ('the king whom of all the kings in Ireland God made most perfect in every good quality'), even to the extent of praising him as 'the king who was the fiercest and harshest towards his enemies that ever lived; the king who most blinded, killed and mutilated rebellious and disaffected subjects'! His son Aedh, no doubt for good reasons of his own, had fought with the justiciar in the war against de Lacy. His father, who held Connacht successfully until the day he died, had tried to secure confirmation of it for his son, though apparently no such charter was issued. Nevertheless Aedh did succeed his father and was even able to call on official support when his position was challenged. But suddenly in the summer of 1226 a change in government policy took place. O Connor was summoned to Dublin where, the summons said, he was to 'surrender the land of Connacht which he ought no longer to hold on account of his own and his father's forfeiture'. This callous treatment can only be explained by ascribing it to de Burgh, who saw his chance to procure O Connor's forfeiture of his kingdom and thereby promote his old claims to the western province. Such an unjust betrayal of a Gaelic ally would not have been tolerated by Marshal or others among the baronage; but Marshal was carefully removed from the office of justiciar before the move against O Connor was made and when he subsequently tried to help, after warning Aedh of the plotting against him, he was prevented by the king from coming to Ireland before he had given guarantees of good behaviour. In due course, then, Richard de Burgh was granted the whole of Connacht, except for the so-called 'King's cantreds' (five cantreds along the Shannon, occupying almost the whole of the modern county of Roscommon and parts of Galway and Sligo, which were reserved for the king), for an annual rent of 500 marks and the service of 10 knights. There can be no doubt that without the help of his uncle in England de Burgh would never have achieved this.

At the same time Aedh O Connor had provided the government with a convenient excuse by foolishly leading an expedition into Annaly in south Longford, shortly after the death of his father, and destroying at least one castle. Furthermore, he did not enjoy the support of all his own people. When the attack on Connacht came, Aedh found himself confronted not only by the feudal armies of the colony but by some of his own relations as well. In the end he was killed and Richard de Burgh, whose hand had been greatly strengthened by his appointment as justiciar in February 1228, was able to act the part of king-maker and had Felim, a younger son of the late king Cathal, inaugurated as king of Connacht. But a year later de Burgh turned on his protégé and had him deposed, imprisoning him in his new castle of Meelick. Another puppet king was to be sent up in his place. In August 1232, however, the king wrote to de Burgh and ordered him to release Felim O Connor who had, he understood, been treated shamefully and grievously by the justiciar.

This unexpected change in attitude was the direct result of a political revolution in England, which saw the fall of Hubert de Burgh and the assumption of personal control by the young Henry III. The disappearance of his uncle from power in England naturally put a halt to Richard de Burgh's expansion in Connacht. But the damage had already been done and it is doubtful if relations with the Gaelic kings could ever again be based on mutual trust after the injustice inflicted on Aedh O Connor. It is no coincidence that shortly after this not only Felim O Connor —who would claim to have a just grievance—but Mac Carthy and O Brien as well attacked the settlements made in Meath, Kerry and Limerick. No Gaelic king could ever feel secure again. He certainly could not depend on it that he held his kingdom from the lord of England in fee, to be passed on to his heir in the normal way. In the normal course these Gaelic kings would have difficulty in establishing their sons as their successors because of the peculiar succession laws which traditional custom imposed. But the disappointment of O Connor was a sufficient demonstration that there was no hope of establishing a rule of primogeniture (as many of them must have hoped) through accepting a dependent relationship with the feudal lord of Ireland. Forfeiture of their kingdoms on a legal technicality was a genuine possibility, so that the claims of land-hungry settlers could be secured. The future was to show that fears such as these were only too realistic.

Meantime there had been a pronounced reaction in Ireland to the fall of Hubert de Burgh in England. For one thing it meant that his nephew, Richard de Burgh, lost office in Ireland and an attack was mounted on him by the new administration. This diverted him from Connacht, where much of what he had achieved was swept away by a rampant Felim O Connor. Favoured by Henry III, Felim had no difficulty in destroying castles built by de Burgh and successfully asserting his own claims to the kingship. Once again, a change in the situation in England was to have important repercussions in Ireland and Felim was to find himself confronted with the prospect of losing all that he had gained in Connacht.

In England the new administration had come under heavy attack. One of the leaders of the opposition was Richard Marshal, who had recently succeeded his brother William as earl of Pembroke and lord of Leinster. He thus earned the bitter enmity of Henry III, who eventually renounced his feudal obligations to Marshal, cancelled his proposed expedition to Ireland, and went to war against him. Marshal retired to Wales and, fearing treachery from Henry, allied himself with the Welsh against the king. Having successfully defended his interests there, he sailed to Ireland in 1234 to look after his lordship of Leinster, now threatened as a result of the machinations of the king. For the war against Marshal was carried into Ireland by an enraged Henry, and the justiciar, Maurice fitz Gerald, and Richard de Burgh and other barons had joined against earl Richard. Some castles had already been taken by the time Marshal arrived. Within a few months, however, the earl was mortally wounded in a cowardly attack on the Curragh and he died shortly after.

There is no doubt that this attack on Marshal in Ireland was a reflection of political change in England following the fall of Hubert de Burgh, and of a great constitutional crisis with earl Richard at its centre. But it should also be seen, in a purely Irish context, as an expression of the more violent forces which could be loosened during this period of expansion, producing bitter quarrels. Lust for land was a powerful stimulant to baser actions. The cowardly attack on earl Richard on the plains of the Curragh, his betrayal by many of his own people, and the fatal wound which brought him to his death on 16 April 1234—called 'one of the worst deeds done in that age' by the *Annals of Connacht*— all left bitter memories. The man who foolishly boasted that he had caused the earl's death, Henry Clement, clerk to Maurice fitz Gerald, was murdered in London by outraged followers of Marshal. That was in 1235. Some of the murderers (led by William de Marisco, son of the former justiciar of Ireland) fled to Lundy island, in the Bristol Channel, where they took to piracy and later even tried to murder the king at Woodstock.

As we saw, one of the people who had joined in the attack on Marshal was Richard de Burgh: he was now to reap his reward. For with the fall of the people in England who had deposed his uncle from power, de Burgh was able to establish good relations with the king and within a few months Connacht was restored to him. To make good this grant a huge army was assembled in 1235. This included the feudal army of the colony, with a large number of individuals who hoped that service would be rewarded with land in Connacht. It was possibly the largest army assembled in Ireland up to this time and it proved invincible as it progressed through the western kingdom like an irresistible tide. Felim O Connor, despite getting help first from O Brien and then O Donnell, was powerless to prevent the conquest of his kingdom. The efficiency of the forces was shown in one of the more colourful episodes in the war, and one of the most important, which was the siege of an island fortress in Loch Key. Small mangonels were mounted on boats and were used to hurl great stones against the fortress. Other boats were tied together to form a great raft, supported by empty barrels, and set on fire. This huge burning contraption was then towed by a special ship towards the fortress, so as to set it on fire. But the defenders got such a fright when they saw this that they surrendered before the incendiary weapon could be put to the test.

O Connor finally accepted the inevitable and made his peace with the king. By way of compensation he was confirmed in possession of the 'king's cantreds', the area which the king had reserved for himself when Richard de Burgh was given Connacht. This conquest of Connacht was a clear indication of the strength of the colony when it could be marshalled and applied. It was also an expansion of feudal Ireland on a grand scale. From 1237 when, as the *Annals of Loch Cé* express it so succinctly, 'the barons of Erin came into Connacht and commenced to build castles in it', new manors were created all over the conquered areas. The Gaelic areas were still at a disadvantage militarily, though this was to be changed before too long. Meantime, however, the colony was being expanded and strengthened. In Ulster Hugh de Lacy was busy consolidating his lordship and in the south further inroads were made into the O Brien kingdom of Thomond. But just when it seemed that most of Ireland was going to be feudalised an extraordinary series of deaths among the great feudatories checked the expansion for good. In 1241 Walter de Lacy died, leaving no son: his great lordship was therefore partitioned among his two grand-daughters. Two years later his brother Hugh, earl of Ulster, died without an heir: his lordship therefore escheated to the Crown. In the same year, 1243, Richard de Burgh of Connacht died, leaving a minor as his heir. And most extraordinary of all, in 1245 the last of the Marshals died without a son, like his brothers before him, so that Leinster was partitioned among five co-heiresses. These deaths, affecting the greatest lordships in Ireland, brought to an end the great momentum towards expansion which the de Lacys and de Burgh personified. More than that, however, they weakened the conquest itself. For there can be no doubt that what had made these lordships strong in the first place was their great size. Partition weakened them; so did falling into the king's hand or that of another absentee, for the lack of immediate supervision by a resident lord who had a personal stake in the land had a bad effect on the settlers and could often lead to the running down of manors. The Gaelic revival which in the next century was to sweep away so much of the settlement did not begin as a result of these deaths. But there is no doubt that because further expansion was checked and Gaelic enclaves were left intact in too great a number and in too many parts of the island, recovery became possible.

Henry III was not the man to seize the opportunity which these deaths presented, despite the keenness with which he pursued royal rights in England and attacked liberties held by his subjects. He had no sustained interest in Ireland and he never seems to have contemplated any real attack on entrenched feudal claims here. Nor did he worry unduly about the aggrandisement of power among certain families. Indeed Walter de Burgh, who became lord of Connacht when he came of age in 1250, was eventually given the earldom of Ulster as well in 1264 and thus became immensely powerful. With the enormous power which control over such land resources gave him, earl Walter's son, the famous

'Red Earl', was in a position to defy the Dublin government. Apart from this spectacular rise of de Burgh power, the disappearance of the great Marshals and de Lacys left the way clear for two other families which were to dominate so much of the public life of Ireland to the end of the middle ages, the Geraldines perhaps the greatest of them all, and the Butlers. These three families, with the lesser satellites which orbited around them, were to become the main contestants for control of privilege and patronage at official level, and first the de Burghs and the Geraldines, and later the Geraldines and the Butlers, were to become enmeshed in savage contests which frequently caused death and destruction in many parts of the island.

The first half of the thirteenth century, then, saw the gradual expansion of the English colony in Ireland until it reached its greatest point when something like three-quarters of the island had been feudalised. It also saw the restoration of the great feudatories to power, after their defeat by King John. At the same time, it witnessed the further development of the royal administration to keep pace with the demands made by the enlarged colony. The exchequer became more sophisticated in its operation, developed new records and added greatly to its personnel. And local government was gradually strengthened not only by the extension of the shire system, but also through the application of the principle that the holder of a franchise was a royal official in the localities. But what was certainly the greatest single administrative development was the creation of an Irish chancery in July 1232, as part and parcel of the great reforms which followed the fall of Hubert de Burgh in England. One major purpose of these reforms was to overhaul completely the system of royal finance, and for this reason every important financial office in England was handed over to Peter de Rivaux, who was thus given the opportunity of carrying out the necessary changes. Peter was given a similar concentration of power in Ireland too, and though he naturally acted through deputies here he was nevertheless able to initiate a programme of reform which was to revolutionise the financial administration of the lordship and generally produce a tightening up in its system of government. Increased efficiency, as always, meant greater control by the king; and one reliable sign of this was the manner in which Henry III was able to make full use of the resources of the colony in his various military enterprises, as he did in 1241, during the campaign in Wales, against David, the son of Llywelyn the Great, or in 1242 during the expedition to Gascony. The best illustration of this, however, is the Welsh campaign of 1245, when a large military force arrived from Ireland to assist the king. What is especially interesting about this expedition is that it included three thousand infantry from Connacht under the leadership of Felim O Connor. This enormous number of men was delayed on its way to the king by a foray into Anglesey, during which they destroyed the island's supply of corn, thus depriving the Welsh of one of their main sources of food. But this did not prevent Henry from losing his temper at their late arrival, so that he cut their wages to ten days instead of the month or so to which they were entitled. Once again the Gaelic leaders had been taught not to trust the king. Before this Henry had summoned a large number of them to an abortive campaign in Scotland, and later they were to be summoned again. But none was to serve, save only some minor northern chieftains who followed the earl of Ulster.

The manner in which the Irish government answered the king's demands for help in 1245 is most impressive. Not only did the justiciar succeed in procuring a huge force of men, but ships, supplies of all kinds (including prefabricated brattices which were shipped from a number of Irish ports) and a large quantity of money were also dispatched. To do this efficiently required a high degree of control by the justiciar over a well organised administrative system, central and local. It is to the government of Henry III that much of the credit for this must go, even if it was building on the foundations laid by King John. But in 1254 Henry granted the lordship of Ireland to his eldest son Edward. From this time forward, until he died in 1307, it was Edward who who responsible for the lordship. And it was under him that it began to go into a decline from which it never recovered in the middle ages.

V Anglo-Irish Society

THE Ireland to which the Anglo-Normans came in the twelfth century was beginning to show features which in the course of time might have brought the island into conformity with the general social pattern of western Europe. Irish society was no longer purely tribal and it can be argued that it was manifesting signs of that 'incipient feudalism' so dear to some historians. Contact with Britain and Europe was having its effect. But Ireland was certainly not feudal. It was the invaders who introduced that complex of customs which goes by the name of feudalism, and they did so suddenly, often violently, planting it all over the land as they conquered it. Feudalism did not develop naturally in Ireland, arising to meet local social needs, as was so often the case elsewhere. It was a foreign intrusion, brought by conquerors, and so not attuned to the Gaelic world which reacted against it. This is important, for it helped to mark off a sharp division between the two societies which henceforth inhabited the island, the one Gaelic and non-feudal; the other Anglo-Irish and feudal. The division was very real, however blurred it may have become in many places with the passage of time, and it was to make the full assimilation of the one society to the othert difficult, and in the end impossible.

The feudalism which the conquerors brought with them was essentially French, just as they themselves were French speaking and the product of a society whose whole culture was French orientated. It involved a system of land tenure which was new, whereby all land in Ireland was held of the lord of Ireland (*dominus Hibernie*), the king of England for most of the medieval period. Those who held their land directly from him were his tenants in chief, no matter how small their holding of land was. They held their land on certain conditions, which were part of the feudal contract between them and the lord. This contract, and the personal relationship which it embodied, was of the essence of feudalism. It was binding on both parties and their successors, in perpetuity, and could only be broken for some few, limited reasons. Part of the bargain was that the recipient of land was able to pass it on intact as an inheritance to his heir, and that he enjoyed the protection of his lord at all times. But he had to perform certain services, the conditions on which he held his land. Generally speaking the most common was military service: depending on the amount of land he held he had to supply a fixed quota of knights (or in some cases fractions of knights, which were calculated in units of fighting men lower in status than the knight) to serve the lord, the service being limited by custom to forty days in the year. For many reasons this military service was from early on usually commuted to a money payment in Ireland, called 'royal service' (known in England as 'scutage'). When the feudal army was summoned to serve in a campaign, the tenants in chief usually paid royal service instead of supplying their quota of knights. With the money raised in this way the government was able to pay troops who would be willing to serve for longer than the customary period of forty days. Consequently, longer campaigns became possible.

The tenant also had to do suit at the lord's court, he had to give him financial aid on certain occasions (limited by *Magna Carta* to three), and he had to give counsel whenever the lord requested it. These last two obligations were most important, for from them developed the idea of a representative parliament and the doctrine of consent, both of them a distinctive contribution of the middle ages to modern Ireland. In addition, the lord had rights of wardship and marriage over an heir who was a minor, and in default of an heir the land became an escheat and returned to the lord.

Such a simple outline can only hint at the complexity of the relationship between the lord and his tenant in chief. Many of these tenants, of course, were given huge areas of land by the king. The grants of Leinster and Meath are obvious examples. Such tenants in chief had to subinfeudate their enormous fief by making grants of land to other sub-tenants and imposing much the same sort of conditions as those under which the tenant in chief held his land of the king. This could often mean a gain for the tenant in chief: for example Leinster, which owed the service of 100 knights to the king, produced 180 through subinfeudation—a very considerable profit to the lord. In this way the tenants in chief themselves usually became the lords of other tenants, who in turn might be the lords of tenants of smaller holdings, and so on. A feudal hierarchy was thus established, with a whole complex of rights and duties, and of mutual obligations, all bound up with the holding of land. The system of land tenure, then, was at the heart of feudalism, for on it the structure of society, outside the towns, was based.

An obvious question arises here: where did these small tenants come from? Recent investigations have suggested that nearly all of them came from outside Ireland and mainly from those areas in England and Wales from which the greater tenants were drawn. They were colonists coming to establish a colony in Ireland. How was it possible to attract them to Ireland, a land which was not only foreign, but hostile and dangerous? It is probable that a rising population and a resultant land shortage, which was becoming acute in the late twelfth and thirteenth centuries, was one fact which helped to bring settlers to Ireland. Indeed it has been argued that land hunger became so acute in the thirteenth century that it was one reason why tenants in England accepted a life of servitude in return for a plot of land: for land, some men were willing to give up their liberty. The easy availability of land has always, in all ages, been a powerful force in attracting people to new settlements. In the case of medieval Ireland, however, we know that an extra inducement was found which encouraged men to settle in an alien and hostile environment. This was the offer of burgage tenure and the many privileges which went with it. It was for this reason that such an inordinate number of small boroughs were created in Ireland during the age of settlement, most of them being nothing more than small villages. There must have been other inducements as well, sufficient to bring colonists in large numbers. For there is no doubt that there was a large-scale migration of peasants into Ireland to populate the manors which were everywhere established as soon as the land was conquered and incastellated.

These manors were also an essential part of the new social structure which was imposed on Ireland. They were modelled, with minor differences, on those with which their lords were familiar in England and Wales. On a typical manor the population was rigidly divided into a number of different classes. The basic division, common to the whole feudal word (and indeed to

Gaelic Ireland as well), was between free and unfree. At the top of the scale was the lord of the manor, who was most frequently a layman, though he could be a bishop, an abbot, or some other ecclesiastic. Immediately below him were the free tenants. They held their lands on normal feudal tenures, which usually involved services of different kinds and, here in Ireland, a money rent as well. Below them were the farmers, who held smaller areas of land on lease for a fixed term, paying a rent for it in money. Gavillers, lower down on the scale, were tenants at will, again paying a money rent. So too did the cottars who held only their cottages and a tiny patch of land with it. The cottars were the farm labourers of the time, finding ready employment on their own or on neighbouring manors. All of these, the farmers, gavillers, and cottars, were personally free, even though they owed suit at the lord's court and had to perform specified labour services at certain times of the year. The unfree tenants were the villeins, called in Ireland betaghs (*betagii*), who were tied to the manor and were bound, in theory at least, to render labour services to their lord at his will. They were intended to provide the basic labour force which the lord of every manor required if he were to work his demesne lands adequately. And this is why we find that one of the clauses of the Treaty of Windsor in 1175 insisted that those of the native population who had fled before the conquerors should be compelled to return to the new manors. Many of them would be betaghs or serfs, the labour force of the manors. Even if many of the native population were reduced to a servile status as a result of the change in their condition following the Anglo-Norman invasion, there were many others who were unfree and even in some cases tied to the land before the settlers arrived. It was probably those whom the settlers were most anxious to have back on the new manors. In the course of time, however, they gained the protection of custom. Many of them became quite well to do, certainly much better off than the cottars, and by the end of the thirteenth century many of the labour services required of them were already being commuted to a money payment.

On most manors the lord had a considerable acreage in demesne, usually separate from the land cultivated by is tenants. At Mallow in 1282, 160 acres were cultivated by the lord—this would be about 400 acres, the medieval Irish acre being the equivalent of roughly two and a half statute acres; at Cloncurry in 1304 the demesne included 125 acres; at Lisronagh in 1333 there were 358 acres in demesne. To work this land the lord relied on the customary labour services of his tenants and on hired labour. Labour services, of course, varied widely; but generally they involved work at ploughing in the spring and reaping in the autumn. For example, a charter of the archbishop of Dublin to the men of Finglas stated that they were bound

to perform the accustomed services to the archbishop and his successors, viz. whoever has a plough ought to plough yearly for the use of his lord one acre at the pleasure of the lord or his bailiff; he who shall not have a whole plough, ought to plough according to his means, and as he is able. Also, they should give the service of one day to carry hay, with horses and carts; and each of them shall find one man for two days to reap the lord's corn in autumn, and besides shall perform the service of one day to carry the lord's corn, with horses and carts.

A lease of 1352 specified that the tenant, who held his land for a term of sixteen years from the prior of Holy Trinity, was to pay thirty shillings rent for the first eight years and forty shillings for the remainder of the term. He was to

plough with his plough for one day at winter seed time, and for one day at Lent seed time, upon the land of the demesnes of the priory at Clonsken; to reap with one man for one day the corn there in harvest; to carry with his cart the corn for one day, or with a car for two days, or with two cars for one day; to give two gallons of ale as often as he brewed; to render suit to the manor court as often as he is summoned.

It is clear that while labour services were an important element of the feudal structure imposed on Ireland, they were never as heavy, for any class of tenant, as they were in England. This was undoubtedly the result of the need to attract settlers to the Irish manors. Furthermore, in many parts of Ireland, from quite early on, such services as existed were often commuted, in part or in whole, to money payments. This can be well illustrated from an important piece of Irish legislation from 1299, a year of exceptional harvests which increased the demand for agricultural labour and thereby not only accelerated the existing tendency towards commutation, but also forced up wages. An ordinance of that year (which anticipated by fifty years the famous English Statute of Labourers) attempted to peg wages and even to reimpose services. It shows us not only the importance of labour services in a period of labour shortage, but also how far the process of commutation had gone. This can be demonstrated in many individual cases. For example, at Grangegorman the cottar Robert le Dryver held his plot at a rent of 12d. per year, with the stipulation that 'he shall hoe for two days with one man and he shall reap for two days with one man'. But a rental of 1326 makes it clear that by then the services had been commuted into a money payment: 'the said services are worth 4d. a year'. The result of this process of commutation was that most commonly the lord of the manor had to rely mainly on hired labour to work his demesnes. The accounts of one Christ Church manor near Dublin for the harvest of 1344 illustrate this well: of a total of 562 days' work by reapers, 471 were paid for and only 91 were the product of required labour services.

The intensive cultivation of the demesne lands made most manors self-sufficient and usually left a surplus which was available for market. The manors supplied a network of markets throughout the colony and these in turn supported a trade in foreign imports and domestic exports which enabled the ports on the Irish coast to survive. Agriculture, of course, was the basis of the economy. The manors made possible intensive agriculture of a kind never witnessed by Ireland before. But for this something more was needed, a stability and order in society which would enable the rural population to invest heavily in agriculture without too much risk (without such an investment a real advance in production was impossible) and capital to make possible the operations which were often necessary, such as constructing larger buildings, clearing and draining land, or purchasing the right equipment. The Anglo-Normans in their settlements provided the first prerequisite, law and order; and Jews to a very limited extent and later Italians provided much of the capital. One does not have to argue for a *Pax Normanica* in Ireland to see that in much of the island the institutions of government which were established by the settlers and the very pattern of the settlement itself (of castles, towns, villages, manors, and the new-style monasteries) gave an order and peace to the countryside which was a guarantee of prosperity and development. The result was a tremendous economic expansion, so great that it can truly be called a revolution.

This is particularly true of the agricultural system, which was suddenly transformed. Basically there were three reasons for this: the new techniques, methods, and even crops which the settlers introduced; the greatly increased area which was brought under tillage; and the development of sheep-farming on a vast scale, producing wool for export. To some extent the Cistercians had begun to show the way after the foundation of Mellifont; but it was the Anglo-Norman settlers who were to revolutionise Irish agriculture. Probably the most important single change which they introduced was the open field system, where great open fields, from 200–500 acres in extent, were employed, with the holdings arranged in long strips, often of 220 yards. Part of this system, too, was three course rotation of winter corn, spring corn and fallow. The arable land was divided into three sections, roughly equal in area. In the winter one section was ploughed and sown with wheat or rye; about Lent the second section was sown with oats, barley, peas; the third lay fallow and was pastured. In 1326, for example, at the manor of Swords 220 acres were under wheat, another 220 were under oats, barley, etc., and another 220 were fallow. At Finglas the proportion was 96, 98 and 103 acres respectively, and at Collon, 50, 48, and 58 acres. The land which was to lie fallow that year was usually ploughed in April, and then was lightly ploughed again at the end of June to destroy the weeds.

This system was designed to preserve the fertility of the land and under the Anglo-Normans the practice of fertilising the land became more regular. On the manor of Old Ross we find sea sand being used extensively for manure. It was taken from the sand banks in the estuary of the river Barrow, which was tidal. But it was a costly method, since the expenses of transporting the sand were high: at the manor of Old Ross the cost came to as much as 8s. an acre. A much cheaper method, and one commonly used, was burning the land. At Old Ross again the cost was given at 16d. per acre, with an additional 4d. per acre for spreading the burned soil. This method was clearly learnt by the settlers from their Gaelic betaghs, since it is described in the accounts as *more patrie* ('after the manner of the country'). Near the coast, of course, seaweed was extensively used and this was the cheapest method of all. But such primitive methods of fertilisation could not make the land fully productive and generally the crop yield per acre was low. For example, in 1297 near Drogheda 22 acres of land sown with wheat produced only 40 crannocks (each crannock, the equivalent of an English quarter, being valued at 4s. 6d.) and 33 acres of oats produced only 60 crannocks (at 4s. each).

Of the grain crops produced oats seems to have been the most common, with wheat a close second and barley a long way behind. It has been estimated, from the frequency of mention of the different crops in manorial records, that the proportion was something like this: oats, 22; wheat, 19; barley, 5. This, of course, is only a rough approximation and would not be true for all manors. At Old Ross in 1283, for example, only 15½ acres were sown in wheat, with 82 acres in oats and 28½ acres in rye. As we saw, the yield per acre was low, something like twice the amount sown. There were many gardens, too, fenced with thorns and producing apples, vegetables and herbs. And always part of the demesne was left in meadow to produce grass. There was great variety from one manor to the next. At Toolooban, near Loughrea in county Galway, there were 32 acres in meadow (compared with the enormous acreage of 570 acres which was under tillage). Many animals were also kept on the manors. At Old Ross in 1283, besides 1,397 sheep, the lord of the manor had after sales and losses 4 heifers, 39 oxen, 1 bull, 29 cows, 14 calves, 5 pigs, 9 swans, and 11 pea-fowl. A much smaller manor at Dunohill in county Tipperary had, in 1295, 300 cows, 120 heifers, 28 mares, 4 horses, 500 sheep, 200 lambs, 100 pigs, 100 goats, 40 kids and 28 oxen.

There can be no doubt that the demesne lands on the manors were worked for profit. Much of the grain produced and many of the animals raised were intended for market. Naturally the home market consumed much of the available surplus, but a surprisingly large amount was exported. Many religious houses in Britain, and even France, procured considerable quantities of wheat and oats in Ireland, often from manors which belonged to them or to their Irish daughter houses. Merchants bought Irish grain for export. There was a particularly lively trade with Gascony, and especially with Bordeaux, where wine provided a profitable return cargo, Perhaps the best indication of the success of the Irish manorial economy in producing a great surplus of agricultural produce for export is the extent to which Edward I and his son were able to use this surplus to supply their armies, especially in Scotland and Gascony. For example, extant accounts (which are by no means complete) show that in 1297 about 11,500 quarters of wheat and 1,850 quarters of oats were shipped from Ireland to the army in Gascony. Ireland had become one of the king's great storehouses of grain, a fact which argues strongly for great developments in agricultural techniques and production earlier in the thirteenth century. Right through the Scottish wars of independence the Dublin government was expected to provide large quantities of wheat and oats, in addition to other produce supplied by the manors of the lordship. In December 1298, for example, the Irish justiciar, John Wogan, was instructed to provide 8,000 quarters of wheat, 10,000 quarters of oats, 2,000 quarts of crushed malt, 1,000 tuns of wine (Ireland had become a centre of trade in wine with France), 500 carcasses of beef, 1,000 bacons, and 20,000 dried fish.

The results, then, of what we may well call an agricultural revolution were spectacular. But without a doubt the most extraordinary development was in sheep farming. With the rise of the great cloth industries of western Europe wool was greatly in demand and the lords of many Irish manors were quick to avail of this growing market. An outbreak of sheep-scab in England in the decade between 1280–90 greatly increased the demand for Irish wool even though it was of poor quality and the number of sheep in Ireland climbed in proportion. This extraordinary rise in numbers can be well illustrated from the accounts of the manor of Old Ross, which show the numbers of sheep at different times within that decade as follows: 1281: 1,182; 1283/84: 1,397; 1285/86: 1,442; 1288: 2,160. So that in seven years the number of sheep very nearly doubled. Other manors would show a similar increase reflecting the same spectacular development. The custom levied on all wool, woolfells and hides exported from Ireland from 1275 onwards will also help to give us some idea of the huge quantity shipped abroad, which suggests large-scale sheep farming by the end of the thirteenth century. The rate of the levy was 6s. 8d. on every sack (of 42 stone) of wool, 6s. 7d. on every 300 woolfells, and 13s. 4d. on every last (or 200 hides) of leather. In a year and a half, between April 1277 and September 1278, the custom amounted to over £2,026. Reducing this to either wool or woolfells, it would represent nearly 7,000 sacks of wool[7] or 1,822,000 woolfells, or 3,039 lasts of leather. It would, of course, be a mixture of all three and it is not now possible to work out the proportion of sacks of wool to woolfells to hides which the total yield from the custom represents. But at least we can get some idea of what large quantities are represented by small sums of money. The tiny port of Dingle in county Kerry yielded a custom of just over £15 in one year, 1287, which would represent 45 sacks[8], or more than 13,500 woolfells, or 22½ lasts of leather. Behind these exports were the entrepreneurs, mainly Italians; and behind them again the sheep runs on many an Irish manor or monastic grange.

This great increase in agricultural produce was partly the result of the growth of a demand in the market towns which sprang up everywhere throughout the settled area. Indeed the rapid proliferation of fairs and markets all over feudal Ireland in the thirteenth century is a sure indication of the expanding commercial activity of the colony. So too is the increasing number of towns which were founded. All over western Europe this was a great period of urban development and Ireland was no exception. It was under the Anglo-Normans that town life became important in Ireland. The newcomers not only took over the ports of Scandinavian origin, but they proceeded to build towns in those parts of the country which they feudalised. It is worth remembering that many of the lords who came to Ireland after the invasion were already experienced founders of towns in England and especially south Wales. Wherever they built their castles a small community formed itself. Many of these were never more than nucleated villages, new to Ireland in any case, even though they may have been given borough status as a way of attracting colonists. But many other such communities grew into proper towns and soon became local commercial centres under the protection and patronage of their lords. Such were Trim, for example, or Kilkenny, Carlow or Nenagh. In the course of time many of them were walled, to protect the inhabitants and offer the kind of

---

[7]Medieval measurements were rarely very accurate. The *sack* of wool was supposed to contain 42 stone, so that 7,000 sacks should contain 294,000 stone of wool. The *last* of hides contained 200 hides, so 3,039 lasts would contain 607,800 hides.

[8]These should contain 1,890 stone and 4,500 hides respectively.

safety which would attract buyers and sellers to market. A well-known poem of the thirteenth century has for its theme the enclosing of New Ross with walls. It tells how the burgesses began to mark out the fosse on 2 February 1265 and hired a hundred men a day to dig it out. They passed a bye law (such as the poet never heard of in France or England) that all the people of the town, grouped by trade or craft, were to help at the work on the wall: the vintners, mercers, merchants and drapers on Monday; the tailors, cloth workers, fullers and saddlers on Tuesday; the cordwainers, tanners and butchers on Wednesday; and so on. They dug a fosse, the poet tells us, '20 feet in depth and its length extended over a league'. When it was completed, it gave complete security. The town had all that was required for its defence, according to the poem: plenty of weapons and more than enough armed men—363 crossbowmen, 'as counted at their musters and enrolled in the muster roll'; 1,200 archers; 3,000 men with lances and axes; and 104 knights. The numbers are hardly credible; but clearly New Ross was well defended and secure from attack.

Very many of these new towns were given the right to hold a market and an annual eight-day fair. They received charters from their lords, and sometimes from the king himself, granting them certain rights, privileges and immunities. For example, the little hamlet of Moone in county Kildare was given a very elaborate charter from William Marshal which conferred on the burgesses the most extensive privileges—their own hundred court, freedom from all tolls and customs, a monopoly of trade, the right to 'contract matrimony for themselves, their sons, their daughters and widows, without licence from their lords', freedom from wardship, the right to have a guild merchant and other guilds, a common in the woods, and other rights besides. Burgesses were thus in a position to manage their own affairs and to provide the sort of guarantees which were necessary for trade. Merchants and traders were attracted from afar to the larger and more important towns which became marketing centres for the districts in which they stood. It is noticeable that each of them was built in a position which was favourable for trade, on a navigable river (and rivers were the main commercial highways of the age) or a main road. New Ross, for example, was called by various names—*Villa Nova Pontis Willielmi Marescalli* ('The new town of the bridge of William Marshal'), or *Nova Villa de Ponte de Ross* ('The new town of the bridge of Ross'), or more simple *Ros Ponte* ('Ross bridge')—in which the common element was the great bridge which first gave the town its importance. By the end of the thirteenth century the whole countryside was dotted with these market towns. In 1299 there were no fewer than thirty-eight in county Cork alone.

But it was the seaport towns, including those of Scandinavian origin, which especially prospered under Anglo-Norman rule and organisation. Dublin, Cork, Waterford, Wexford and Limerick were enlarged, strengthened and given a new vigour under royal charters. New ports, like Drogheda (which was really two ports, one on each side of the Boyne), Galway, New Ross and Carrickfergus were similarly developed. All of this, of course, had an important effect on external trade, for these ports not only provided an outlet for the exportable produce of Ireland, but also gave the kind of facilities which attracted foreign importers and greatly increased the flow of goods into Ireland.

Increasing urbanisation and an expanding trade went together. The one depended on the other. Most of the towns had been built, as we saw, at points favourable for commercial activity, while the older Scandinavian ports were already linked with the main trade routes in Europe. The majority of the larger towns enjoyed the privileges which Bristol possessed in England, or else what were known as the 'customs of Breteuil'. These latter were first granted to that little town in Normandy in 1060, brought to England after the conquest, and introduced from there into Ireland. They conferred certain basic municipal rights, such as freeing all burgesses from villein status, and granted the town at least the elements of self government. They were granted by Walter de Lacy to his town of Drogheda on the southern banks of the Boyne in 1194, and many other Irish towns were similarly honoured, some of them small places like Duleek in county Meath, or Rathcoole in county Kildare. Here the burgesses enjoyed the enormous privilege of self-government, with their own court (the hundred court), a monopoly of trade, the power to legislate and to tax themselves, and later the right to elect representatives to parliament.

Within the large towns the mercantile community was probably organised into a typical medieval guild. Nearly all our information comes from Dublin, which was very much larger than any other city in Ireland, so that it would be dangerous to generalise. But before the end of the twelfth century Dublin already had its Guild Merchant, to which all who wished to engage in trade must belong. In the Lord John's charter of 1192 to Dublin, one of the privileges granted to the citizens was that 'they shall have their rightful guilds, as fully as the burgesses of Bristol have or are accustomed to have', and this he later confirmed as king in 1200 and 1215. By 1226 the Guild Merchant was flourishing, since no less than 224 members were admitted in that year, most of them from England, Scotland and Wales, though some came from much further afield. In 1256, sixty-five new members were admitted and the following year 140 more. Those admitted represented more than fifty different occupations and the number grew yearly. Soon there was need for diversification and out of the Guild Merchant grew the more specialised craft guilds. By the end of the fifteenth century, in a remarkable regulation governing the order of the great pageant on Corpus Christi (when a series of miracle and morality plays was performed) no less than twenty-eight craft groups were listed, each playing its part:

Glovers: Adam and Eve, with an angel following bearing a sword; Weavers: Abraham and Isaac, with their altar and a lamb and their offering; Skinners, House-Carpenters and Tanners and Embroiderers: the body of the Camel and Our Lady and her child well apparelled, with St Joseph to lead the camel, and Moses with the children of Israel, and the Porters to bear the camel. And Stainers and Painters to paint the head of the camel.

Each guild was highly organised under a master, two wardens and a council, elected annually. They had a monopoly over the craft (or crafts, since sometimes more than one craft formed a guild, such as the barbers and surgeons). Moreover, since the municipal council was frequently elected from among the brethren of the guilds, they had a virtual monopoly of town government also. The guild looked after its own, helped them in distress, settled their quarrels, saw to their funerals, but above all regulated carefully the practice of their craft. Admission was carefully controlled and Gaelic Irish were excluded. In Dublin, for example, no one was to be admitted 'without he be of English name and blood, of honest conversation, and also free citizen of the city'. In 1355 the archbishop of Armagh, the famous Richard fitz Ralph, preached a sermon in Drogheda in which he condemned the guilds for the sin of excluding 'a certain nation' from membership. But evidently this exclusive character was not always maintained. There is evidence, for example, of Gaelic apprentices being admitted in Dundalk in the mid-fourteenth century. Apprenticeship normally lasted seven years and upon execution of his 'masterpiece' in some guilds, a candidate was fully admitted and given the freedom of the city.

Each guild was under the patronage of either Our Lady or a saint, just as the Guild Merchant was under the patronage of the Holy Trinity. For example, in Dublin the Guild of Carpenters, Millers, Masons and Heliers (Tilers), was under the patronage of the Blessed Virgin and St Thomas, and attached to the Lady Chapel of Thomascourt abbey; the Tailors under the Blessed Virgin and St John the Baptist, attached to the church of St John the Baptist in Fishamble Street: the Barber-Surgeons under St Mary Magdalene, and attached to the chapel of St Mary Magdalene in the Hospital of St John outside Newgate. The feast of the patron was celebrated annually with great ceremonies, with attendance at mass compulsory on all the brethren, followed by a feast.

The guilds, of course, were composed of the well-to-do citizens. The majority of the inhabitants of any town were unskilled labourers, who lived in squalid and overcrowded conditions, at the mercy of poverty, plague, fire and the not infrequent attacks of enemies and vagabonds. Every famine sent swarms to the towns and the unsettled condition of the Irish countryside often resulted in refugees seeking protection in the towns. Beggars were everywhere and not only were they a problem because of their numbers, and their frequent assaults on citizens, but also because they were carriers of plague. So, too, were the pigs which were kept in enormous numbers in every town. In Dublin they ran wild in the streets. Small wonder that the oath of the provost of Dublin made him promise 'not to suffer any cattle to be slaughtered within your walls; neither to suffer any swine to run about the streets, and to banish all beggars in time of sickness and plague'. The picture which emerges of the condition of Dublin in 1489 from a letter of the earl of Kildare is grim indeed:

The king has been informed that dungheaps, swine, hogsties, and other nuisances in the streets, lanes and suburbs of Dublin infect the air and produce mortality, fevers and pestilence throughout that city. Many citizens and sojourners have thus died in Dublin. The fear of pestilence prevents the coming thither of lords, ecclesiastics and lawyers. Great detriments thence arise to his majesty, as well as dangers to his subjects and impediments to business. The king commands the mayor and bailiffs to cause forthwith the removal of all swine, and to have the streets and lands freed from ordure, so as to prevent loss of life from pestilential exhalations. The mayor is to expel all Irish vagrants and mendicants from the city.

Outside the towns, life was often violent and in Ireland, where in the later middle ages so much of the land was disturbed by war or the threat of war, there was little to encourage the arts of peace. But in the thirteenth century feudal Ireland was comparatively peaceful. Travel was easy and communications rapidly improved. This no doubt helped the expanding commercial life of the colony—indeed good communications were necessary if trade were to prosper. The Irish government caused new roads to be built, ordered passes in the woods to be cleared, and bridges or causeways to be constructed, or old ones to be properly maintained. Rivers, of course, were widely used, mainly because water transport was always cheaper and easier. Frequently, therefore, we find that old weirs and other obstacles were removed from rivers to facilitate traffic. In 1220, for example, the Liffey was ordered to be freed from obstructions, so that ships and barges might use it 'as they did of old'.

There were two other developments which certainly helped to revolutionise Irish trade. The first and more important of these was the provision of an adequate coinage, acceptable to foreign merchants and exchangeable abroad. A beginning had been made in Dublin before the Anglo-Normans came, but it was after the invasion that a series of mints was established, with expert officials and a system of checks, and an official coinage regularly produced. The principal mint was naturally in Dublin, but at various times royal mints existed elsewhere, such as Limerick, Waterford, Kilkenny, Carrickfergus, Cork, Galway, Drogheda, and Trim.

The other innovation which was important was the attempt to standardise weights and measures. The wide variation in these from place to place was always a problem in the middle ages. In Ireland, although the reform measures were never permanently successful, the most glaring discrepancies were removed and a greater uniformity than ever before was brought into existence throughout the colony. In 1268 the Irish council ordained that London weights and measures should be uniformly followed throughout the lordship. A special official, a 'keeper of weights and measures', was also added to the administration, with the standard weights and measures kept in the exchequer in Dublin.

All the conditions were present, then, for a great expansion of trade in the thirteenth century, and long before the end of the century commercial prosperity was evident throughout Anglo-Ireland. One sign of this prosperity is the building activity which was widespread throughout the colony. In particular, the enclosing of many towns with walls is evidence of the new affluence. In order to pay for these walls, towns were often given the right to levy tolls (called 'murage') on certain goods for market entering or leaving the town. These murage grants are interesting because they list the principal commodities likely to be bought or sold within the town and in this way they give us some idea of the character of the trade of that town. A good number survive, listing a bewildering variety of agricultural produce, imported luxuries, and manufactured goods. None can be picked out as typical, but that for Fethard in 1292 may help to illustrate the kind of commodities in which a small Irish vill of the period traded. For every quarter of wheat for sale, the burgesses might levy ½d; each horse and mare, ox or cow, ½d; each hide of horse, mare, ox or cow, fresh, salt or tanned, ¼d; each cart carrying salt meat, 1½d; 5 pigs, ½d; 10 gammons, ½d; each fresh salmon, ¼d; each lamprey before easter, ¼d; 10 sheep, goats or hogs, 1d; 10 fleeces, ½d; 100 woolfells, skins of goats, stags, hinds, bucks, and does, 1d; each 100 skins of lambs, kids, hares, rabbits, foxes, cats, squirrels, ½d; each cartload of salt, 1d; each horseload of salt, by the week, ¼d; each horse--load of cloths, ½d; each entire cloth sold, ¼d; each hundred of linen cloth, each hundred of Irish cloth sold, ¼d; each cloth of silk with gold, samite, diaper, and Baudekyn, ½d; each cloth of silk without gold, ¼d; each cartload of sea fish sold, 4d; each horse-load of sea fish sold, ½d; each hogshead of wine sold, 1½d; each horse-load of cinders for sale, ½d; each horse-load of honey,

1d; each hogshead of honey, 3d; each sack of wool, 2d; each truss of cloths brought by cart, 3d; each horse-load of cloth and other diverse and minute articles coming to the vill, ½d; each cartload of iron, 1d; each cartload of lead, 2d; each horse-load of tan, by the week, ½d; each hundred of avoir-dupois, 1d; each wey of soap and grease, 1d; each quarter of woad, ¼d; each hundred of alum and copperas, ½d; 2,000 onions, ¼d; each horse-load of garlic, ½d; each 1,000 herrings, ¼d; each 100 boards, ½d; each millstone, ½d; each quarter of salt, ¼d; each quarter of flour, ½d; each wey of cheese and butter, 1d; each dozen horse-loads of coal, ½d; each cartload of firewood by the week, ½d; each bale of cordwain, 3d; each 1,000 nails for roofs of houses, ¼d; each 100 horse-shoes and tires for carts, ½d; 2,000 of all kinds of nails, excepting nails for carts and roofs of houses, ¼d; each truss of any kind of goods coming to the vill and exceeding the value of 2s, ¼d.

Above all, it was overseas trade which prospered and flourished under the influence of the settlers and the foreign merchants who were soon attracted to the expanding market of Ireland. The kings of England always encouraged Irish commerce. Henry II granted the burgesses of Dublin freedom from tolls throughout his lands of England, Wales, Normandy, and France. King John in 1204 helped to establish some great fairs, to attract foreign traders, and Henry III in 1221 encouraged trade between Dublin and La Rochelle. Before long many foreign merchants were trading with Ireland and, most important of all, the great Italian merchant and banking companies found their way to Ireland. More than anything else, their presence testifies to the expanding character of Irish commerce, for the Italians were to be found only where the pickings were good. They were first employed as collectors of papal revenues in Ireland, but soon they were active in every aspect of the commercial life of the colony. As money lenders they provided much of the capital which an expanding economy demanded. But they were heavily involved in trade as well. Foremost were the great companies of Florence and Lucca, like the Frescobaldi and the Ricardi. But lesser companies and many individuals were also involved. Through them Irish produce found better markets abroad, for not only did the Italians have the contacts which enabled new markets to be opened up, they had (what was possibly more important) the ability to provide credit facilities abroad through their network of houses. The Italians were in a dominant position in Irish trade in the thirteenth and early fourteenth centuries, being particularly prominent in the wool trade. But the more important of them were ruined by their credit dealings with the English king and gradually their influence in Ireland waned and the initiative passed to the local merchant families which arose to take their place. The Italians were still coming in the fifteenth century, however. In 1413 several Florentine families were settled here and one of the most important narratives of a pilgrimage to St Patrick's Pugatory in Lough Derg was left by a Florentine merchant, Antonio Mannini. There was still a flourishing trade with Italy, especially in the hides which went to supply the leather industry there. Enormous numbers of hides were exported annually, reflecting the huge herds of cattle which were such a dominant feature of the Irish country scene.

Ireland's main markets, however, were much nearer home in Britain and the north-west of Europe. Some of the necessities which she lacked had naturally to be imported. Of these salt was probably the most important, since it was essential for preserving meat, fish, and to some extent hides as well. It remained a major, though seasonal, import right through the middle ages. Iron, too, was constantly in demand (though every attempt was made to exploit Ireland's meagre mineral resources, including silver, copper and lead, in addition to iron). Both of these were useful return cargoes on ships carrying Irish goods abroad. But far more important was wine, which was so valuable as a cargo that Ireland became an entrepôt for a time. Great quantities were shipped from France, especially Gascony, though some came from Spain and Portugal as well. In the thirteenth and early fourteenth centuries much of this was re-exported to England. In the first instance these exports of wine from Ireland were intended for royal armies on campaign and through this trade useful links were established with small ports in Scotland and Wales. But in the later middle ages this side of the Irish wine trade declined and for the most part only what was required for domestic consumption was imported. All sorts of manufactured articles were brought in, armour, nails, knives, pots and pans. But on the whole Ireland was able to supply her own needs through domestic manufacture and it was mainly luxury goods of foreign manu-

facture which were imported. Soft leather goods from Europe, fine jewellery from Spain, silk, cloth of gold, spices and dried fruit, perfumes, drugs, almonds, pepper, and all sorts of fine cloth. Since the many churches, especially those in the towns, required rich cloths and precious objects to adorn their altars and shrines, there was a thriving trade in ornaments and costly cloth and vestments. When the archbishop of Tuam died in 1393, he had

a chasuble of red samite, a great cross of pearls, two precious embroidered choir copes, a clasp for a cope with an image of the deity and precious stones, a gilt crest for the head of the cope with divers shields and precious stones, and an amice with pearls, of varied work.

John of Sandford, an archbishop of Dublin, left when he died (amongst other chattels), three silver ewers, five silver vases of large size and another vase, two gilt cups, six silver plates, twenty-three spoons, forty-two silver dishes, twenty-eight silver salt cellars, and a plate with a cover. This was exceptional. The average man possessed only a small quantity of silver or plate. The will of Hugh Gilliane, a fairly prosperous citizen of Dublin, shows that in 1474 he owned four brass pots to the value of 16s; one bell, value 3s. 4d; one skillet, value 4s; four brass candlesticks, value 8d; two silver cups, value 40s; four maser cups (made of wood, often used for drinking and sometimes given names), value 16s; one 'nut' (or cup made from half a coconut, mounted and covered), value 3s 4d; ten platters, eight dishes and four saucers of pewter, value 4s; three basins with one ewer, value 2s; one silver girdle worth 4s; twelve silver spoons worth 16s; household furniture to the value of 6s 8d.

Another important item of import was cloth. Ireland developed her own cloth industry and many Irish trained weavers found ready employment in England. But the coarse Irish wool was not suitable for weaving fine light cloth and great numbers of English woollen cloths were shipped to Ireland annually. Most of these came through Bristol, which was always the leading English port in Anglo-Irish trade. During one winter Ireland received a third of Bristol's total export of cloth.

In return for all of these expensive imports, Ireland was able to offer a wide variety of goods. For example, even then Irish horses, small, light and fast, were prized. Henry II took some horses with him after his expedition to Ireland, and thereafter there was a steady export of them not only to England, but to the continent as well. Hawks and other birds of prey were also in steady demand. But these were only minor commodities in Ireland's expanding overseas trade in the thirteenth century. Raw wool was shipped in large quantities, even though its poor quality meant that many of the continental factories would not use it. In the fourteenth century, however, a native cloth industry began to expand when a demand grew for the Irish mantle (or *fallaing*), for which the Irish wool produced a coarse, heavy cloth. In the winter of 1479–80 nearly 400 were shipped to Bristol alone and in 1504 well over 2,000 went to Bristol and about 500 to Bridgewater. Irish frieze was also popular in England and the continent, where it was cheap and therefore in demand in the poorer and colder areas. The needs of the home market therefore meant a decline in the export of wool and in the fifteenth century linen became a major export. During one year alone over 20,000 yards of Irish linen were shipped to Bristol. Hides, too, were being sent out of the country in great numbers from early in the thirteenth century and were in demand as far away as Italy. Many a leather manufacturer depended on Irish hides. But probably the most important export of all was fish, whether fresh, salted or smoked. Herrings especially went overseas in great numbers, mainly to England, where Bristol was the main port of entry. A well known English proverb of the fifteenth century said: 'Herring of Sligo and salmon of Bann has made in Bristol many a rich man'. But in addition to salmon and herrings, cod, hake, ling, whiting, pollock, and even whale, seal and porpoise were exported. Comparatively little meat was shipped abroad, which is a clear indication that in sharp contrast to today cattle were reared mainly for their hides.

For a time in the thirteenth and fourteenth centuries Ireland was a great producer of corn, beans, and peas, with a huge surplus for export. It was possibly the demands of the royal purveyors trying to feed the armies of England which stimulated this great production of grain crops. Many a lord grew rich on the profits. But for one reason or another tillage declined in Ireland in the fourteenth century and much land went back to pasture. The gradual disappearance of the betaghs, the loss of labour services, the great scarcity and high cost of labour after the Black Death, which was made worse by the continual emigration of farm labourers to England—all this undoubtedly helped to bring about the change. It was cheaper to raise stock than to plough. It was also safer, and there can be no doubt that the growing insecurity of life in the fourteenth century, the result of war and the general unsettled conditions of the time, helped the change. There was less danger of loss of cattle than of too easily destroyed crops. At any rate, the change took place. One can see it in the early fourteenth century on a de Burgh manor in county Meath, where an inquisition revealed that there were '370 acres which used to be under the lord's plough and were worth per acre in time of peace 10d., but now, because they lie waste and untilled and in the march among the Irish, each acre is worth for grazing 1d. per annum'.

The effect, then, was that corn production declined, the number of cattle grew and the export of hides became a most important commodity in Ireland's overseas trade. A certain amount of fur and skins was also sent abroad; sheep, lamb and kid were common enough, and less so rabbit, fox, otter, and even wolf. Irish timber, too, was shipped to England for military purposes, often in a manufactured state. For example, in 1225 the justiciar was ordered to make 200 ashen oars for galleys and to ship them to Winchelsea, together with two cargoes of boards. Galleys were built in Ireland for the king in the thirteenth century, at Dublin, Drogheda, Cork, Limerick and other ports, and wooden brattices were shipped from here on a number of occasions. Right through the medieval period Irish oak was much prized in England and France.

Irish trade, then, was thriving in the middle ages. It was by no means confined to England: many of the most important markets were in Europe. And after the great age of the Italians it was mostly in Irish hands. It is clear, too, that by the fifteenth century the balance of trade was very much in Ireland's favour and that the country was getting more prosperous by the year. No wonder the author of the *Libelle of English Policy* could say in the 1430s:

> And, as men say, in all Christendom
> There is no ground nor land to Ireland like,
> So large, so good, so plenteous, so rich.

This prosperity is reflected in surviving fifteenth-century wills. A group of fifty-six wills of small farmers, mostly from north county Dublin, shows them to have been holders of small acreages, paying good rent for the land they held. Most of them had wheat, oats and barley sown, and owned horses, oxen, sheep, lambs and pigs, as well as carts, ploughs and miscellaneous farm implements. They were all comfortable and were able to provide in their wills for their wakes, funerals and burials as well as masses for the future. This was common throughout Ireland at the time. John Chever, a wealthy citizen of Dublin, in his will in 1474 left '£6 13s. 4d. for a thousand masses to be celebrated for my soul'. Others left wax for candles: Richard Donogh of Dublin in 1443 left 'five pounds of wax, to make candles to be placed around his corpse at wake and funeral'. He also left 6s. 8d. 'for bread and ale on the night of his wake and day of burial, to be distributed to the poor'. In 1420 John Blake left the large sum of 40s. and a pipe of wine for his burial. Then, as now in rural Ireland, wakes were social occasions, with food and drink available to pass the night.

If the poor benefitted in this way, they were not forgotten by many people in making their wills. A sixteenth-century bishop of Meath left one of his best pans to be used in common by the poor of Dunboyne, 'to serve their turns', with the portreeve of the town in charge of lending the pan so as to prevent quarrels. But usually the poor were remembered in a more practical way, by gifts of money, clothes or food. This was done for the good of the deceased's soul. For the same reason the Church and clergy were remembered in most wills, receiving not only money, but houses, land, and all sorts of other bequests. Money was left to provide candles for altars, for gilding or repairing chalices, for adorning shrines, or for helping to construct or repair churches. The religious fraternities which were attached to many parishes were frequently the recipients of bequests and chantries were often endowed by people on the point of death.

All of this is a reminder of how closely integrated the Church was with the lives of the people in medieval Ireland. Even their wills were administered by the ecclesiastical courts, which claimed exclusive jurisdiction in the matter. No man lived outside the Church. He was born into it and he died in it. His whole life was governed by rules laid down by the Church. Religion was everywhere much more in evidence than it is today, with shrines, religious processions, pilgrimages and religious houses a common feature of everyday life. Feast days and holidays were frequent and new ones were constantly being added. In Dublin, for example, the feast of St Laurence O Toole was made a holiday of obligation at a provincial council in 1339, and others were added by later councils. Indeed in 1367 Archbishop Minot was forced to reduce the number of feasts, because 'experience and actual fact make it plain that the multiplication of feasts beyond what is customary hinders work in the fields and in the city'.

No institution was more important than the Church, which dominated men's lives from birth to death. As an institution, it had a life of its own. In Ireland it had a history which began in the fifth century, during which it developed a character and shape which was unique in the western world. But by the time of the Anglo-Norman invasion a series of great reforming synods had established a new diocesan structure within the Irish Church. At Kells, in 1152, the island was divided into four provinces: Armagh (the seat of the primacy), with ten suffragans; Dublin, with five; Cashel, with twelve; and Tuam, with seven—a total of thirty-eight dioceses in all. This structure remained virtually unchanged through the middle ages, although some modifications were introduced. For example, a new diocese was established at Annaghdown in the late twelfth century, only to be absorbed by Tuam in the fourteenth. Connor was joined to Down as late as 1453, Cloyne to Cork in 1429, Glendalough to Dublin in 1216. Such changes were part of the continuing development of the Church, so that the programme of the twelfth-century reformers was carried out by the generation of bishops which followed the Anglo-Norman invasion. Despite the racialism which frequently manifested itself, particularly among the religious orders, and more especially the Cistercians and Franciscans, the new foreign bishops were no less zealous in the interests of the Church than their Gaelic predecessors had been. Even when attempts were made to intrude English bishops into Irish dioceses, which neccessarily soured relations for a time with the Gaelic clergy, prelates of both races continued to work together in defence of ecclesiastical liberties. At the fourth Lateran council in 1215, for example, which was attended by eighteen bishops and two bishops-elect from Ireland, no racial animosity was allowed to interfere with the business of defending ecclesiastical liberties in Ireland.

It was within each diocese that the real work of reorganising the Irish Church took place. Once the territorial limits had been fixed, it remained to supply the bishop with the apparatus of government and administration. It is difficult to see how far this process had gone by the time of the Anglo-Norman invasion, but there seems to be no doubt that it was the new arrivals who introduced the diocesan system with which they were familiar. Armagh, for example, did not acquire a dean and chapter until well into the thirteenth century. A dean and chapter are first mentioned in Waterford in 1210. The chapter at Limerick was instituted by Bishop Donatus c. 1205. Meath does not seem to have any formal chapter organisation at all. It appears, then, that during the period of Anglo-Norman expansion the elements of an English organisation were introduced in those areas which came under foreign influence. This meant, in practice, most of the cathedrals of the provinces of Dublin and Cashel, and some in Tuam and Armagh. Here the chapters were secular, with four principal offices of dean, precentor, treasurer and chancellor. Each canon was given a prebend, usually a parish rectory, for his support and was able to draw on a fund (the 'common fund') while he was acutally in residence at the cathedral. In fact many of the canons were non-resident, and were frequently pluralists as well, so that they were unable to give counsel to the bishop, play a part in the administration of his diocese, or maintain a noble liturgy in his cathedral. For example, in the fifteenth century John Stack held canonries (with prebends) in Cloyne, Limerick, Tuam and Ardfert, as well as being the archdeacon of Limerick, dean of Ardfert and rector of Dungarvan.

There were some cathedrals, mainly in the Gaelic areas, which retained an older and looser form of constitution, derived from the rule of Arrouaise which was brought to Ireland by St Malachy. It survived most notably in Christ Church Dublin, where the chapter remained regular, whereas a short distance away in the rival cathedral of St Patrick the chapter was secular and consti-tuted on the English model. This difference naturally worsened the rivalry which existed for so long between the two cathedrals.

The canon law of the Church prescribed that it was the cathedral chapter which elected the bishop and here, too, the procedure adopted in Ireland was more or less the same as in England. It was laid down in the concordat of 1215 between Pope Innocent III and King John, confirmed by Gregory IX in

1227 and Innocent IV in 1246. The electors must first obtain the royal licence to elect and must then procure the consent of the king to the candidate elected. In addition, during the vacancy the king was to have the temporalities (or the material possessions of the see), which naturally tempted him to prolong vacancies as long as possible. Naturally, too, disputes arose over elections and it was only in such cases that the pope could intervene, when he could 'provide' a candidate with the see. In the thirteenth century this was rare enough, only twelve such provisions being recorded during the reign of Edward I, for example. But in the later middle ages it became more normal.

Although this system of electing bishops could obviously be abused by the king, he does not in fact seem to have brought pressure on chapters to elect his own nominee in the thirteenth century. Licence to elect was commonly sought, even though the king's rights could be enforced only in those areas where the power of his government was effective. The position in Ireland was also further complicated by the two-culture situation which persisted in many parts of the island to the end of the medieval lordship. This often resulted in a diocese being divided into two parts, one *inter Anglicos* ('amongst the English'), the other *inter Hibernicos* ('amongst the Irish'). A good example is Kerry, or Ardfert as it was more properly called, which reflected the cultural division perfectly. The northern part of the diocese, based on the cathedral city of Ardfert, remained dominated by the Anglo-Irish; the southern part, ruled by Mac Carthy or O Sullivan, remained Gaelic to the end. Naturally there was only one bishop, living in Ardfert and usually Anglo-Irish. But there were two archdeacons, instead of the customary one, reflecting the division of the diocese: one at Ardfert and the other, acting as a sort of vicar general for the south, living at Aghado, near Killarney.

The Irish diocese was generally subdivided into rural deaneries, the dean being responsible for the churches in his division and for seeing that the decrees of diocesan synods or provincial councils were promulgated there. It was by means of such councils and synods, held regularly, that the metropolitan and his suffragans legislated for the clergy and laity. Sometimes the decrees were copied from those of other bishops, especially in England: but often they were purely local in character, designed to deal with local problems and needs. For example, those of

Meath, from the synod of Trim, organised the diocese into rural deaneries in 1216. Primate Colton held a provincial council at Armagh in the fourteenth century, the decrees of which will serve as illustration. Some deal with the rights of the Church in relation to wills and last testaments, land held in chief from ecclesiastics, the practice of annual confession and communion, the sale of church property. Each bishop of the province should confer holy orders within his diocese 'at least at the three times of the year determined for celebrating orders' and should administer confirmation in each deanery at least once a year, adding the sinister proviso 'if he can safely approach them'. Another decree ordered that 'any cleric of Armagh province who is a notorious keeper of concubines or harlots or has or holds a concubine in court or in care, (shall) expel her within a month of the publication of the present constitutions'. Excommunication was pronounced against those who imposed taxation on ecclesiastics or their tenants without their consent. Another decree renewed old statutes against 'mimes, jugglers, poets, drummers or harpers, and especially against kernes'. Each bishop was ordered to 'labour to reform, hold and preserve peace between the English and Irish of Armagh province according to his power and preach peace between the same and compel all his subjects by all ecclesiastical censures to hold the peace'. The faithful were to abstain from servile work on the sixth day after Easter, the feast of the Preparation, and they were to give up the 'perverse vulgar error' which held that 'the flesh of a hare on the feast of the Preparation is an excellent medicine against various diseases'. The game of *galbardy* (which some historians, for no good reason, have presumed to be hurling) was forbidden, because 'mortal sins and beatings and often homicides are committed'. The feast of St Patrick was to be celebrated as a double greater feast; that of St Brigid was also to be celebrated yearly on 1 February, which was also the eve of the Purification of the Blessed Virgin, a day of abstinence—a dispensation was to be given, as was already the custom elsewhere in Ireland; the feast of St Colmcille was to be celebrated throughout the province, and that of Ss Feghin and Ronan in the diocese of Armagh only. Marriage might henceforth be solmnised on all days of the year except from Palm Sunday to the Sunday after Easter, provided the banns were properly proclaimed. The supreme jurisdiction of the archbishop's court was redefined. It was decreed that Urban VI should be recognised as the legitimate pope.

Decrees of this kind were frequent enough in the medieval Irish Church and often give the impression of great abuses being widespread. This impression is on the whole confirmed by other evidence, especially for the later middle ages when the failure of the two cultures to be assimilated to each other split the Church into two. The unhappy situation of divided dioceses, and sometimes even parishes, did not make it easy for any bishop to maintain proper standards among his clergy. For this reason alone, abuses multiplied as the years passed, a situation which was gravely aggravated by the disaster of the great schism at the end of the fourteenth century. But pluralism, which was rampant, absenteeism and ignorance were even more responsible for the neglect of the people by the clergy in too many parishes. The kind of accusation which was brought against Donald Cremin, the perpetual vicar of Aghabulloge, in 1484, that he allowed one of his flock to die without the sacraments, was all too frequent. The system of papal provision, which should have been employed as an instrument of reform, was itself frequently the occasion of abuse, leading to pluralism and absenteeism. In the fifteenth century especially many clerics were provided with benefices in Ireland merely to sustain them in one position or another in England or elsewhere. Others led dissipated lives which were a scandal. The great quarrel between the friars and the seculars didn't help, since too much energy was devoted to issues which were of no real value in the important business of the care of souls. The violence of the long quarrel often caused scandal, as when the Franciscan archbishop, Philip Torinton, was violently assaulted by the bishop of Limerick in 1375.

Small wonder that standards slipped so badly in so many places. Too much time was devoted to the material world and too little to the spiritual. It is a curious fact that the only real fragments of wall paintings to survive from medieval Ireland come from abbey churches: Abbeyknockmoy in county Galway and Holy Cross in county Tipperary, both Cistercian and both therefore showing a decline from the austere tradition of the early days of the order in Ireland. What is even more curious, however, is that both paintings are completely secular in character, an appropriate commentary on the worldliness of many monastic houses in the later middle ages. In 1290 the abuses of the ecclesiastical courts were highlighted in the diocese of Emly, where responsible clerks were charged with demanding excessive fees for making wills, of which they had a monopoly; taking fines from weavers who worked on holidays; imposing outrageous penalties on usurers, and so on. It is easy to understand how failure to teach the people even the elementary facts of the life of Christ could lead to this entry in the *Anuals of Ulster* for 1447: 'And a son of maledictions for malice and a devil for evils (was) that Furnival and what the learned of Ireland say of him is that there came not from *Herod, by whom Christ was crucified downwards*, one so bad for ill deeds'.

It was the regular clergy who manifested some of the worst abuses, partly because of a decline in standards which resulted from the difficulties of finding suitable persons after the Black Death, and partly because of the increased worldliness which inevitably followed from the smaller numbers who had to look after the temporalities of each house. It is a staggering fact that after the outbreak of the Black Death in 1348 not a single new monastery was founded. But in other directions there was a great manifestation of religious fervour during the same period, with the foundation of nearly sixty new houses for mendicant friars and, more significantly, the setting up of large numbers of houses for members of the Franciscan Third Order. It was the growth of the Third Order and the introduction of the Observant reform, especially in the west, which marked the great revival and which indicates that the friars at least were determined to prevent a complete degeneration from the ideals of the early brethern.

The arrival of the mendicant friars in the thirteenth century was one of the most important events of that time. The first to come were the Dominicans, in 1224, and they spread rapidly. By the end of the century they had twenty-four priories in Ireland and thirty-eight by the sixteenth century. Even more popular were the Franciscans, who arrived c.1230, and had thirty-one houses by the end of the century and no fewer than fifty-eight (the same number as in England) by the time of the reformation. The Carmelites, who came c.1270, had twenty-seven houses in all and the Augustinians, the last to arrive c.1280, had twenty-two friaries. Such figures indicate more than anything else the great popularity which the friars enjoyed in Ireland. They were closely integrated into local communities everywhere, mainly in the towns where they went first of all. But in Ireland the friars went to the countryside as well, which had the effect of bringing them into close contact with Gaelic Ireland, and before very long the Franciscans in particular were involved in the politics of the Gaelic revival. Inevitably racial divisions emerged and from early in the fourteenth century the Franciscans had to be organised accordingly.

The popularity of the friars can also be seen in the fact that they were not given harsh treatment in a famous fourteenth-century satire, the so-called 'Satire on the people of Kildare' (though it is more likely to refer to the people of Dublin). By way of contrast, the author is savage about some of the older orders, notably the Benedictines:

> Hail, ye holy monks with your corrin[9]
> Late and early filled with ale and wine.
> Deep ye can booze, that is all your care,
> With St Benedict's scourge oft ye are disciplined.

In fact however, there were very few Benedictine houses in Ireland. It was the Cistercians, brought to Ireland by St Malachy, who had captured the imagination of the Irish. By the time of the Anglo-Norman invasion there were twelve abbeys founded and before the end of the thirteenth century there were thirty-five. The Cistercians were particularly affected at an early stage by the unfortunate cultural division which had such disastrous effects generally within the Church. The so-called 'Conspiracy of Mellifont', which in the years 1216–31 saw a number of abbeys in virtual open revolt against the general chapter of the Cistercians, did the order in Ireland no good. Long before the end of the century many of the abbeys were in need of reform and though some effort was made at revitalising the order, especially in the fifteenth century, the abbot of Mellifont, in a letter of 1495 to the abbot of Citeaux, had to write of 'the ruin and destruction of the order in Ireland'. Some time later a detailed report on the order showed that in Ireland only two houses, Mellifont and Dublin,

[9]A pot or can.

followed the rules, with the monks wearing the Cistercian habit.

Surprisingly enough it was the Augustinian canons who seem to have been the most popular of all in Ireland, if one is to judge from the number of houses which they had. There seem to have been well over a hundred foundations in all. After the Anglo-Norman invasion the two great military orders, the Knights Hospitallers and Templars, were introduced, the latter being suppressed by Edward II. Only one Carthusian priory (Kinelahin) was founded, and it had failed by the mid-fourteenth century— all the more surprising considering the great tradition of asceticism in the Irish Church. It is impossible to say how many convents of nuns were founded. The majority seem to have been Augustinian, though some were Benedictine, Cistercian and Franciscan.

During the middle ages, then, Ireland was dotted with an enormous number of religious houses of all kinds and sizes, mainly poor and often degenerate, but at least serving a useful function in society as hospices or hospitals, occasionally as schools, always as places for the worship of God. Not unnaturally many of them became involved with the pastoral care of people in the locality, especially the friars, who thereby earned the bitter enmity of the secular clergy. But in the Gaelic tradition, where monks had served the spiritual needs of the people and the local monastic church had been the church of the people, it was easy for the religious to slip back into old ways. All the more so since a parochial organisation was slow to develop in Ireland and can hardly have existed before the Anglo-Norman invasion. The very word *paróiste* (parish) itself is French and seems to have been introduced by the newcomers. At any rate there is no doubt that it was they who set up parishes as they settled the country, the parish usually being coterminous with the manor and endowed to provide for the priest and his church. The trouble was that with the growth of pluralism and therefore absenteeism, hired priests had to be put in charge of many parishes. These, naturally enough, were not always suitable. At one time the standard stipend for a hired priest was three marks a year, which was hardly likely to attract properly qualified men to fill the office. So in many parishes the duties of the priest were very inadequately discharged and abuses of all kinds multiplied.

Even at the best of times, finding a man qualified to be a priest must have been difficult. Education was always a problem and in the absence of even the most elementary kind of seminary organisation, it was difficult for a young man with a vocation to the priesthood to prepare himself adequately. What education was available was provided by the Church. Fosterage (or its equivalent) may have provided sons of the nobility with an education of sorts. And some towns, like New Ross, may have had schools of their own. But most children, if they received a formal education at all, received it at the hands of the regular or secular clergy. Chantry chapels were commonly employed as schools, the chaplain being the teacher. When Richard de Burgh proposed in 1305 to establish a chantry in Loughrea or Ballintubber, heavily endowed for the service of no less than twenty-five chaplains, an inquisition revealed 'that it would be much to the advantage of the king and country if such a chantry should be established in one or other of those places, if for no other reason for teaching the boys of those parts where learning is very scant'. In the towns religious guilds, which were usually endowed to support one or more chaplains, often looked after the education of members. In Dublin, for example, the chantry priests of the guild of St Anne, attached to Audoen's, looked after education and had a 'college' for the purpose in Blakeney's Inns in what is now Schoolhouse Lane. The friars, of course, were great believers in schools and while these were primarily intended for their own people, they were generally open to other clerks as well. The Franciscans had houses of study at Nenagh, Armagh, Ennis, Galway, Dublin and Drogheda; the Dominicans had theirs at Dublin, Athenry and Limerick. Many went abroad to complete their studies, especially to the schools at Oxford. In order to support them while they were abroad, they were normally beneficed in Ireland. John Walsh, for example, was given the rectory at Ballyby in the diocese of Cloyne in 1413 to sustain him at Oxford while he was studying canon law. It is clear that canon law was also taught in Ireland, though it is impossible to say how widely it was available. But those who wished to study at an advanced level had no option, because of the lack of a university in Ireland, but to go abroad. Some became famous, like Richard fitz Ralph, who was chancellor of the university of Oxford for a time; William of Drogheda, who taught at Oxford in the thirteenth century; Peter of Ireland, who taught the great Aquinas. But these were exceptions and no

Irish school of theology, philosophy or canon law was ever developed in the middle ages.

Most surprising of all is the failure to establish a permanent university here. The attempt was made in the early fourteenth century, when a petition to Clement V requested that a university should be established here. One argument which was put forward in support of the petition was that only by 'crossing the sea at grave risk' could one get to a university from Ireland. The pope granted the petition in 1312, when Archbishop Leche of Dublin was authorised to found a university in Dublin. Nothing was done, however, until 1321 when a new archbishop, Alexander Biknor, inaugurated the university of St Patrick's. We don't know what caused the delay, but it is possible that Leche had been unable to procure the consent of all his suffragan bishops, as the pope had ordered. At any rate it was ominous for the future, since the project was never properly supported. Only two faculties were instituted, theology and law, though elaborate statutes were provided by Biknor. It rapidly went into decline. Writing of it some years later, the Kilkenny chronicler Clyn said that it was 'a university as far as its names goes, would that it were so in fact'. Its later history is obscure. It is possible that it never completely died, for there are occasional references to it in later years. Even as late as 1494 a provincial council in Dublin voted certain sums of money for the support of lectures in the university, which kept life of sorts in it. But it can never have functioned as a proper university, so that Ireland was left without that most medieval of all institutions. An attempt to found one in Drogheda in 1465 was still-born.

It is hardly surprising, then, that an adequately educated clergy was not really available to look after people at parochial level. There was a literate public, to be sure, for whom literary compositions had to be provided. Not much has survived of the literature of medieval Anglo-Ireland, but there is sufficient to show that works in Latin, French and English were provided to satisfy a demand from patrons willing to buy. Many were imported. When Walter of Islip, treasurer of Ireland, had his goods seized in 1326, he owned three books—a bible, a copy of the *Roman de la Rose* and of the 'liber de seint graal' (which could be one of a number of French works dealing with the holy grail). But there were many other compositions which originated here,

8

the most famous being those associated with the name of Friar Michael of Kildare, including a delightful satire known as *The land of Cokaygne*. Bishop Ledrede of Ossory composed sixty latin songs, to be sung to the popular airs of the day, in order to counter the pernicious influence of the secular ballads in which the people of Kilkenny delighted. Even today the catchy rhythm and rhymes of some of them make an instant appeal:

> Da, da nobis nunc
> Da prompte fundere potum,
> Da sobrie bibere totum:
> Da, da nobis nunc.

Three English songs survive from Kilkenny, though none of those against which the bishop fulminated. One lovely fifteenth-century lyric begins: 'Graceful and gay, on her is set all my thought. Unless she have pity on me today she will bring me to death'. Completely different is another fifteenth-century poem from Armagh, which viciously satirises the fashions of the times, especially the horned headdresses worn by the women: 'May God, who wears the crown of thorns, destroy the pride of women's horns for His precious Passion'.

Most monasteries and religious houses had libraries and show the great interest that was taken in the secular compositions of the age. It was in Christ Church that the monks hurriedly copied down a morality play, now known as *The Pride of Life*, on the back of an account roll, thus preserving a copy of the earliest known morality in the English language. The British Museum manuscript Harley 913 was compiled in an Irish Franciscan friary, possibly Dublin, in the early fourteenth century and contains a miscellaneous collection of Latin, French and English prose and verse. Included are some Latin parodies, most notably the notorious *Missa de Potatoribus* (or 'Drunkard's Mass'), one of the most blasphemous parodies of all.

The impression one gets is that religion sat lightly on the people, cleric as well as lay, and was not either oppressive or an inhibiting factor in their lives. That is not to say that there was a great deal of insincerity. So far as the evidence goes, people seemed to be sincere in their religious devotions, of which there were many. Shrines were everywhere, relics were common, and pilgrimages were frequent. A very popular one was to the Holy Cross and the *Bachail Íosa* (or 'staff of Christ') in Christ Church. Many religious houses were frequented by pilgrims, who were often protected by the king while their pilgrimage lasted. A parliament of 1454 enacted that the king's protection should be extended to 'all people, whether rebels or others, who shall go in pilgrimage to the convent of the Blessed Virgin of Navan'. Much legislation of a similar nature survives. Wonders were supposedly worked at some of the shrines, which was no doubt one reason why they were so popular. The statue of Our Lady of Trim, for example, attracted large numbers of pilgrims, and no wonder. In 1444 it was said of it that 'it gave his eyes to the blind, his tongue to the dumb, his legs to the cripple, and the reaching of his hand to one that had it tied to his side'.

As might be expected, places associated with the national apostle, St Patrick, claimed many pilgrims. Croagh Patrick in Mayo was climbed by many and then, as now, the recommended day for the pilgrimage was the last Sunday in July. It was 'St Patrick's Purgatory', in Lough Derg, which was the most famous of all, attracting pilgrims from all over Europe and finding a place in the literature of England, Spain, France and Italy. Until it was closed by the pope in 1497, the Purgatory continued to claim the attention of Europe.

Irish pilgrims naturally travelled abroad, to Rome, to the Holy land (we are lucky to have a long narrative written by a Franciscan pilgrim, Simon fitz Simeon, who left Ireland for the Holy Land in 1322 with a companion, Hugo Illuminator), and, above all, to the great shrine of St James of Compostella in Spain. A special hospice was maintained in Dublin for pilgrims to the latter place, so numerous were they. Like all pilgrims, they wore a special pilgrim's cloak—a 'fringed cloak', as it is described by a Gaelic poet of the thirteenth century, who probably went to the Holy Land, carrying a cross (most likely marked on the cloak) which he offered to the Creator: 'I am carrying it assiduously for thee, o thou of the slender brow, it has been two years on my back without encountering anyone from Ireland'.

It was probably because they were not morbid about their religion that the excesses so noticeable elsewhere are not a prominent feature of the religious life of the Irish at this time. Archbishop Minot of Dublin, when reducing the number of feast days in 1367, complained that they were occasions of sin to workmen, 'many of whom never or rarely enter their parish church at hours when masses are celebrated, but spend almost all the feast-day or at least the greater part thereof in taverns and drunkenness and other illicit acts of pleasure'. For many the churchyard was a place for holding dances, playing games, wrestling, and holding what the archbishop described as 'theatrical pageants and wanton spectacles'. For others it was nothing out of the way to do their threshing in the church, or to use it as a safe place in which to store their valuables (including grain and wool as well as money). Others grazed their animals in the cemetry. To many the church was a place of sanctuary, where they were supposed to be assured of refuge. For all, there was an easy familiarity with their church, which was in a very real sense the centre of the community. It was perhaps this which made them treat their religion so lightly. They were as super-stitious as most people in their age—we have the evidence of diocesan synods and provincial councils for that. But religious beliefs and practices were conservative and orthodox. There was little of the dissent which in Europe found expression in heresy and there is no trace at all of the messianic eruptions or the pursuit of the millenium which were so common elsewhere, expecially in times of stress, among people who suffered hardship from war and famine, so that an escape was sought in a belief in the second coming of Christ and the kingdom of the saints. Indeed, given the uncertain pattern of life in Ireland, it is ex-traordinary that dissent and anti-clericalism did not manifest themselves more violently. There is evidence of dissent in the diocese of Raphoe in 1256, where according to the bishop, in a report to Pope Alexander IV, some laymen of the diocese 'have been spurred on by the devil to such a pitch of insanity that they not only worship idols but also marry their own kinsfolk and relations'. Worst of all, when rebuked or excommunicated, 'they have the timidity to argue, like sons of perdition, against the Catholic Faith and against the authority which has been divinely bestowed upon the Apostolic See'. Much more serious was the assertion of Pope Benedict XII in 1335, in a letter to Edward III, that certain heretics had arisen in Ireland, some of whom 'asserted that Jesus Christ was a man, a sinner, and was justly crucified for his own sins'.

But the most significant fact is that there are only two recorded instances of heretics being burnt in Ireland, and one of these (Adam O Toole, who was burnt in what is now College Green in Dublin in 1327) is dubious. The other is hardly any more credible. Two Gaels were convicted of heresy ('a gross insult to the Blessed Virgin Mary') in Bunratty castle in 1353 and burnt. It is very likely that politics more than religion was responsible for bringing the pair to the stake. Politics, too, seems to have played a part in the only recorded case of execution for witchcraft in Ireland, during the notorious Kyteler affair in Kilkenny. It is probable that Bishop Ledrede was quite sincere in his belief that heresy and witchcraft were rife in his diocese and in his attempt to have Alice Kyteler and her accomplices tried and burnt at the stake. But there seems to be no doubt that so far as the leading figures were concerned (and none of them were executed in the end—it was the servant Petronilla who was tortured and then burnt publicly in Kilkenny) the whole thing was as much a reflection of the contemporary Mortimer—Despenser struggle in England as anything else. In any event the whole thing was a nine days wonder and quite unique. Many years later, in 1447, an Irish parliament took the very sensible view that sorcery was impossible. It appears that someone had been slandered by being accused of practising black arts, 'as in ruining or destroying any man by sorcery or necromancy, the which they (i.e. the members of parliament) decided that the king should be told that "no such art was attempted at any time in this land, known or rumoured among the people, nor any opinion had or entertained of the same by the lay men in this land until now"'.

Some provincial or diocesan decrees laid down strict rules concerning how the laity were to conduct themselves in church. The synod of Limerick in 1453, for instance, in enjoining attendance at mass and rest from all servile work on Sundays, under pain of excommunication, forbade men and women, even husbands and wives, to sit in the same stall together. Other synods made the laity responsible for whitewashing the church and for its general maintenance. It is doubtful, however, if the general body of people in any parish played much of a part in either the building or upkeep of their church. The impression one gets is that it was wealthy patrons who were responsible and it is their munificence which is recorded.

Many of the churches, especially in the towns and those attached to the larger abbeys or friaries, were richly endowed and preserved a wealth of ornamentation of one kind or another of which hardly any trace now remains (apart from carving in stone). The Dominican friary chapel at Athenry was presented with a painting (*tabulam bene depictam et deauratam*—a 'panel well painted and gilded') from Flanders which showed the death and burial of the Blessed Virgin. Indeed this church is a very good example of how a local benefactor could initiate a building and how others could co-operate subsequently to see it finished. Meiler de Bermingham purchased the site, for 160 marks, and gave money to cover the cost of building. He also made various gifts to the brothers— English cloth, wine, horses to cart building materials—and he persuaded his own people, including even the knights, to help in the work. Subsequently we find Gaelic and Anglo-Norman lords co-operating to finish the friary. Felim O Connor built the refectory, Eugene O Heyne endowed the dormitory, Walter Husgard the cloister, Cornelius O Kelly the chapter- house, and two other local Gaelic lords the guest house and the infirmary.

Ecclesiastics, too, could act as patrons. A notable one was Bishop Ledrede, who filled the east windows of his cathedral church in Kilkenny in the mid-fourteenth century with beautiful glass showing 'the entire life, passion, resurrection and ascension of Our Lord'. Rinnucinni admired these windows so much in the seventeenth century that he wished to purchase them to take back to Italy. Another church in Kilkenny, St John's Augustinian priory, still preserves some of its marvellous windows: the Lady Chapel was known by the beautiful name of 'the lantern of Ireland', because it had so many lights. The win- dows in Galway's collegiate church of St Nicholas were equally famous and many another church must have had fine stained glass of which no trace remains, save for a few fragments of broken glass in Kilkenny and Holy Cross. The benefactor who endowed the Franciscan friary church in Ennis with 'bluepainted windows', in addition to vestments, furniture and carved book- cases, was not unique. But the wanton destruction of the centuries has left no trace of them. In Dublin the shrine of St Anne in St Audoen's had a fifteenth-century fresco which showed the Trinity (usually depicted as an old man, with a dove and the figure of Christ resting in his lap), with angels playing harps on each side and the figure of St Anne below, teaching Our Lady at her knee. Most churches had rood screens, separating the nave from the church, which would support statues and were often richly carved. Sometimes, too, the partition over the screen was used for a painting. In Christ Church, for example, in the mid-thirteenth century, the story of the Passion was painted over the screen. But none survive. Shrines, too, were often richly endowed with precious objects. Images of patron saints of churches or of craft or religious guilds were common.

Many of the objects which adorned the churches and shrines of medieval Ireland were undoubtedly imported. But there were native craftsmen with the skill and genius to create beauty. The painters, masons, smiths, weavers and others who took the trouble to form themselves into guilds must have produced many works of art of which no trace remains. The Church was the great patron, but many laymen had the means to commission objects of beauty and value to adorn their homes. Not all of the domestic silver which is so commonly mentioned in surviving wills was imported. Some of it must have been of local origin. But now it is difficult to be sure, since nothing identifiable has survived. Indeed, the Anglo-Ireland of the middle ages has left few material remains, apart from its ecclesiastical and domestic architecture, to show how rich and variegated that society was.

VI Edwardian Ireland:
The Beginning of Decline

THE grant of Ireland to the Lord Edward in 1254 bears an obvious similarity to the earlier grant to John by Henry II. There were, however, some important differences. For example, Henry III reserved to himself his rights in relation to the Church, together at first with the cities and counties of Dublin and Limerick, and Athlone, though these were later granted to Edward. But most important was the reservation in the grant which stated that it was made 'so however that the land of Ireland shall never be separated from the Crown of England'. There was to be no independent lordship of Ireland in the future, nor was any land to be permanently alienated by the new lord of Ireland. This was no idle proposition, as was made plain in 1268 when the reservation was quoted in justification of direct interference by the king in the administration of Ireland: he ordered the resumption of crown-lands which had been alienated by Edward without royal licence.

In due course Edward would succeed to the throne in England and his lordship of Ireland would once again be merged with the English Crown. Meantime Ireland was now his responsibility. It had been his father's intention that the young Edward should visit his new acquisition and plans were accordingly made in the summer of 1255. He was to voyage to Ireland from Gascony and settle the state of the land. It need not surprise us that the visit never materialised. The king himself had defaulted on a number of occasions when an Irish visit had been proposed. In 1233, after most elaborate preparations had been made, he changed his mind at the last minute. In 1240 and again in 1243 a royal visitation was announced, the last being the occasion for the building of a new great hall in Dublin castle, richly decorated to suit the king's extravagant taste. But Henry never came. Indeed after 1210 no lord of Ireland came until Richard II arrived at the end of the fourteenth century, a neglect which was to encourage the dissident elements in the lordship.

The Lord Edward had no real interest in Ireland at this time. He was young, only fourteen when the grant was made, and he had other interests to guard. Besides Ireland and lands in England and Wales, he had the Channel Islands and the whole of Gascony, an inheritance which altogether was expected to yield him an income of 15,000 marks annually. In that context Ireland must have seemed of no very great importance. There was another reason, too, why Gascony should claim so much of his attention: it was in danger of being lost. By contrast, Ireland was safe. This accounts for Edward's obsession with Gascony and neglect of Ireland. By the time he woke up to the internal dangers which threatened Ireland, it was too late. The obsession with France, which seemed to be ingrained in all Plantagenet kings, had done its damage.

This lack of interest in Ireland is very evident and it was responsible for the serious deterioration in the quality of government once Edward became lord. Nor is it a coincidence that the same period marks the beginning of the Gaelic revival which was to have such a catastrophic effect upon the colonists and their settlements. The comparative stability of government under Henry III when two justiciars, Maurice fitz Gerald and John fitz Geoffrey, successively ruled Ireland for twenty-four years is in marked contrast to the steady decline of the sixteen years after Edward assumed personal responsibility for Ireland, during which period no fewer than eight filled the office of chief governor. Local government suffered in particular and this naturally gave rise to an increase in lawlessness. This situation was aggravated by the outbreak of quarrels among the magnates and the growth of factions, all of which seriously disturbed the peace. This was partly the result of the civil war in England, for the greatest of the Irish magnates were naturally involved in it, and that involvment was reflected in groupings in Ireland.

The most spectacular of these quarrels, and one which was to last until near the end of the century, was that which involved the de Burghs and the Geraldines. When Maurice fitz Maurice seized the justiciar in December 1264 it plunged the lordship into civil war. Writing to the archbishop of Dublin in February 1265, the English government expressed concern about the situation in Ireland, especially the 'discord prevailing among its great men and magnates, whereby great danger and expense may threaten

the king and Edward his son'. A month later the archbishop had
replied that 'great dissensions had arisen between the nobles and
the magnates'. So serious was the disturbance that the citizens of
New Ross hurriedly decided to enclose their town. The poem
composed in 1265 in commemoration of this event tells us that
they were moved to this because they were 'alarmed by the war
existing between two barons, whose names you shall see written,
Sir Maurice and Sir Walter'.

But by June of the same year the quarrel was healed and some
degree of order seems to have been restored. Nevertheless the
irritant which caused the breach in the first place remained—
very likely de Burgh jealousy of what must have seemed a
threatening Geraldine aggrandizement in Connacht. At any rate
outbreaks were intermittent during the next thirty years, cul-
minating in the seizure of the earl of Ulster by John fitz Thomas
in December 1294 and his imprisonment in the castle of Lea in
Offaly. As a result, according to the Annals of Loch Cé, 'all Erin
was thrown into a state of disturbance', which is hardly surprising
considering that the quarrel must have involved the greater part
of Anglo-Ireland and had serious repercussions in parts of Gaelic
Ireland as well. Indeed the official records of the time make it
plain that disorder was widespread. A receipt roll of the Irish
exchequer, recording the receipts for Hilary Term 1295 from the
tax on moveable property (a fifteenth) granted to the king bears
the rubic: 'Nothing in this term, on account of the war and the
capture of the earl of Ulster'. It took a session of parliament,
sitting at Kilkenny in March 1295, to effect the earl's release and
it wasn't until the arrival of John Wogan as justiciar in the following year, 1296, that a truce was negotiated. Even then, a final
settlement was to take another two years: agreements made in
1298 and 1299 saw fitz Thomas surrendering all his lands in
Connacht and Ulster, leaving the earl the undisputed master with
an increased power based on his greatly augmented landed
wealth.

This great quarrel, which caused such havoc while it lasted,
was the more dangerous because it involved the principals in the
politics of Gaelic Connacht, each trying to place an O Connor
of his choice on the throne. Fortunately for the colony, for most
of the time the internecine war among the O Connors made the
Connachtmen incapable of taking advantage of the situation.

Another complication was the activity of William de Vescy, lord of Kildare, which provoked fitz Thomas into yet another quarrel. The fact that de Vescy was justiciar made no difference to the Geraldine, especially since de Vescy seemed prepared to use the prerogatives of his office in his own interest. Finally, after complaints had been made against de Vescy in the English parliament of 1293, a sensational charge was made before the council in Dublin. Fitz Thomas accused de Vescy, who was still justiciar, of having said that if the people of Ireland 'knew as much of the king as he knew they would value the king very little, for he is the most perverse and dastardly knight of his kingdom'. This was bad enough, but perhaps no less dangerous were the words which fitz Thomas swore had been uttered by de Vescy: '. . . the people of Ireland were the most miserable he knew, for they would be, if they willed anything, great lords, and would well maintain the lands and franchises of Ireland, notwithstanding the king'. The result was a wager of battle; but before the date appointed for the duel, both parties were summoned to appear before the king at Westminster. The court record tells how on the appointed day 'William appears as an armed knight with military arms, namely, an armoured house, a lance, a shield, a poniard, a coat of mail and other military arms, and offers to defend himself against John as the court shall adjudge'. John failed to appear and de Vescy claimed to have won his case by default and, says the record, he 'prays that if he has more arms than are proper, he may by licence of the court lay them aside, and if fewer that he may take more'.

Quarrels of this kind usually had a background of disputes over land and ambitions to power. The successful man was **not** necessarily he who could successfully prosecute his claims in court, as indeed the case of de Vescy illustrates since fitz Thomas won out in the end. Rather it was he who should command the greatest resources, especially in manpower. So we find the great magnates building up retinues of armed retainers, the raw material of what in modern times has come to be known as 'bastard feudalism'. Men entered the service of a lord and received in return not land, as had usually been the case in the age of classical feudalism, but money. The signs of this new kind of quasi-feudal relationship were *feode et robe*, 'fees and robes'. A man took another man's wages, wore his livery, and was thereby retained in his service. In this way private armies were maintained. It is no accident that the earliest (1289) surviving example of an indenture of such service in Ireland has as one of its parties John fitz Thomas, at a time when he was building up his power. Indeed the *Red Book of Kildare*, a cartulary of the Leinster Gerald-ines, contains from this time a number of such agreements of retinue with fitz Thomas.

Already, then, the appearance of armed retainers and the growth of factions was producing the conditions which were to lead to a collapse of law and order in many parts of the medieval lordship. The real beginnings of this change must be sought in the period before the Lord Edward became king in England. It is no coincidence that it was this same period which produced the first manifestations of the Gaelic revival, with the attempt of Brian O Neill to revive the high kingship, the success of O Donnell in west Ulster and the great Mac Carthy recovery in Munster. Edward's neglect of his responsibilities in Ireland was an important fact in helping to produce the kind of situation in which that revival could take place. For while Edward did not hesitate to make the fullest possible use of such financial and material resources as he could procure from Ireland—for example, in 1257 he employed in Wales Irish foot soldiers, a variety of food supplies, and a huge sum of money—it is clear that he lacked any real interest in the affairs of Ireland. He devoted no serious attention to the growing problems of the lordship and this negligence was carried forward to the early years of his reign after his return to England from his crusade in the East. Politically it had serious repercussions in that it contributed to the growing independence of some Gaelic chieftains and to disputes among the Anglo-Irish, such as that between the Mandevilles and William fitz Warin the seneschal of Ulster. So, in a letter written in August 1275, in which he requested the bishops and the people of Ireland generally to exert themselves in the pacification of the land, the king could say that Ireland was 'impoverished by war and discord'.

There was to be no quick or easy improvement, however. The long years of neglect had their effect and, as before, the instability of the Irish government is reflected in the frequent changes of chief governor from 1272 until the appointment of John Wogan in 1295. Lack of control from the centre is well illustrated by the considerable decline in the numbers coming to account at the Dublin exchequer—indeed it was believed at the time that many sheriffs and bailiffs did not even know how to compile accounts or answer at the exchequer. There was a corresponding decline in the normal revenue, a much more serious matter. For example, where Geoffrey de Tourville as treasurer could show a receipt of more than £5,000 for the year 1251, the bishop of Meath could only show £4,000 for the the two years ending Michaelmas 1272, or just £2,000 a year.

The appointment of Geoffrey de Geneville as justiciar in August 1273 began an attempt to infuse new life into the Irish administration and to cope with the growing disorder. He had been a close companion of the king and had long since been rewarded with the hand in marriage of Maud de Lacy, one of the co-heirs of Meath. He is interesting in another way, too, since he was French born, a younger brother of that famous Sire de Joinville who was both friend to and biographer of Louis IX of France. Geoffrey is therefore a living reminder to us of the continuity of the French cultural tradition in Ireland. While he eventually made his home in Meath, he was frequently in the service of his king abroad, and not least in France. For example, he was sent to Paris in 1282 to help arrange peace between France and Castile and in 1298–9 he was one of those who treated for peace with France and represented Edward I at the treaty of Montreuil. Twice he was sent to Rome, in 1290 and again in 1300. He also accompanied the young Edward on his crusade to the Holy Land. For Geoffrey was a man of piety, a true knight who in many ways reminds us of another great knight who came to Ireland before him, William Marshal. After his wife died in 1307 he surrendered all his Irish lands to his grand-daughter Joan and her husband Roger Mortimer. He entered the Dominican friary at Trim, his own foundation, the following year and died there in October 1314.

It was no ordinary man, then, who was sent to Ireland in 1273, a clear sign that the English government hoped for some definite improvement in Ireland. When appointed Geoffrey was given wide financial powers, 'the king now reflecting that the perturbation of those parts is of long standing and not settled, and that it is expedient to do so for the prosecution of the king's affairs'. Despite this he achieved little and in 1276, at his own request he was released from office. Although the new justiciar, Robert de Ufford, had some success in repressing the Leinster Irish, his health failed him and incapable of carrying on he was replaced in November 1281 by Stephen de Fulburne, bishop of Waterford and already treasurer. There had been a growing concentration of power in Bishop Stephen's hands and since he now retained the treasurership he was in complete control of the administration—dangerously so, it might be thought. But the Irish situation was such that a desperate remedy was needed. As treasurer Bishop Stephen had already shown his capacity as an administrator and during his tenure of office there had been a sharp increase in revenue, so that by 1278 the income of the exchequer had climbed to more than £7,000 a year.

With so much power in his hands the justiciar was bound to make enemies. Complaints began to reach the king and he was compelled to listen. One writer told Edward that 'by default of the chief keeper and of the ministers of the exchequer (of Ireland) the king's land there is desolated and impoverished, bowed down with the universal pestilence of war'. On more than one occasion Bishop Stephen himself expressed concern about the sheriffs who were sent from England and who used their office to their own advantage. 'How to bring them to judgement is a question', he said himself. And not only sheriffs, but all other classes of officials, even within the exchequer where standards of probity were supposed to be particularly high, were corrupt and guilty of peculation. Inefficiency was now made worse by official corruption and there was little anyone could do about it.

At last, in 1284, it was said that 'the whole clergy and people and the common rumour of the country' demanded an investigation into the condition of the lordship and the king was forced to act. A commission of four was established with wide terms of reference—but their primary concern, as the members said on arrival, was to examine thoroughly the state of Ireland. One result of their investigation was a series of charges of malpractice against the justiciar. While most of these were eventually shown to be false, other charges were sustained. For example, it was said of Bishop Stephen that he filled offices only on receipt of a substantial bribe: 'almost no one can be in any office in the exchequer, nor in any shrievalty or custody of a castle, unless he gives or sells land to the justiciar, or bestows on him a moiety of his fee'. He was also accused of buying up provisions when rumour of a war in Wales reached Ireland, so that when the royal army needed supplies the highest possible price had to be paid; buying wines with the king's money and then selling them to the king for the highest price; selling bad corn to the king; enriching himself by taking fines from mariners whom he imprisoned and accused of carrying badly preserved grain to the army in Wales, though the corn was his own from his lands at Swords and Santry; being buyer and seller of nearly all the wines coming to Ireland (for which he used the king's money) and of selling the worst wine to the king at the dearest prices; retaining the money due to merchants, native and foreign, for wine, corn, meat and other victuals taken from them for the king's use and extorting from them a percentage of this before paying them. The list of charges, in fact, reads almost like a catalogue of crime. In the end Bishop Stephen was found to owe the king the huge sum of £33,000. Part of this debt can be accounted for by the fact that the accounts presented by the bishop were so altered and erased that the auditors in England could make nothing of some of them and refused to make adequate allowance to Fulburne for money he had spent on instructions from the king. But there seems little doubt that at least £13,000 was a genuine debt, which may be taken as a measure of the bishop's insufficiency in keeping proper accounts and running an efficient exchequer, as well as his sharp practice while in office. A royal pardon was forthcoming, however, and Bishop Stephen was deprived of the office of treasurer but was retained in office as justiciar until his death in 1288. He was impossible to replace satisfactorily, a sad comment on the state of affairs in Ireland at the time.

This inquiry had exposed the insufficiency and corruption in the Irish administration, which may be why an Irish writer in 1286 castigated the degradation and corruption of the people in general, but was particularly venemous about the misgovernment of Ireland. He was the Franciscan, Friar Michael of Limerick, who in his tract *De Veneno* (which dealt with the seven deadly sins) pointed out that one special blessing of Ireland was the absence of poisonous animals; but, he said, the poison which God denied to the spider or the land, he allowed to rule in human nature there. As an instance of this, he cites the ministers and bailiffs of the king! He might well have quoted the example of

William le Prene, 'king's master of works and master carpenter throughout Ireland', who embezzled money intended for works at various castles, stole nails and other building materials, and generally made profitable use of his office. The record of the case against him, for instance, tells how he 'took £20 of the lord king's money to build Limerick Bridge and by reason of the faultiness of his work on the aforesaid bridge 80 men were drowned, and in this way he defrauded the king of his money'.

In any case, after 1285 some attempt was made to bring about improvements. But the justiciar in Ireland was to prove ineffectual now and many of his officers in Dublin were themselves hostile to any reforms. Once again, too, Ireland was neglected by the king (or rather by his regent, the earl of Cornwall) during his absence abroad bewteen 1286 and 1289. Laxity of control, of which Irish officials took full advantage, led to widespread abuse in the lordship. Soon complaints were being made against the conduct of government officials and local officials such as sheriffs. The situation was rapidly getting out of hand when Bishop Stephen died in July 1288. He was succeeded by a remarkable man, John of Sandford, archbishop of Dublin, an experienced royal official and devoted servant of the king, typical of many churchmen who climbed to high ecclesiastical office through service of the Crown. But what makes him remarkable is the vigour with which he tackled the worsening condition of the administration of the lordship and the measure of success he achieved. He is superior to many a more notable chief governor of Ireland, especially the much vaunted John Wogan.

Sandford quickly began his attempt to restore order. He caused more than fifty inquisitions to be taken regarding the conduct of the king's ministers in Ireland and in addition gave all persons who had cause for complaint the opportunity of laying their grievances before him as he moved about the country. He summoned a number of parliaments to regulate the state of the lordship and he issued new orders, based on the work of those parliaments, to the king's ministers on how they were to carry out the duties of their office. In 1289 he sent two of the king's sergeants to arrest sheriffs and other local officials who had refused to obey the orders of the exchequer to render an account or pay in revenues. Not the least important part of the work he did was to survey the royal service of Ireland—that is, the feudal service owing to the king in time of war—the details of which had been lost when the book in which they had been preserved (called Doomsday Book in obvious imitation of the more famous English compilation of that name) had been accidently destroyed.

One of the results of Sandford's reforms was the long list of complaints and petitions laid before the king in the English parliament of 1290, at which members of the Irish council were present. Among these were many charges of peculation, extortion and oppression against the treasurer Nicholas of Clere, some of which were sustained—such as destroying documents which might incriminate him, selling offices to the highest bidder, issuing false writs, altering the words of writs to his own advantage, and other practices so bad that his judges in England speak of 'the low cunning of the man'. An investigation of his accounts followed and many dubious and irregular entries were discovered. Like Fulburne before him, Nicholas was discovered to owe huge sums of money to the king, his lands and goods were confiscated, he himself was imprisoned in the Fleet prison in London, and his brothers and other relatives were compelled to pay back as much as they could of the money owed. He was, of course, dismissed from office and at last the English government was compelled to take a hard look at the serious defects in the Irish administration. Reforms followed: the well-known ordinance of 1292 tried to bring the Irish exchequer, at least in its officers, into line with practice in England; and the following year another ordinance virtually ended the independence of the Irish exchequer by requiring the Irish treasurer to have his account audited annually by the officers of the English exchequer. Despite such ordinances, however, corruption was still rife and complaints against officials continued until well into the fourteenth century, when the situation in Ireland deteriorated rapidly. Scandals in the exchequer remained almost commonplace. In 1306, for example, one of the chamberlains, Henry of Walton, had to be removed from office because of the charges of embezzlement brought against him.

Yet despite this, reforms of the 1290s had one important result in that they made the administration, at least for a time, more efficient. In particular financial administration was much improved and the exchequer transacted its business with a greater degree of skill and expertise. This was particularly important now, for King Edward was anxious to make the fullest possible use of the resources of Ireland in his wars and for this he required a fairly efficient (however corrupt) civil service in Ireland. Indeed so great was the strain which the war years imposed on his government that it can be said that Edward needed whatever he could get from Ireland. The appointment of John Wogan as justiciar in October 1295 indicates what was in the king's mind, for on the day he received his commission Wogan was ordered to raise 10,000 foot in Ireland, in addition to cavalry 'at his discretion', for service with the king in Scotland. It is quite clear that Wogan was appointed, somewhat like Wentworth in the seventeenth century, to make the Irish colony as productive as possible in aid of the king's wars. In this task he did not fail his master, and under his direction the Irish government was geared to the great war effort which was designed to win Scotland for the king. Men, money, supplies of war, ships—all were demanded by Edward in a never-ending list of orders. So effectively did Wogan meet the demand that he virtually reduced the Irish government to a state of bankruptcy, precipitating a crisis in the exchequer from which it never really recovered in the middle ages.

It is important to remember that as lord of Ireland the English king was fully entitled to utilise the resources of his lordship in whatever way he thought fit. From the time of King John it had became the practice that all surplus revenue in Ireland should be available for the use of the king and in time of war in particular the government in Dublin might be requested either to send such money to the king, or to apply it to the purchase of war supplies, the furnishing of troops, or the provision of ships. No king would seriously contemplate leaving the Irish government short of the finances necessary to carry out its work, and both John and Henry III were fairly moderate in their employment of Irish resources to help their war efforts. During a crisis, however, discretion might be put on one side and the order could come to Dublin that 'all the money accruing from the issues of Ireland' should be applied to a particular enterprise, such as the building of the Welsh castles, the defence of Gascony, or the war in Scotland. During the Welsh campaign of 1245, for example, the Irish justiciar was compelled to send large sums of money before, during, and immediately after the campaign, most of which went to help pay the cost of the great fortress at Degannwy.

In addition he had to furnish supplies of all kinds: food, especially corn, beef and pork; wine, which was transhipped from Gascony; rope; arms; and brattices, which were shipped in a prefabricated state to Anglesey and thence to Degannwy, where they were used by builders. Then, too, he provided an army, which had a large Gaelic element since Felim O Connor of Connacht led no less than 3,000 troops. All of this meant an enormous drain on the resources available to the Irish government and naturally placed a nearly intolerable strain on an already hard-pressed government. The loss of revenue was bad enough; but the absence of the tenants in chief on service overseas was especially dangerous. For the most part Henry III appreciated the danger only too well. In 1230, for example, when making preparations for an expedition to Poitou, he sought military assistance from Ireland. Summonses were despatched ordering the forces to muster; but later the king decided that some of the levies should remain in Ireland 'for the security of the land of Ireland while the justiciar is absent'. Again in 1253, on the occasion of a campaign in Gascony, the Irish justiciar was once more ordered to muster an army for service with the king. But just before the expedition was due to sail, the king received word that Gaelic chieftains were 'restless' and adopting a threatening attitude: they were, he was told, 'over-elated at the departure of the magnates for Gascony'. Henry therefore decided that a proportion of the magnates should remain in Ireland to see to its defence and he further ordered that if the danger was really pressing, then the justiciar himself should stay behind.

Such moderation in the face of possible danger did not charactise Edward I's use of his Irish resources, once he embarked on his all-out efforts to conquer Scotland. And even earlier in his reign, when he was engaged in his Welsh or French wars, he tended to make excessive demands on Ireland. War was now waged on a scale beyond what earlier kings had attempted. Winter campaigns not only made war less of a seasonal and more an all-year business, but also necessitated the employment of paid rather than feudal levies. It also required a better organised commissariat to feed the troops and a much more professional approach to the problems of transport and communication. This demanded an ever-increasing expenditure, and during the last decade of his reign, a period of incessant warfare, Edward I found that the effort was beyond what his English resources could supply, and in addition to borrowing heavily from Italian bankers, he was forced by his needs to over-exploit his Irish lordship. The administrative machinery of the colony was geared to keep pace with his increasing demands, so that there should be as little delay as possible in supplying the king's needs.

This was bound to have a disruptive effect on the business of government, since it meant that too often attention was diverted from the routine administrative problems which should have preoccupied the justiciar and the king's ministers. But even more serious were the financial losses which the Dublin government sustained, for in the end there was not sufficient revenue available for the maintenance of law and order, a fact to which Edward II drew attention in a memorable letter early in his reign. Not only did Edward I draw huge sums of money from Ireland—certainly more than £40,000 between 1278 and 1306, and as much as £11,000 recorded in one year, 1305—but he forced the government there to incur an expenditure of a kind it could not really afford, so that it had to borrow and put future revenue in pawn. To appreciate the significance of the sums mentioned, it is important to remember that the normal revenue of the Irish exchequer during this period would have amounted to only about £5,000 per annum (though in the early 1290s, as a result of taxation, it was inflated to about £9,000 a year). Yet despite this, the Irish government was able to supply nearly £30,000 of the total cost (approximately £80,000) of the great system of fortifications which Edward built in Wales. Indeed throughout the Welsh wars a regular stream of supplies was shipped from Irish ports to victual the Welsh castles and to supply the English army, all at the cost of the Irish exchequer. That this involvement in Wales was producing repercussions in Gaelic Ireland seems evident from a letter which Thomas fitz Maurice wrote to the bishop of Bath and Wells in 1282. In it he said that because of the war in Wales the Irish 'are more elated than is their custom; some make war and others are moved towards war'. Yet King Edward ignored signs of this kind that his war policy might produce an adverse effect in Ireland and from the time John Wogan was appointed in 1295 he recklessly exploited the colony, regardless of the consequence. Three times major expeditions left Ireland for Scotland: in 1296, against Balliol, nearly 3,200 men served at a cost of £7,500; in 1301, against Wallace, the number fell to nearly 2,500 and the cost to £6,800; and in 1303 it went up to about 3,500 men, at a cost which must have been well in excess of £8,000—shipping alone cost more than £1,000. There were other smaller expeditions regularly each year, including naval forces which were sent against the west coast of Scotland and the isles. And on top of all that the Dublin government had to maintain a constant supply of food, wine, and the necessities of war, all at its own cost. For a time the Irish lordship was made largely responsible for all the supplies needed in the western theatre of war based on Carlisle. The figures available in the accounts of the Irish exchequer show the astonishing fact that during these years sometimes as much as half the annual income of the government went on supplies for Scotland.

Clearly the Irish government could not continue to over-spend like this and at the end of the reign of Edward I a financial crisis developed in the Irish exchequer. For a time Edward II made a serious effort to solve the problem, helped by the fact that the confiscation of the property of the Templars in Ireland eased the situation somewhat. He also attempted to collect bad debts in Ireland and, more important, took the important decision that all Irish revenues were to be left in Dublin at the disposal of the government there. But soon he too was deeply involved in Scotland and once again the English government resorted to the old practice of employing Irish resources in the Scottish wars. That Gaelic Ireland was now reacting in a positive way to this was ignored, despite the fact that in 1306 and later Gaelic Ulster actively supported the Scots and finally invited Edward Bruce, brother of King Robert of Scotland, to accept the high kingship of Ireland. Even when Bruce landed at the head of an army in 1315, Edward II was still foolishly trying to get further Irish supplies away to Scotland. But already the effect of this policy was all too apparent in Dublin: there was no money available to the government to raise an adequate army to resist the invasion, which partly accounts for the easy success of the Scots during the early stages of their war in Ireland. So bad was the situation now that for the first time an appeal had to be sent to England for financial assistance. This marks a momentous change and a sign of what was to come, for Ireland was now no longer an asset to the English Crown and was gradually to become a heavy liability.

The Irish government could no longer afford to pay the cost of maintaining an adequate defence against Gaelic Ireland, or even of sustaining the scale of operations which had become normal in the thirteenth century. From now on it was to become more dependant on the English exchequer and ultimately on the English taxpayer.

This policy, then, had disastrous effects on the Irish revenues. It can also be argued that it was one of the principal facts in bringing about the collapse of that feudal settlement which had been made in the century after the arrival of the first Anglo-Normans. For there is no doubt that in weakening the government and making it less effective, it made it easier for Gaelic Ireland to begin a revival which was to sweep away much of the colony. Further, it hastened the process of disintegration by contributing to the growth of lawlessness and disorder which becomes so evident in the early fourteenth century.

We have already observed that the Irish government was involved in a huge expenditure on the king's war, far beyond anything which it could afford. This situation was worsened because of the policy of pardoning debts in an effort to persuade people to undertake service overseas. Such pardons, and they were many and frequent, represented a serious loss of revenue to the exchequer. The result was disastrous and there exists no better exposition of the evils which followed from this misuse of Irish revenues than a long letter which Edward II wrote to the Irish treasurer in 1312. In it he explains that in past times a wrong use had been made of these revenues which, he says, 'for the most part have been converted to our use in Scotland and England and have also been spent on divers victuals bought in Ireland for our expeditions to Scotland . . . so that the residue of money of the issues of Ireland has so far not sufficed for preserving the peace there'. He thus expresses clearly and positively the effects which the policy produced. He then enlarges on this in the section which follows: day by day, because of the lack of money, and because of their own warlike nature, the Irish burn, kill, rob and commit other transgressions against the peace in an intolerable manner. He has therefore decided that henceforth all Irish revenue is to be spent in Ireland 'to preserve the peace there and to carry out the other arduous duties of government'. The implication is clear: what the king calls 'default of money' had prevented the Irish government from carrying out its 'arduous duties' and thereby had helped the growth of lawlessness.

This increase in disorder also resulted in another way from the policy which we outlined earlier. In order to procure sufficient supplies, the royal prerogative of purveyance was used widely in Ireland. This was normal practice and simply meant that the king's ministers were entitled to use what was in theory merely a form of preemption. They were expected to pay the current market price for whatever they seized. Lack of money, however, frequently meant that payment had to be postponed indefinitely and this was what aroused opposition. Exercised reasonably, the right of purveyance gave no real ground for complaint. It was hard, but necessary, and every member of the community had a recognised obligation to help the king in his necessity. But exercised as it was under Edward I it caused alarm, provoked resistence, and often made the victims resort to force. The frequency of these impositions, on a wide scale; the failure of the exchequer to reimburse the victims; and above all the peculation it encouraged not only among the purveyors, but also among local officials of the government—all this roused the anger of the people and thereby contributed to the growth of lawlessness. Local records in England give ample proof of the way in which local government was adversely affected by such purveyances: how much worse must the effect have been in Ireland, where the situation was far more delicate. Ireland contained strong elements of disorder within her borders. The general situation there can best be compared to that of the borderlands of Wales and Scotland. Local subsidies and local purveyances were constantly being employed for the local warfare which prevailed. Any undue pressure on the local officials, any excessive demands which could be met only by sacrificing local needs, would upset the delicate balance of power which obtained outside the vicinity of the land of peace. Apart, then, from the financial embarrassment which these purveyances caused to the central authority in Dublin, they had repercussions in widespread localities which had an even more dangerous effect. Purveyance imposed an undue strain on sheriffs and their underlings, for a large part of the work was pushed onto them. They in turn used the opportunities provided to reimburse themselves for the trouble they had to take. Especially did they use the threat of purveyance as a form of blackmail. To this, and to purveyance in general, the victims retaliated by whatever means they could—at first, in the courts, until they found that it was difficult to procure redress. If they were high ecclesiastics, they could resort to excommunication. So effective indeed was this, despite all prohibitions by the king, that some who had no power of excommunication nevertheless employed it against some ignorant servants of the royal purveyors. One amusing example of this occurred in county Meath in 1309, when the archdeacon of Meath and his chaplain by a ruse successfully prevented the servants of the purveyors from threshing the corn in the chaplain's haggard. What they did was to enrol the services of two other chaplains, together with three clerks, who had come to officiate at a funeral, and to persuade them to march in solemn procession to the haggard. This they did, bearing a cross before them and two candles, reciting aloud 'certain words in Latin' and giving the impression to the credulous laymen that they were hearing the solemn words of excommunication. When the candles were ceremoniously extinguished (the customary form in excommunication) the laymen took fright and fled from the haggard, leaving to the chaplain his corn. Subsequently court proceedings revealed that what supposedly had been the sentence of excommunication was, in fact, part of the well-known grammar of Donatus, 'such as adverbs of place and the like'.

But there was nothing amusing about the normal working of purveyance during this period of crisis in Ireland and all too often the only redress the victim had was to resort to force. It had an adverse effect, too, on trade: the citizens of Dublin complained to the king that frequent purveyance within the city 'deters many persons from bringing victuals, goods, and merchandise to the city', and we know that here, too, even the mayor was prepared to countenance the use of force in order to prevent the royal purveyors from doing their work. This sort of action helped to create the kind of climate in which lawlessness thrived. So, too, did the facility with which general pardons were obtained from the king in return for service overseas. Great numbers of these were issued to all and sundry and clearly they helped to promote crime. On the records of the Irish courts it is common to find the accused producing pardons which had been procured in advance of a crime being committed. For example, during the session of the justiciar's court at Cashel on 17 December 1317, a man was accused of the theft of one crannock of flour, valued at 32s. He came to the court and said that he was not guilty, but that in any case he had a pardon from the king which freed him from the liability of prosecution for all breaches of the peace, transgressions against the law, felonies, and so on. The pardon covered the period up to 18 December, during which time the theft had taken place. He produced the relevant letter patent out of the Irish chancery, properly sealed and authenticated, and this the court had to accept. The jury agreed that the theft had taken place within the time covered by the pardon and therefore the man was acquitted. This sort of pardon was often produced, even in cases of homicide, and was always successful. Finally in 1317 and again in 1323 Edward II found that he had to curtail grants of such general pardons, because 'others have been encouraged to commit crimes on account of the facility of obtaining such pardons'. Indeed when Edward I's need had been really pressing, he released criminals from Irish gaols on condition that they joined his service in Scotland.

In addition to weakening central authority and helping to increase disorder, these wars had reverberations in Gaelic Ireland. This is reflected, for example, in the amount of attention given them in a Franciscan chronicle which mirrors the Gaelic revival. Chieftains were quick to take advantage when the Anglo-Irish were away on service overseas. As we saw, there were occasions when Henry III was conscious of this danger and acted with caution. Even Edward I, when he first began to seek military assistance from Ireland, seemed well aware of the possible danger and always insisted, in his orders to Dublin, that the country 'remain sufficiently well guarded'. But when the difficulties of maintaining war on two, and even three, fronts began to sap his resources and the troubles which are so marked a feature of the last years of his reign became practically insurmountable, he quickly lost sight of the adverse effect which his policy might have in Ireland and omitted to take the necessary precautions. The Gaelic leaders therefore seized their chance when the Anglo-Irish were diverted from their lordships by service overseas. They invaded the lands of the settlers, seized their property, burned their castles, and in general caused havoc among their inadequately protected holdings. All of this probably would have happened in any case; but the policy of Edward I made it that much easier.

The growth in lawlessness and disorder is reflected in many aspects of the state of Ireland at the end of the thirteenth century. In 1297 a parliament was summoned 'in order to establish peace more firmly', the record tells us, and its legislation shows not only some of the problems of defence in the localities, but also the difficulties of keeping the peace. A letter from Edward II in June 1308 describes the situation:

We have been informed by some that very many of our enemies and other evildoers and disturbers of our peace, frequently committing homicides, burnings, robberies and other very serious injuries, by night and day in Ireland, wander from county to county, and run to and fro, by reason of the default and negligence of most men, who have hitherto refused and do refuse to turn aside from the parts in which they live to the neighbouring part in which such evils are committed, to aid their neighbours who dwell there.

Two years later, in 1310, the Kilkenny parliament concluded that current prices were so high because 'merchants, strangers, and others passing through the country are robbed of their goods by those of great lineage, against whom they have frequently heretofore had small means of recovery'. They were often imprisoned and held to ransom. Such malefactors 'take, as well in the town as in the woods, bread, wine, beer, flesh, and other victuals and things for sale, wherever they be, without making reasonable payment, by reason whereof merchants dare not pass through the country, to convey or expose their merchandise any more in the town than in the wood'. For this kind of disorder there was no real remedy forthcoming and it is clear from the legislation of subsequent parliaments, and from petitions of grievance from individuals and communities, that lawlessness increased with the years.

It should not be thought, however, that Ireland was unique in this. For this growth of disorder was part of a pattern in Europe, where the traditional feudal structure of society was beginning to crumble and disruptive forces were asserting themselves. There is, too, another side to the picture which shows the more constructive elements in society at work. So far as government is concerned there was a further advance made in the shiring of feudal Ireland. More significant, however, was the development of parliament, one of the truly characteristic contributions of the middle ages to our civilisation. The emergence of the principle of representation was the crucial fact and three Edwardian parliaments in Ireland illustrate very well how this happened. In 1297, as we saw, the problem of peace-keeping and defence in the localities was acute; so that when parliament was summoned to suggest a solution, it was natural that the localities should be represented in order to give advice. The counties and liberties therefore elected knights to represent them, thereby widening the composition of parliament to include the local communities. Two years later, in 1299, representatives of towns were summoned to a parliament in Dublin in order to debate the problem of 'false moneys which divers foreign merchants bring into this land' and to advise on currency regulations. In 1300, for the first time so far as we know, parliament included both kinds of popular representatives, from towns as well as counties and liberties, this time for the specific function of discussing taxation. It is clear that the commons were summoned only occasionally and always for a limited purpose. Not for many years did they establish their right to be a constituent element in a parliament which was still a meeting of the great men of the land. But a real beginning was made in Ireland at the end of the thirteenth century. The representatives summoned to the parliament of 1297 were required to come with 'full power' (*plena potestas*) to bind the communities which elected them; and in 1300 counties and boroughs were ordered to elect representatives who in parliament would have 'special power as if all were present'—in other words the commons in parliament were to be in the very fullest sense the plenipotentiaries of their communities. This meant, for example, that if (as indeed happened from now on) the representatives granted a subsidy in parliament, the whole community of the lordship was bound to pay it. Few more fundamental principles were ever devised in the middle ages than this one of popular representation and its appearance in Ireland at such an early date is a sign not only of the influx of ideas into the lordship, but of the constructive achievements of the *communitas Hibernie* (the community of the lordship) which must be taken into account in any estimate of the age. There was a more constructive side to life at the end of the thirteenth century than we might suppose from reading the annals of the time. For some, Ireland possessed a peace and a tranquillity which aroused a nostalgia such as that expressed in an exquisite lyric by an unknown poet of the time:

> I am of Ireland,
> And of the Holy land
> Of Ireland.
> Good sir, pray I thee,
> For of *saint charité*,
> Come and dance with me
> In Ireland.

Nevertheless, looking back we can see this as an age of violence, when life was as uncertain as it always is under frontier conditions and the fear of death was ever present. Raids by Irish enemies or English rebels, not to mention the activities of 'common thieves' and criminals who roamed the countryside, made terror a common experience in many a community. The little hamlet of Haughstown in county Kildare could be plunged into terror on a night in 1310 by a crowd of mischief-makers who, as a court record tells us, 'of malice shouted in a loud voice *Fennock aboo, Fennock aboo*, which is the war cry of the O Tooles, and by this cry of malice made all the men and women of the town fly out of their houses', because they feared that the Irish were descending on them.

But it wasn't only the Irish who could make life a burden, for often the feudal lords were just as ruthless in their demands. Such a one was Richard de Burgh, the 'red' earl of Ulster and lord of Connacht. He was by far the most powerful man in the lordship, often taking precedence over the chief governor himself, and controlling vast resources in land and manpower. He was close to the king, who once sent him a remarkable message in which he said that he 'relies on him more than any other man in the land for many reasons'. But for all his power de Burgh was typical of the other Irish magnates in helping to maintain the conditions in which lawlessness flourished. He constantly interfered in the internal affairs of Gaelic chieftancies, levied non-feudal imposts on his tenants, and altogether behaved almost as if he were an independent potentate within his vast lordship. It was typical of the *Annals of Connacht* to record that in 1310 in the extensive Irish territory of Síl Murray, in the present county Roscommon, 'there was not one of their townlands without its permanent quartering, nor a tuath free from exaction, nor a prince free from oppression, so long as William Burke was in control of them after the death of Aed'. It is not, therefore, altogether surprising that Earl Richard should have proved unpopular with some elements in the population, most notably the towns, which seem to have developed a deep hatred for the Anglo-Irish magnates before the end of the thirteenth century. This in a way was perfectly natural, for the towns relied on settled conditions and trade for their very existence, and too often the feudal aristocracy had been responsible for disturbances that threatened to wreck trade. There were many instances of fights between the two classes, between the town and the manor as it were. When the *Annals of Connacht* recorded in 1252 that during a military expedition to Ulster 'strife arose at Dundalk between the Meath and Munster contingents and some of those of Munster were killed', the annalist was silent about how the townsmen reacted. But we know that they could use violence against soldiers passing through their town. In the early fourteenth century, for example, Peter de Bermingham and his men were trapped by the citizens of Drogheda on a bridge leading into the town and in the resulting skirmish three of his men were killed. Maurice de Carreu lodged his contingent in the Coombe while passing through Dublin on his way to serve with the king in Scotland. He was attacked by a number of citizens, some of his men were slain, and goods to the value of £100 were lost. So bad did relations become between Dublin and the Anglo-Irish magnates, that in 1317 Edward II was compelled to order the parliament which had been summoned to Dublin to meet elsewhere, because he feared 'that damage may be done if the magnates of Ireland and their men enter that city, on account of the disputes between them and the men of that city'. He further ordered that in future the magnates should not be allowed to 'house their men within the city against the will of the community, nor to cause victuals within the city to be taken without their consent'. Here we undoubtedly have the cause of the bad feeling, probably stretching back over a long period of time during which troops were billeted on an unwilling population, but almost certainly referring in particular to events associated with the Bruce wars in Ireland only a short time before. During the difficult years which followed the invasion of Edward Bruce in 1315, troops frequently passed through or near Dublin, leaving a trail of damage behind them. To suffer at the hands of the Scots was bad enough; but to suffer because of the Anglo-Irish magnates was intolerable. Small wonder, then, that the Dubliners felt venomous towards the magnates.

Such bad feeling was partly responsible for the great outburst of 21 February 1317, when the citizens seized the earl of Ulster and threw him into prison. In normal circumstances such an action would have been inconceivable, so powerful was the earl. It was panic at the imminent approach of a Scottish army, coupled with the deep suspicion that de Burgh was a traitor and was in league with the invaders, that precipitated so drastic a step. It was on the same occasion that, with the defences of Dublin in a hopeless state in the face of the advancing Scots, the citizens took matters into their own hands and on one memorable night they set fire to the bridge across the Liffey, burned the suburbs, destroyed Thomas Street, and tore down the belfry of St Mary's so as to provide some of the material necessary to repair breaches in the walls of the city. The activities of that night, we are told, were enough to deter Edward Bruce. As he watched the burning suburbs from his camp at Castleknock, he decided that a siege of the city would prove too costly and so he pressed forward on his circuit of Ireland, leaving Dublin for a later date.

The presence of Edward Bruce in Ireland, the fact that he was on a circuit of the country with a large army, the panic which his approach to Dublin engendered, and the wild rumours that some of the greatest men in the lordship (including the justiciar of the time, Edmund Butler, and some other royal officials) were assisting him, all indicate the low state of the lordship in the early fourteenth century—so bad, indeed, that in 1311 the Ordainers in England complained to the king that Ireland 'was on the point of being lost, unless God improve the situation'. It was, in fact, a manifestation of the Gaelic revival which brought the Scots to Ireland, since the Ulster leaders clearly felt that the time had come to revive the old high kingship and restore the Gaelic order. At the same time the great success of Scottish arms at Bannockburn in 1314 made an extension of the war against England into Ireland a logical proposition, especially since raids southwards across the border into England became more daring, penetrating, and effective, and since it was also believed that a combined attack on Anglo-Wales was in the mind of the king of Scotland. There was, too, the fear in King Robert's mind that his brother Edward might yet prove ambitious in Scotland; far better to divert him to Ireland, where his ambitions might be satisfied and where he could at the same time strike a blow against England. Bruce had personal experience of the extensive use made of Irish resources by the king of England in Scotland and he knew well that by sending his brother Edward to Ireland he would be calling a halt on this exploitation of the Irish lordship as a source of supply. In addition, by opening up a second front in Ireland he would be forcing the English government to divert some of its energy towards meeting the crisis across the Irish sea, which indeed is what eventually happened.

The initiative seems to have been taken by the king of Ulster, Donal O Neill, and the chieftains under him, who invited Edward Bruce to Ireland at some time after the victory of Bannockburn. That event had naturally excited Gaelic Ulster, for the Scots were mostly Gaelic too (a fact to which Robert I adverted in a letter which he wrote to 'all the kings of Ireland', when he said that 'we and you and our people and your people, free since ancient time, share the same natural ancestry') and it must have raised hopes that Gaelic Ireland could free herself from the Gall. The king of Scotland later said that his brother was sent 'so that with God's will your nation may be able to recover her ancient liberty', a hope expressed later in the *Annals of Loch Cé* which recounted the landing of King Robert himself 'in aid of his brother . . . and to expel the Foreigners from Ireland'. The cultural link between Ulster and Gaelic Scotland was strong —indeed culturally they formed one region and for years before 1315 traffic was continuous across the narrow channel which divided them. The links had been strengthened by the influx of gallowglasses, Scottish mercenary forces, into Ireland from the mid-thirteenth century onwards and by the involvement of some northern chieftains in the Scottish war of independence. Robert Bruce had close connections, too, although with feudal Ulster, since he was married to Elizabeth de Burgh, daughter of the earl of Ulster and had visited that province on a number of occasions. James the Steward of Scotland had married a sister of the earl and many other Scottish families had close connections with Ulster, some since the plantation of part of the province by Scots in the time of King John. It is not altogether surprising, then, that Edward Bruce should have accepted the invitation from Ireland.

He landed near Larne on 25 May 1315, with what contemporaries describe as an army of 6,000 and a fleet of 200 ships. We must regard these figures as an overstatement, but they do suggest that Bruce had with him a sizeable force of veterans, a sure indication that his purpose was not merely exploratory. Indeed his army, amplified no doubt by the Gaelic forces which joined him, was large enough to give him control of Ulster. By the end of June he had taken and burned Dundalk, and finally on 10 September he defeated the earl of Ulster at the battle of Connor. The Gaelic chieftains of the north had quickly supported Bruce after his landing, thus repudiating the lordship of the earl of Ulster. Soon afterwards Felim O Connor did likewise, plunging Connacht into catastrophe for the next few years. Thus the military superiority of Bruce was quickly established, and the loss of Ulster and Connacht reduced the great earl of Ulster to impotence, so that, as an annalist puts it, he was 'a wanderer up and down Ireland, with no power of lordship'.

There seemed to be no stopping Bruce now. The king's special agent, John of Hotham, reported that the Scots 'with their allies puffed up with pride were doing all damage as they wished'. He invaded Meath, where he defeated Mortimer of Trim, then marched into Leinster early in 1316. The government seemed powerless, partly because lack of money hampered it in its efforts to put an adequate army into the field. But the fault lay mainly with the magnates who were jealous of each other and refused to co-operate. The earl of Ulster had learnt a hard lesson when he refused to accept the assistance of the justiciar and insisted on fighting Bruce on his own, meeting with crushing defeat. In his defence it can be argued that not only did he feel that Ulster was his special responsibility, but (what was more to the point) as the *Annals of Innisfallen* tell us 'because he had feared the ruin of his lands' by a government army, he was not willing to allow them through his land—a more reasonable fear, as we have already seen. The same annals, after recounting the damage done by the Scots at Dundalk, add that 'excepting homicide, however, deeds no less evil were done by an army drawn from different parts of Ireland to do battle with them, in the districts through which the units passed'. The magnates who were summoned to oppose Bruce in Leinster, however, had no such excuse. They assembled as ordered, but the leaders quarrelled among themselves and they allowed the Scots to escape unchallenged. Perhaps the most serious result of this particular failure to deal with Bruce was the effect it had in Munster, where it encouraged the O Briens and others to rise out in rebellion.

Bruce now returned to Ulster and there, in the early summer of 1316, he was inaugurated high king of Ireland. After the fall of Carrickfergus in September he made it his capital. There he held his court, offering justice to all. He also summoned parliaments, hanged lawbreakers and began to prepare for an attempt to win the whole of Ireland. His position had been considerably weakened by the great defeat of O Connor at the battle of Athenry on 10 August 1316, though it was to be some years yet before Connacht was once again settled into its old relationship to its lord, the earl of Ulster. Bruce had secured a firm hold on Ulster, where not only Gaelic chieftains but Anglo-Irish, too, accepted him. His very presence there and his acting the part of a high king, were a threat to the English lordship in Ireland. Yet he clearly realised, probably from experience gained during his perambulations of 1315–16, that he was in no position to attempt to win all Ireland. Outside Ulster Gaelic support was for the most part either tepid or wholly lacking, and the forces of the government would regroup sooner or later. So he returned to Scotland, succeeded in persuading his brother Robert to come to help him in Ireland, which he did late in the winter of 1316.

Edward Bruce was very much in the position of an old-style high king 'with opposition'. He needed to impose his rule, even on most of Gaelic Ireland. This meant undertaking a great circuit of Ireland in the traditional style, forcing submissions, procuring hostages, taking tribute. He would also have to bring about the downfall of the Dublin government and dispossess all those magnates who might refuse to acquiesce in his rule. All of this required careful preparation and it was not until early 1317 that he moved out of Ulster and made his bid for power. By then it was too late. Whatever Gaelic enthusiasm there may have been at first was now blunted. Only O Neill remained constant and it soon became obvious that without active Gaelic support success was impossible. His army starved as it moved through Meath, Kildare, Kilkenny, Tipperary and as far west as Limerick in February, March and April of 1317. Everywhere the Scots burned, destroyed or plundered what they could, committing atrocities as they moved. They finally retreated to Ulster in early May, and Robert Bruce returned to Scotland.

By now the English government had realised the seriousness of the crisis in Ireland and offered belated help. A measure of their alarm is the arrangement made to ship 1,000 mercenaries from Genoa to fight in Ireland in the summer of 1317. Money, too, was provided and a new chief governor, Roger Mortimer, lord of Trim and one of the greatest men in England, arrived in April with extensive powers. It was probably because of this English reaction, coupled with the departure of his brother, that Edward Bruce remained in Ulster for the next year and a half. He had missed his chance and he was not now anxious to try a second time. Then, for no apparent reason, he moved out of Ulster again in October 1318. This time he was soon opposed by a colonial army and at a pitched battle at Faughart, just north of Dundalk, he was defeated and killed. So ended the greatest single challenge so far encountered by the lordship of Ireland.

Bruce went within an ace of toppling that lordship. Had circumstances been more propitious and had more of Gaelic Ireland supported him he might well have succeeded. As it was, he exposed for all to see the shaky state of the lordship, the weakness of the government, the strength of many of the Gaelic chieftains, and the disloyalty of many of the settlers. According to a contemporary writer Ireland, while he was there, 'became one trembling wave of commotion'; and when he died he was universally condemned by the annalists, one of whom wrote that 'he was the common ruin of the Galls and Gaels of Ireland . . . for in this Bruce's time, for three years and a half, falsehood and famine and homicide filled the country, and undoubtedly men ate each other in Ireland'.

There is no doubt that Bruce and his army destroyed much in Ireland. Yet the responsibility for the terrors of those years was not entirely his, for his invasion coincided with one of the worst

famines of the middle ages, when the whole of Europe was
gripped by hunger in the years 1315, 1316 and 1317. In Ireland,
where the famine lasted until 1318, the terrible weather of 1314
and the year following was to produce the same effects as elsewhere in Europe: bad harvests, high prices, starvation, followed
by disease, violence and death everywhere. A simple statement in
the *Annals of Connacht* under 1315—'many afflications in all parts
of Ireland: very many deaths, famine and many strange diseases,
murders and intolerable storms as well'—hides a terrible story.
More than anything else, this famine defeated Bruce in the end,
and it is surely ironical that by the time he died, and in popular
tradition ever since, he was held to be entirely to blame for all
that Ireland had suffered during those years.

This invasion has often been seen as a great turning point in the
history of the medieval lordship, a watershed in the middle ages.
Remembering all that happened during those years, it is difficult
to escape that conclusion. During the war so much had been
destroyed that many manors never recovered, land fell back into
waste, and great areas became depopulated. Even as late as 1327
it was proposed that Welsh or English colonists be introduced to
reoccupy waste lands near Carrickfergus which had been unoccupied or uncultivated since 1315. In many ways, too, it
contributed to the gradual breakdown of central authority in
Ireland. There was a great moral collapse in the face of the
invasion, not only because of the numbers of Anglo-Irish who
defected, but also because of the bishops and other clergy (not all
of them in Gaelic Ireland) who preached rebellion and urged co-
operation with the Scots. But the true significance of the invasion
is that it exposed the essential weakness of the king's government
in Ireland. In itself the Bruce war was not the major cause of that
weakness, though it did contribute to it. A financial crisis had
long since emerged at the Dublin exchequer, so that when Bruce
landed the Irish council found that it had insufficient money to
pay the wages of an army to send against him. Without adequate
financial resources no government could properly discharge its
duties and in Ireland from early in the fourteenth century a
noticeable decline in revenues had taken place. Again, while the
Bruce war may have contributed to the acceleration of that
decline, it certainly did not cause it. Nor was disloyalty among
the Anglo-Irish new: it had manifested itself before and would do

so again throughout the medieval period. As for Gaelic Ireland, the Bruce invasion failed to act as the catalyst it might have been. Friar Clyn, the Kilkenny chronicler, in referring to the invasion says: 'There adhered to them (the Scots) while they were in Ireland almost all the Irish of the land, and few kept their faith and loyalty'. This is an exagerrated estimate of the situation, for the greater part of Gaelic Ireland either held aloof or else used the situation created by Bruce to benefit themselves.

Yet there is no doubt that while the common belief reported by Clyn is not true, it is a fact that many Gaelic leaders repudiated the lordship not only of the fedual magnates, but also of the king himself. This is made clear not only by their actions, such as those of O Neill in Ulster or O Connor in Connacht, but also in the reports of writers of the time. A well-known Gaelic tract, *The Tribes and Customs of Hy Many*, while extolling the ruling O Madden for keeping faith (he thereby 'taught truth to the chieftains and kept his people from treachery', according to the writer), condemned O Neill and others who sided unjustly with 'foreigners less noble than these our own foreigners'. More important, an appeal addressed to Pope John XXII by the king of Ulster, writing on behalf of Gaelic Ireland, attempted to justify a repudiation of the lordship of the king of England: it was necessary to make war on him in Ireland, because of his bad government here, the wrongs done by him, his 'evil ministers and barons born in Ireland', and the failure of all the kings since Henry II to fulfil the terms of the original grant of Adrian IV. 'And as it is free to anyone to renounce his right and transfer it to another, all the right which is publicly known to pertain to us in the said kingdom as its true heirs we have given and granted to him (i.e. Edward Bruce) by our letters patent, and in order that he may do therein judgement and justice and equity which through default of the prince (i.e. Edward II) have utterly failed therein, we have unanimously established and set him up as our king and lord in our kingdom aforesaid'.

Some years later, when royal agents were making proposals to the pope for the reformation of the Irish Church, they complained that 'the people of the Irish nation do not deem our lord the king to be the true lord of Ireland but only lord by usurpation', to which the pope replied that both in the pulpit and in the confessional the clergy of Ireland must defend the king's dominion.

None of this can be ascribed directly to Edward Bruce, though Gaelic Ireland undoubtedly gained from the upset he caused in the feudal lordship. He gave added momentum to a movement which had already made much progress, a great Gaelic revival which aimed at restoring ancestral rule and traditional institutions and recovering lost lands. In the history of this Gaelic revival Scotland had an important part to play, mainly because she supplied the mercenaries who helped to tip the military balance in favour of many Gaelic chieftains, but also because of the shock given to the king's administration in the localities by the Bruce invasion and its aftermath.

VII The Gaelic Revival

THE Bruce invasion and the widespread Gaelic revival associated with it mark a turning point in the history of the medieval lordship. From now on the English colony was in steady decline and everywhere Gaelic chieftains were recovering ancestral lands and authority. The Dublin government found that it was unable to cope with this great Gaelic recovery and slowly began to narrow the effective range of its authority until in the fifteenth century it found that it was largely confined to a small defended area in the east known as the Pale. Here, and in a few towns outside, the king's writ effectively ran. Elsewhere the Gaelic chieftains or the powerful Anglo-Irish lords virtually ruled supreme in a complex network of lordships. And almost everywhere the Irish language, and with it the culture of Gaelic Ireland, was the norm.

It is true that all this is most discernible in the fourteenth century, when the government made frantic efforts to halt the spread of Gaelic culture and the territorial expansion of Gaelic Ireland. There is a temptation to see in the Bruce invasion of 1315 and the events associated with it the root cause of this great decline of Anglo-Ireland. As we have seen, however, the beginnings of that decline antedate the Bruce wars, and there were other factors at work in the thirteenth century which in the long run were to undermine the colony. The basic fact, of course, was the existence of many independent Gaelic enclaves all over Ireland, places which had never been conquered, settled and feudalised, and therefore Gaelic strongholds from which military or cultural assaults might be made. Nearly all of the land over about six hundred feet remained Gaelic, as did a good part of the west, north-west and south-west. And all through the feudal area, even where English settlement was thickest, there survived a very pronounced Gaelic element in the population which, however loyal and however feudal, had remained the custodians of the language and culture of Gaelic Ireland, which in turn they transmitted to their Anglo-Irish neighbours.

Territorially and culturally Ireland was, from the beginning of the Anglo-Norman invasion, divided into two areas, mutually antagonistic towards each other. The Treaty of Windsor of 1175 had first recognised this division and had tried to fix a frontier between Gaelic and Anglo-Norman Ireland. For a number of reasons this attempt failed and subsequently the expansion of feudal Ireland saw the creation of a constantly shifting frontier heavily fortified (indeed one of the first of the kind in western Europe) and carefully guarded. It is impossible to delineate this frontier exactly at any given time, though its broad course can be plotted. Behind that frontier lay what was called the *terra pacis* (the 'land of peace') and outside was the *terra guerre* (the 'land of war'). In between, where the frontier land was in dispute, where boundaries were vague, and where life was more uncertain than usual, lay the 'march land'. These terms are self-explanatory and their usage gives us a clear idea of how the government and inhabitants of feudal Ireland viewed their situation in the thirteenth century. Probably more than two-thirds of Ireland lay within the land of peace (in theory, at any rate) by the time Edward I came to the throne in 1272. Here lived not only the feudal lords and the settlers from England, but the Gaelic population of many manors, and the Gaelic chieftains and people who had accepted the lordship of the king and the mesne lordship of the great feudatories. Outside lived those whom Richard II was later to call 'the wild Irish, our enemies', frequently referred to simply as 'the Irish enemies' (*Hibernici inimici*) in the earlier period; within lived the *fideles Anglici* ('loyal English', a phrase which presupposes the existence of not-so-loyal English). To keep the 'Irish enemies' at bay posed a great problem of defence which at first was well within the resources of the Dublin government and the local communities of the colony or the feudatories in their lordships. But, as we saw, the resources of the government were too often diverted abroad from the needs of Ireland, while many of the lordships were weakened by partition and absenteeism, internecine strife, or sometimes bad management. The result was that in many places the defence of the frontier broke down and Gaelic Ireland began to infiltrate the land of peace, first in a trickle and later, in places, in a flood. It is difficult to say when and where precisely this began to happen; but the trend was under way long before the end of the thirteenth century. First the expansion of Anglo-Ireland was checked; then its frontiers were pushed back.

There are two aspects of this great revival of Gaelic Ireland which are best treated separately, though in truth such a separation is highly artificial since both are very closely intertwined: the first we might call the political rally, through which land was regained, lost Gaelic lordships re-established, and some great kingships effectively revived; and the second is its cultural phase, which manifested itself not only in an extension of Gaelic culture, but in the assimilation of many of the settlers to it. The political phase itself can also be divided into two movements, the one which had as its aim the restoration of the high kingship, and the other which was confined to the recreation of local lordship. The first was national, or pseudo-national, in that it was supposed to embrace the whole of Gaelic Ireland. Ireland would rise again and the shame of her bondage would be forgotten—so the poets wrote at the height of the revival: 'Ireland is a woman who has risen again from the horrors of reproach . . . she belongs to Irishmen after all that she was owned by foreign churls'. The bardic poets of the fourteenth and fifteenth centuries frequently in praise poems, or inauguration odes, promised the high kingship to the patron whom they addressed, or urged that it should be seized. A poem from the mid-fourteenth century dedicated to an O Connor says: ' . . . our hope is fixed on another Fair on bright-surfaced Teamhair', referring to the festival which only the high king could summon. The other phase of the revival was purely local in its ramifications. The first was a failure, the second a success.

Before, however, we examine these different aspects of the Gaelic revival, it would be well to suggest what forces were responsible for it. There is no doubt that the very weaknesses inherent in the colony, which the passage of time exposed, where an invitation to the Gaelic chieftains to attack the settlements and win back land. Military superiority had enabled the Anglo-Normans to defeat most armies thrown against them in Ireland. But this advantage was lost in the thirteenth century, mainly because the importation of foreign mercenary soldiers into Gaelic Ireland supplied the professionalism and the military expertise which had been lacking before. These were the gallow-glasses (*gall-óglaigh*, or 'foreign soldiers'), from the western islands of Scotland, a mixture of Norse and Gael by blood, and still nominally under the lordship of the king of Norway. They seem to have come first to the north-west of Ulster in 1258, and subsequently spread to many parts of the island. With their armour and fearsome axes, and their extraordinary courage and daring in battle, they quickly proved more than a match for the soldiers of the colony. They cancelled out the grave military disadvantage which Gaelic Ireland suffered and the result was quickly seen in local Gaelic victories where formerly there would have been defeats. The availability of these mercenaries, and soon too of their Gaelic counterparts (*buannadha*, or men in permanent service), undoubtedly spurred on Gaelic chieftains to take military risks. But there must have been other, less tangible factors, which induced Gaelic Ireland to make this comeback, some hidden force which persuaded the chieftains to react against what they had earlier peaceably accepted, the lordship of a Butler, a fitz Gerald, or some other feudatory, or even in extreme cases to reject the lordship of the king of England. It has been suggested that this force was 'national sentiment, intensified and supplied with a more definite political form under a sense of national oppression'.[10] It is easy to dismiss such an argument as anachronistic, on the ground that nationalism could not have existed in Ireland at that time. But the example of emergent nationality in Europe in this period, or shortly afterwards, should warn us against too quick an assumption that a sense of nationality was not present in Ireland. There was no doubt that there was a Gaelic nation, recognisable through its language, laws and customs, and self-conscious, at least in its literature. Indeed the Anglo-Irish were hardly any less self-conscious, aware of being a race apart (a *media natio* or 'middle nation', as they were so aptly described in the fourteenth century). But it is doubtful if national self-consciousness in Ireland ever became an agent for political action, at least during this period of the middle ages. The attempt was made, on more than one occasion, to make national sentiment a force for action. In a letter which he wrote to a Mac Carthy of Desmond, urging him to join Edward Bruce in the war against the English, Donal O Neill, king of Ulster, made an impassioned appeal to national sentiment

[10]E. MacNeill, *Phases of Irish History*, Dublin, 1920, 325.

as a reason for attacking the 'sacriligious and accursed English', the 'worst of all people', and he pointed out that the chief weakness of Gaelic Ireland was that its people were divided against each other: 'so that we, being weakened by wounding one another, may easily yield ourselves a prey to them. Hence it is that we owe to ourselves the miseries with which we are afflicted, degenerate and manifestly unworthy of our ancestors, by whose valour and splendid deeds the Irish race in all past ages has retained its liberty'. On another occasion King Robert I of Scotland tried to form a confederation against the English, comprising the Scots, Irish and the Welsh. Once, before 1315, he made an appeal based on their common Celtic ancestry; and again, in 1327, he joined their common hatred of the English to their racial kinship as a basis for common action. Indeed in a letter to 'all and every one of the kings of Ireland, the prelates and clergy too of the same, and the inhabitants of all Ireland, our friends', he appealed for a 'confederation of special friendship' based on common language and common descent. Long afterwards, in the early fifteenth century, Owen Glyndwr of Wales made a similar attempt to involve the Irish and the Scots in his rebellion against the new Lancastrian dynasty in England and, like Bruce, he based his appeal on common kinship and oppression by the common enemy, the 'Saxons'.

Appeals of this kind to national sentiment did not succeed in producing the kind of reaction they were designed to achieve, though the very fact that they were made in the expectation of some response is significant. The horizon of most men was still limited to the *patria*, the locality, and for a long time in Ireland local particularism (or 'patriotism') was to remain too strong a force to give way to any kind of real sense of nationality. However strong such a sense may have been among the men of letters, the professional jurists, or the greater churchmen (who were always conscious of the Irish Church as a national institution within the wider framework of an international body), the local rulers can never have been moved to action by any such sentiment. But a sense of oppression there undoubtedly was, which prompted some local rulers at least to strike out for independence. Sometimes the feeling of oppression was justified, at other times not. But what matters is that it existed and that it prompted a reaction. When, for example, there was a Geraldine attempt to expand into Donegal in the 1240s, the O Donnells rightly felt aggrieved and at the first opportunity struck back. A similar reaction can be seen in Thomond when the kingdom was granted to de Clare over the heads of the O Briens, or in Desmond when further advances by the Geraldines there threatened what little the Mac Carthys still held. Many Gaelic kings, such as the O Connors of Connacht, quite rightly felt that they had been betrayed by the feudal lord of Ireland who instead of protecting them, as he should have done, too often ignored their rights in making speculative grants of land to newcomers. Poets often urged their patrons not to rely on charters from the king, but to ignore them and trust instead to their own strength. A poem addressed to an O Reilly Lord of Breifne repeats this almost as a refrain: 'Thou shalt seek no other charter except thy own reliance on thy gallantry; to charge against the sharp spears that pierce thee is thy true charter to thy land'. And again: 'The sharp spear in thy hand, the blade from Vulcan's smithy, the spear if it be nearer thee, thy sword—these are thy charter'. Indeed, apart from the so-called 'Five Bloods', the descendants of the old provincial dynasties, the Gaelic race as a whole was left outside English law, was denied its use and appeal to its courts, except for those who purchased charters of denizenship. Within the Church attempts were made to exclude the Gaelic element from office. None of the Gaelic chieftains was ever made a baron, summoned to parliament, or made to feel in any way the equal of any of the feudatories of Ireland. The fact is that officially the Gaelic race, and its language and institutions, indeed its whole culture, was regarded as at best second class, and often as depraved: the typical attitude of the conqueror towards the conquered. No wonder, then, that Gaelic Ireland felt oppressed and had a strong sense of grievance.

To illustrate this it is only necessary to look at the famous 'Remonstrance' addressed by the king of Ulster, in the name of Gaelic Ireland, to Pope John XXII during the Bruce invasion. There is every reason to doubt the truth of much that is said in this remarkable statement of grievance against both the king of England and the feudatories of Ireland. It contains a great deal of special pleading, in an attempt to justify the war of Bruce against the English. But when every allowance is made, there is no doubt that this document gives us a fairly accurate insight into the Gaelic mind and the reasons for rebellion. The king of England has not fulfilled his obligations in Ireland and therefore his lordship can be repudiated. But the really venomous part of this document is reserved for the Anglo-Irish, from whom Gaelic Ireland suffered most. These were the English of 'the middle nation' and they were 'so different in character from the English of England and from other nations that with the greatest propriety they may be called a nation not of middle (*medium*) but of utmost perfidy'. Examples of their perfidy are quoted, such as 'lusting eagerly for our lands' and thus promoting endless war in which more than 50,000 of 'each nation' have been killed; inviting neighbours to banquets so as to murder them easily; or preaching the heresy that it is no more a sin to kill an Irishman than to kill a dog. It is impossible to live in peace with them. 'For such is their arrogance and excessive lust to lord it over us and so great is our due and natural desire to throw off the unbearable yoke of their slavery and to recover our inheritance wickedly seized upon by them, that as there has not been hitherto, there cannot now be or ever henceforward be established, sincere good will between them and us in this life. For we have a natural hostility towards each other arising from the mutual, malignant and incessant slaying of fathers, brothers, nephews and other near relatives and friends so that we can have no inclination to reciprocal friendship in our time'. The same sort of language, expressing the same sort of grievance, is used by O Neill in his letter to Mac Carthy, from which we have already quoted: ' . . . the sacrilegious and accursed English, who, worse than the inhuman Danes themselves, are busy heaping injuries of every kind upon the inhabitants of this country'.

Whatever chance there had been then that the two races in Ireland might have been assimilated to one another, or at least have learned to live in peace together, was destroyed by the genuine sense of oppression which Gaelic Ireland soon felt. At least one king of England, Richard II, recognised that Gaelic Ireland had some justification for feeling aggrieved. He wrote from Ireland in 1395 that 'to us and our council it appears that the Irish rebels have rebelled in consequence of the injustice and grievances practised towards them, for which they have been afforded no redress'. When this sense of grievance was translated

into action, the Gaelic revival was under way and the lordship
of Ireland was repudiated. This was symbolised in a most unusual
event in 1258, when a meeting was convened at Caoluisce on
the river Erne, near Beleek in county Fermanagh, at which an
O Connor and an O Brien made peace and gave what an annalist
calls 'the kingship of the Gaels of Ireland' to Brian O Neill, king
of Ulster. Thus was the high kingship restored—in 1260 King
Henry III, writing to his son Edward, remarks that O Neill
'presumptuously bears himself as king of the kings of Ireland'—
and the feudal lordship of Ireland rejected. The most remarkable
feature of this episode is that the offer to O Neill seems to have
been made spontaneously. That it was made at all is extraordinary enough in itself, when we remember the bitterness
which the struggle for the high kingship had engendered in the
previous century. It should not be thought, however, that this
in any way represents a nation-wide movement to restore a
national monarchy. O'Brien and O'Connor were both the
descendants of two of the great dynasties which had claimed the
high kingship and they could thus in theory be said to be speaking
on behalf of a great part of Gaelic Ireland. But the realities of the
situation in 1258 must make us realise that neither of those two
could in practice represent anything more than a small part of
that which was still in Gaelic hands. Furthermore, it is instructive
to notice that among the many who were not present at this
meeting were two kings who could be said to represent in real
terms far more than either O Brien or O Connor. One was
Mac Carthy, king of Desmond, who at this very time was leading
the most successful rally against the Anglo-Irish in the south;
the other was O Donnell, king of Tirconaill, who was also
enjoying a spectacular success against the settlers in the north-
west. Indeed not only did the O Donnells refuse to recognise
the high kingship of O Neill, they even repudiated his claims
to have rights over them and others as king of Ulster.

This first attempt to restore the high kingship ended in disaster,
though not before it had caused the government some moments
of anxiety. Troops had to be rushed northwards to defend Ulster.
Finally in May 1260 O Neill made his big effort, marching on
Downpatrick, the capital of the earldom. But there he met his
end, defeated by local levies. His death, according to the lament
composed by his court poet Giolla Brighde Mac Con Midhe,

was the result of an unequal contest between Gael and Foreigner, the unarmed against the armed:

> Unequal they engaged in battle,
> The foreigners and the Gael of Tara,
> Fine linen shirts on the race of Conn
> And foreigners in one mass of iron.

Earlier in the poem he had described the army of the colonists coming

> In a blue-grey mass thither
> In gold and iron armour.

After his death, King Brian's head was sent to the king in England, together with messages announcing the great victory. This savage, though common, custom caused the poet to burst forth in a great cry of grief:

> Death of my heart! The head of Brian
> Is in a strange country under cold clay!
> O head of Brian of Sliabh Sneachta,
> Ireland after thee is an orphan.

> It equals all the evils the foreigners have done
> To have taken the head of Brian to London!
> It is a sore consummation of his fate
> That his head should be in a stranger's church.

This defeat of O Neill was so significant that for the poet it cancelled out all the earlier triumphs of the king. In reciting some of these previous victories the poet makes one savage boast which if true might seem to justify the contemporary opinion that the Irish were a 'bestial' people:

> A chess-board of the shin-bones of the Leinstermen
> In our wordshop was constructed
> Carved chess-men on this board of our ancestors
> Of the bare Leinstermen's bones.

At any rate, such a great defeat had to be explained and the only reason the poet can find is that the Ulstermen insisted on fighting on a Sunday. But he was nearer the truth when he recounted how the massive armour of the colonists gave them the advantage. For O Neill does not seem to have employed gallowglasses, and his own army was neither professional enough nor sufficiently well armed to be able to stand up to a colonial army in a pitched battle.

There is no doubt that O Neill's pretensions to power were responsible for this attempted revival of the high kingship. His court poet referred to him as 'Eire's high king', and his immediate successor, Aedh, styled himself 'king of all the Irish of Ireland'. It is true also that the attempt was centred on Ulster. This Ulster character of the enterprise, if we may so term it, is also a prominent feature of the other two attempts at restoring the high kingship, which again should make us wary of regarding them as in any way national movements. The first of these took place within a short time of O Neill's death in 1260. An invitation seems to have been sent to King Hakon Hakonsson of Norway, in 1263, to assume the kingship of Ireland. It is almost as if those responsible for this invitation realised that old antagonisms were slow in dying in Ireland and that after the failure of Brian O Neill the descendants of the former contenders for the high kingship would not again agree to suppress their own claims in favour of any one of themselves. So they looked abroad. Hakon was a fairly obvious choice, because he happened to be in the vicinity (he came to the Scottish isles in 1263) and because it could be said that he had inherited an interest in Ireland from his Viking ancestors. It is most likely, however, that the gallowglasses now coming into Ulster had a hand in this, since Hakon was the suzerain of the islands from which they came. The scheme came to nothing, however, for Hakon died in the Orkneys in December. Not for another fifty years did anyone attempt to revive the high kingship, when Edward Bruce was invited to accept it in 1315. Again the invitation originated from Ulster, with another O Neill as the leading spirit behind it. As we have seen this attempt was by far the most successful, since Bruce was not only inaugurated as high king, but established his own machinery of government and went within an ace of overthrowing the king's authority in Ireland. But it failed in the end, mainly because it did not enjoy the full support of Gaelic Ireland. It seems that Gaelic Ireland was incapable of uniting, or of being united, behind any one leader, not even behind one who bore the great name of Bruce.

The real victories of the Gaelic revival were won in the localities, in battles fought by local chieftains and occasionally in greater victories achieved by confederacies. While it would be impossible to recount here the full story of this military recovery, it can be summarised by confining attention to significant events in different areas. For there are a few battles which may be taken as symbolic of this great Gaelic rally and there are some especially important manifestations of the assault on the frontiers of the feudal world in different regions.

Perhaps the most important sign in the thirteenth century that the expansion of feudal Ireland was about to be halted was the check given to Geraldine thrusts into Gaelic Ireland in the north and southwest. There had been a Geraldine attempt to lead an expansion into Donegal in the 1240s. Castles had been built at Coleraine at one end of the long frontier of feudal Ulster and at Sligo at the northern limit of expansion in Connacht. Other fortresses in between were to be not just frontier castles, but jumping off points for an expansion into Tyrone and Donegal. In 1247 Maurice fitz Gerald crossed the Erne and proceeded into O Donnell's country, killing the chieftain when he opposed him and setting up another in his place. The attempt was premature and in the following year the legitimate O Donnell line was restored. Until his death in 1257, however, fitz Gerald continued to lay claim to land in Donegal. But his death was the occasion for a great O Donnell attack on the Geraldine castles, during which some were destroyed and a memorable defeat was given to the Geraldine forces at the battle of Credran. This was one of the first great victories of the Gaelic revival, because not only did it check Geraldine expansion into the north-west corner of Ulster, but it enabled the O Donnells eventually to assert a lordship which ranged widely into Breifne and Fermanagh. It is significant that this was achieved with the help of gallowglasses: when O Donnell returned to Ulster from Scotland in 1258 he brought a troop of these mercenaries with him and from then on the O Donnells were never without a company of them. If, then, the O Donnells accepted some sort of tenurial relationship with the earl of Ulster (and there is some evidence to suggest that this was the case) it was of the most formal kind and never seriously interfered with their autonomy in their lordship.

At the other end of Ireland, in Desmond or south Kerry, the battle of Callan, in 1261, ended all hope of an effective Geraldine lordship over the country of the Mac Carthys. From quite early on in the century attempts were made to infiltrate and to gain control over the whole of Desmond. In this forward movement through Kerry the Geraldines were most prominent. On the whole, there seems to have been remarkably little fighting, new settlements being gained gradually. Sometimes they came as a reward for services rendered to local chieftains, or again as a result of intermarriage (which seems to have been common). The position of the Mac Carthy chieftain appears to have been recognised: he was clearly regarded by the government as occupying the position of a magnate, and for his part he seemed willing to fulfil some of the obligations of a tenant in chief—for example, in 1224 Dermot Mac Carthy joined the feudal levies against the rebel Hugh de Lacy. Relations between the settlers and the Mac Carthys were generally amicable and indeed the whole history of this expansion of feudalism in Kerry is a very good example of the way in which both races could have learnt to co-exist. But one of the factors which soured relations between the two was that the settlers took sides in the internal disputes among the Mac Carthys about the chieftainship. Retaliations followed and castles were attacked. Violence became endemic and reached a climax when in 1251 the reigning Mac Carthy was killed by John fitz Thomas. Then in 1259 fitz Thomas managed to procure from Edward, son of Henry III and now lord of Ireland, a charter for 'all the lands of Desmond' (and incidentally Decies as well) and this seems to have been the final straw so far as the Mac Carthys were concerned. New attacks followed and it soon became clear to fitz Thomas that if his charter were to have any value he must put an end once and for all to the nuisance of these Mac Carthy raids. It wasn't until 1261 that he was ready to lead an expedition, of which the Munster Geraldines formed the backbone, though the government allowed the feudal host to be used and some notable magnates participated. The army which marched against Mac Carthy was therefore no mean one, and even though it was to be financed by 'the barons of Desmond', it included many who were in no way connected with the Geraldines of Munster. Given the military superiority which the Anglo-Normans had enjoyed since they came to Ireland, it could confidently be predicted that this feudal army would easily win the day in a pitched battle. Yet victory went to the Gaelic army, even though the feudal army was strengthened by the inclusion of a Mac Carthy claimant to the kingship of Desmond. The

11

Annals of Loch Cé relate that John fitz Thomas 'and his son and fifteen knights and eight noble barons along with them were slain there, besides several young men and soldiers innumerable'. Worse than the loss of the head of the Munster Geraldines and his heir, however, was the check this defeat gave to Geraldine ambitions in Desmond. Although Mac Carthy subsequently overreached himself in following up this victory by extending far into county Cork, where he was killed by Miles de Cogan, the victory of Callan was nevertheless to mark the real beginning of the decay of Anglo-Norman power in that part of Ireland. Referring to the period immediately after the battle, a later chronicler was to remark that 'the Carties plaied the Divells in Desmond, where they burned, spoiled, preyed, and slue many an innocent'; and in the inquisition taken as to the lands of John fitz Thomas in 1282, it is said of some that they are 'now worth nothing, for they all lie in the power of the Irish', or of others that 'the greater part is destroyed by the war of the Irish'. By the end of the thirteenth century the Mac Carthys had succeeded in establishing themselves not only in the south of Kerry, but in west Cork as well.

In Connacht the situation was much more complicated and no easy picture can be given of the complex and confusing succession disputes among the O Connors and their relations with the settlers and with the de Burghs in particular. Nor was there a great Gaelic recovery here during the second half of the thirteenth century such as occurred elsewhere. Nevertheless the battle of Athankip, near Carrick on Shannon, in 1270, does typify some features of the Gaelic revival and has a peculiar significance in the history of the Anglo-Norman occupation of Connacht. The *Annals of Ulster* say of it that 'no greater defeat had been given to the Foreigners of Ireland up to that time', and while this is an exaggerated estimate of its importance it does suggest that to Gaelic Ireland Athankip was a noteworthy victory in the history of the Gaelic rally. There seems to be little doubt too that the battle was won with the help of a large force of Scottish gallowglasses, who were subsequently to play such an important part in the Gaelic revival. And the battle not only established the heroic reputation of Aedh O Connor as 'a king who emptied and wasted Connacht' and 'the most formidable and triumphant king of the kings of Erinn', but it also dealt a great blow to the military prestige of the feudal aristocracy at a time when it was suffering similar blows in other parts.

Dissensions among the magnates, which were to be a potent cause of weakness in the colony in the future, had already begun to appear. There is no doubt that the civil war in England was reflected in these dissensions in Ireland. Perhaps the most significant incident in all these faction fights occurred in 1264 when Maurice fitz Maurice and other Geraldines seized the justiciar, Richard de la Rochelle, and held him prisoner for a time. This was connected, if only remotely, with the greatest dispute, and one which affected Connacht intimately, that between the de Burghs and the Geraldines. Of this quarrel the *Annals of Loch Cé* say in 1264 that 'a great war arose . . . so that the major part of Erinn was destroyed between them'. This outbreak of civil war in Ireland provided an opportunity for Aedh O Connor, king of Connacht in 1265, though even before that he was king in all but name, to raid and burn, especially in the Geraldine districts. But by 1267 the de Burghs had come to realise how serious a threat was posed by O Connor and they began to retaliate. In the struggle which followed the main victory lay with O Connor. By the time Robert de Ufford was appointed justiciar in 1269, Connacht posed a grave problem of defence and the government had little choice but to decide to try to cope. A castle was built at Roscommon, that at Sligo was rebuilt by fitz Maurice, and finally in 1270 the government sent a large force into Connacht to bring O Connor to submission. This was joined with the army of de Burgh, so that, say the annals, 'they had all the foreigners of Erinn with them'. But the army was harried to great effect by O Connor, 'as a furious, raging, tearing lion goes about his enemies when killing them, so that he permitted them neither to eat, sleep nor be at rest'. And finally at the ford across the Shannon at Athankip O Connor completely routed the feudal army: 'their courage was confounded in this place and nine of their principal knights were slain on the spot . . . and it is not known how many men were lost there; and one hundred horses, with their mail coverings, and with their saddles, were left there'. O Connor followed up his victory by destroying many castles and thereby shaking the English hold on Connacht. He even raided into Meath as far as Granard, and burnt Athlone, the gateway to Connacht, destroying the bridge across the Shannon. But he died in 1274 and there was no one among his successors strong enough to emulate him. Indeed, during the next fifty odd years there were no less than fourteen kings of Connacht, a good indication of the terrible succession disputes which helped to immobilise the O Connor kings. It was not until the last earl of Ulster was murdered in 1333 that the feudal lordship of Connacht collapsed in earnest and the Gaelic rulers there, together with the gaelicised Burkes, began to assert their full independence.

Nevertheless Athankip deserves attention as one of the great military triumphs of resurgent Gaelic Ireland. In this respect it ranks with Callan, even though it did not produce the same decisive results. Among those who fought with O Connor was Turloch O Brien, who was later killed in single combat by the earl of Ulster, Walter de Burgh. He was probably a son of the O Brien king of Thomond, Brian Rua, who in the same year as Athankip was fought was to lead a rebellion against the English. King Brian took the castle of Clare near Ennis and went on the rampage. Hostages were taken from him two years running, in 1272 and 1273, but he still remained a problem. Then in January 1276 Edward I granted the whole of Thomond, for the service of only ten knights, to Thomas de Clare, a younger brother of the earl of Gloucester and a close friend of the king. Moreover he was already in Ireland in the king's employment, was a descendant of Strongbow, and was recently married to Juliana, the daughter of Maurice fitz Maurice. This connection with the Geraldines was to be important to the man whom the king had chosen to be the conqueror of Thomond, for not only did it give him the expectation of the support of one of the most powerful families in Ireland, but it brought him the enmity of the other great family, the de Burghs. This was to be partly responsible for the intervention of the de Burghs against Richard, the son of Thomas de Clare, during a critical period of the wars resulting from the attempts to colonise Thomond. And in a way that intervention was fatal to the English cause and helped to turn the tide in favour of a final Gaelic victory. For the attempt to conquer Thomond failed and the O Briens won one of the great victories of the Gaelic revival which was to secure to them their patrimony right down to the end of the medieval lordship.

This success of the O Briens and defeat of the de Clares has been celebrated in a great chronicle, written almost in the style of the old epics, where the protagonists are cast in heroic mould and the events surrounding them are all of great moment. This is the *Caithréim Thoirdhealbhaigh* ('The triumphs of Turloch'), written in the middle of the fourteenth century by a court poet who if not an eyewitness himself at least could draw upon the memories of many of the participants in the wars. His hero is Turloch O Brien, king of Thomond and victor over the de Clares. When in 1284 he succeeds in becoming undisputed master over the whole of Gaelic Thomond, the writer eulogises him as follows:

For Turloch the sun put on a brighter and a newly burnished face; the firmament for him unveiled a visage freshly beautified. At news that Turloch was made lord of all, the wild rude wind of hoarse and inarticulate utterance hied him back swiftly to his sleeping-house; the sea left her loud booming, stilled her raving noise, out of her skirts extruding on the shores that held her the fish in shoals, until all strands were filled with this her produce so cast up. In Turloch's favour the kindly fruitful woods, conceiving and bringing forth abundantly, grew variegated; and the men of this our Ireland in general participated in the copious blessings which, at his accession, by operation of the elements and of benignant planets were showered upon Turloch. In a word, but that the oversea folk were in a way to hinder him of becoming monarch, the Irish were well inclined to have him for their noble head.[11]

This is how the poets often eulogised the good ruler, since a sign of his worth was the fertility of the land. For example, an O Connor was addressed in the fourteenth century as 'a hero for whom in the south from smooth-plained Codhal the fruit and mast of gentle Mumha have grown bright of colour; owing to our prince red are the fair-branched hazels and the fruits of the pleasant sloe-trees laden down and dark-crested'. The old pagan link between the king and the land, the idea of the king as an agent of fertility, was still kept alive.

At no time, however, did Turloch ever seek to win any kind of lordship outside Thomond; indeed he was hard put to it to maintain his own place as leader of the O Briens. Nor was the real Turloch very like the character depicted in such glowing terms in the *Caithréim*, for he was a ruthless man, vicious and at

[11]*Caithréim Thoirdhealbhaigh*, translated by Standish Hayes O'Grady, London, 1929, 25.

times savage, until he had won what he wanted and was able to reign in some sort of security. He was, in fact, the kind of man which the times demanded, a worthwhile adversary for the equally ruthless de Clares. But it was not he who won the final victory for the O Briens, but his son Murchertach, who in 1317 at the battle of Corcomroe established the supremacy of his line among the O Briens, and in the following year at the battle of Dysert O Dea routed the de Clares and thereby ended all hope of an English colony in Thomond.

Looking back now, with a knowledge of the final outcome of the wars, it is easy to jump to the conclusion that the beginning of it all was the grant of Thomond to de Clare, in 1276. In fact, however, as so often happened in Ireland at that time, the real origin was a succession war among the O Briens in which Thomas de Clare, ever an opportunist, participated. Indeed it is also true that until near the end the wars retained more of the character of a civil war among the O Briens than a crusade against the English. When the Mac Namaras and O Deas revolted against Brian Rua and set up his nephew Turloch in his place as king, the two O Brien factions which were to promote the civil war were created. Brian Rua called in de Clare, made a bargain with him regarding possession of lands in Thomond, and in 1277 a great army of de Clares, Geraldines, Butlers and the followers of Brian left Limerick to recover Thomond. Subsequently Turloch had to fly to Connacht where he got help from the O Maddens, O Kellys and, most significantly, the de Burghs. This time of disturbance was used by de Clare to take possession of lands, build Bunratty castle, and settle Englishmen on his manors. He also earned for himself a permanent niche in the Irish hall of ill-fame by murdering Brian Rua while he was under his protection at Bunratty, an event which was subsequently used to impugn the honesty of the feudal lords in the appeal of Gaelic Ireland which was addressed to Pope John XXII in 1317.

In 1284 Turloch murdered Brian Rua's successor and was thus enabled to rule the O Briens virtually unchallenged until his death in 1306. Occasionally he found scope for his ambition by raiding abroad, as for instance in 1287 when he devastated Butler lands in Limerick and Ormond. But on the whole he ruled peacefully and maintained good relations with the settlers.

His death was the occasion for another outbreak of civil war which was to make of the land, in the words of the *Caithréim*, 'a shaking sod'. Once again the settlers took sides, the de Clares on one side and the de Burghs on the other. Attempts to settle the matter by a partition proved useless. Then in 1315 the Bruce invasion gave a new twist to the wars in Thomond and for the first time they really assumed an anti-English character: 'they (the O Briens) unanimously voted rather to make war on the English and their domains', though it is quite clear now that in fact they cautiously waited until the Scots enjoyed a remarkable success and they felt that they were backing the winning side. Two years later the battle of Corcomroe settled the issue of the civil war in favour of the family of Turloch and now the O Briens were free to deal wholeheartedly with the de Clares. At Dysert O Dea, on 10 May 1318, the de Clares were completely routed. Only a few escaped the slaughter and when their pursuers came in sight of Bunratty, the *Caithréim* tells us that they found the castle and town

deserted, empty, wrapped in fire. For upon his wife's and household's receiving of the tidings that de Clare was killed, with one consent they betake them to their fast galleys and shove off on the Shannon, taking with them the choicest of the town's wealth and valuable effects, and having at all points set it on fire. From which time to this, never a one of their breed has come back to look after it.

The battle of Dysert O Dea and its aftermath thus made the O Briens masters of Thomond and their lordship remained intact until the end of the middle ages. But they never were, and indeed never wished to be, fully independent. They accepted the lordship of the king of England, a distant figure who never seriously interfered with them. For example, an O Brien did homage to Lionel of Clarence, son of Edward III, in the mid-fourteenth century, while another did homage to Richard II when he came to Ireland. What they were not willing to accept was the lordship of someone else, someone between them and the king, a mesne lord in feudal terminology. Such were Thomas de Clare and his son Richard, who must therefore be repudiated. Elsewhere in Gaelic Ireland the same impatience with mesne lords was to be observed, even though for much of the thirteenth century the chieftains had little choice but to accept them. Nowhere is this better illustrated than in Ulster, where the O Neill kings of Tyrone (which covered most of the modern counties of Tyrone, Derry and Armagh) claimed to be the overlords of other Gaelic kings in the north and indeed asserted their rights to the high kingship of Ireland as the true descendants of the royal line. As we saw, Brian O Neill tried to secure his title of 'king of the kings of Ireland', and later on Donal O Neill, in the famous appeal to Pope John XXII, styled himself 'King of Ultonia, true heir by hereditary right of all Ireland'. And yet in the thirteenth century these O Neills had been forced to accept the mesne lordship of the earls of Ulster. A remarkable document of 1269 records how the reigning O Neill, Aedh, 'is bound to the nobleman, his lord, Walter, earl of Ulster' and it concludes: 'If he breaks the agreement, the earl may drive him from his regality, which he (O Neill) is bound to hold of him, and may give or sell it to anyone else'. Attempts to break free always failed in the end. As always, full use was made of any civil war among the settlers. Early in the reign of Edward I, for example, fitz Warin, the seneschal of the earldom of Ulster, and the Mandevilles quarrelled and resorted to force. The O Neills and others joined in on the side of the Mandevilles and according to a complaint of the mayor and community of Carrickfergus they 'burned five vills, 2,000 crannocks of wheat and three mills' belonging to the seneschal. 'They took hostages from the king's English subjects, proposing to destroy and lay waste the land, but they were driven to confusion by the valour of the seneschal, Hugh Byset, and their friends. Many of them were taken and confined, one of them died in prison, and the remainder obtained the king's peace more leniently than they deserved'. But despite such incidents, the earldom of Ulster normally kept the O'Neills closely confined and it was not until after the murder of the last de Burgh earl of Ulster in 1333, and the passing of the great lordship into absentee hands, that the O Neills got their great chance. By 1344 one branch of the family had succeeded in gaining permanent ascendancy, thus ending a century of internecine contests which, as always, gravely weakened the Gaelic position. Towards the end of the fourteenth century the O Neill king of Tyrone had extended his influence over much of Ulster, his suzerainty being acknowledged by most of the smaller chieftaincies. And in 1394, when Ireland first heard of the impending visit of Richard II, envoys from O Brien, O Connor, MacCarthy and many others of the Gaelic parts of southern Ireland urged O Neill not to go to the king's court, implying that he had a special position among the kings of Gaelic Ireland. Even Richard II accepted the primacy of O Neill, referring to him in letters as 'The Great O Neill' (Le Grand Onel).

Much closer to Dublin, and therefore much more dangerous to the government, another Gaelic recovery was taking place. South of the city of Dublin stretches the great massif of the Dublin and Wicklow mountains, and here the settlers never succeeded in establishing a really firm foothold. The deep valleys, difficult of access, became strongholds of resurgent Gaelic chieftains and many an expedition of government forces set out from Dublin only to meet disaster in the narrow defiles of the mountains. During most of the thirteenth century, however, this area did not seriously menace the settlement achieved in Leinster by Strongbow and his successors. The ruling Mac Murrough dynasty had been deprived of the kingship and instead had been given the office of seneschal of Gaelic Leinster, which became hereditary in the family. As long as the great lordship of Leinster lasted, the Gaelic and feudal areas enjoyed a peaceful co-existence. But when the last of the Marshals died in 1245, and Leinster was partitioned among five co-heiresses, a new relationship was established between the Mac Murroughs and the Bigod lords of Carlow, one of the five new divisions. By 1306, however, with the death of Roger Bigod, the lordship of Carlow fell into the hands of the king and this was to make it easier for the Mac Murroughs to reclaim their lost lordship and to assume once again their old title of 'high king of Leinster'. Why precisely they should have thus reasserted their old claims is not quite clear. Pride, certainly, and a natural desire to be independent played a part. But, as so often, a sense of oppression may have supplied the motivation. In 1281 Art Mac Murrough was murdered in Arklow by the settlers, his head being sent to Dublin and the usual bounty claimed from the government. Such decapitations were common enough and the government regularly paid bounties on the heads of rebel Irish. In this particular case, however, Art was at peace and, worse still, possessed a safe conduct from the king when he was murdered. Again in 1305 four leading Mac Murroughs were murdered at Ferns, even though they had come under the safe conduct of the justiciar. Incidents such as these may have sparked off the revival. In any event the Mac Murroughs now began to re-establish their position as the chief dynasty in Leinster and a number of other chieftains, notably the O Byrnes and the O Tooles, looked to the ruling Mac Murrough as their real lord. Finally in 1327 Donal Mac Murrough was elected king of Leinster, the first since the conquest. By 1395, as the submissions to Richard II show, the Mac Murrough kings of Leinster had recovered their old sovereignty over much of the province.

Long before that, however, Leinster had become a military problem to the government, a running sore which refused to be healed. The O Byrnes and others, 'rebels and enemies of the king' as they are usually called, occupied the mountains and the long valley of Glenmalure in particular became a stronghold which proved impossible to take. In 1274 the first of a succession of expeditions set out under the prior of the Hospital of Kilmainham, though it met with no success. The prior himself was taken prisoner and was only released in exchange for hostages held by the government in Dublin. There were more expeditions in 1275, 1276, which ended in complete disaster, and 1277, when the government at long last enjoyed a success. There was no more trouble for some years, but by the 1290s the situation was again becoming serious, and by the early fourteenth century it was rapidly worsening.

One aspect of this new Gaelic menace which was especially sinister was its propinquity to Dublin. Not even the city was safe: on at least one occasion the enemy broke into the castle itself, the very seat of government. The suburbs were always open to raiding parties and further out along the coast, or across the plain towards the foothills, manors and centres of population were subject to frequent attack. A very good illustration of the precarious condition of life south of the city, compared with the greater peace and security of the area to the north, is provided by some of the manors of the archbishop of Dublin. Those on the north, or safe, side of the city, such as Finglas and Swords, were still comparatively prosperous in extents taken in 1326. But those on the south side were in a perilous condition. The manor of Castlekevin, up in the mountains, was entirely lost. On the remaining manors most of the betaghs had disappeared.

Of two townlands on the manor of Tallaght formerly held by betaghs it was said that no tenant dared to inhabit them, while three others were said to be too near the Irish to be habitable. During the 1270s there were complaints from Saggart that forty men had been killed during a raid, when they were working in the fields. As might be expected, the disturbances caused by the Bruce invasion made the situation even worse, and a pitiful complaint of 1316 illustrates this well. It was said that 'all Englishmen and other faithful subjects of the king, who were wont to remain between the vale of Dublin and the county of Wexford in times past, by the malice and wantonness of the Irish of the mountains of Leinster, felons of the king, they have been expelled and removed from their fortresses, manors and houses . . . '. The Lawlesses, who made the complaint, said that they were hemmed in between the sea and the mountains, at the mercy of the 'Irish felons . . . whose malice they cannot resist . . . nor can they live or remain any longer in those parts except by the will of those Irishmen unless provision is quickly made for them by suitable succour'. They were allowed to parley with the Irish and to grant them 'munificence', so 'that they may be able to save and preserve themselves'. Clearly the 'suitable succour' requested was not going to be made available. It rarely was, so that the Gaelic revival was able to proceed virtually unchecked.

While it is probably an exaggeration to say, as the complainant did, that all Englishmen had been expelled from that area stretching south to Wexford, this Gaelic revival did have important consequences in Leinster. First of all the settlers abandoned the highlands and receded to the river valleys. But then these valleys themselves were threatened, lines of communication were cut and settlements isolated. Most important of all, probably, was the attack on the line of the Barrow, the great river linking the south to the Liffey valleys of the north. All through the fourteenth century this highway, thickly populated and extensively colonised, was under pressure from resurgent Gaelic Leinster under the ruling Mac Murrough. From the east O Byrnes and O Tooles were a constant menace; from the west the O Connors of Offaly and the O Mores of Leix were no less a danger. So desperate did the situation become that in 1372 the government actually offered Donachad Mac Murrough twenty marks as a reward for 'the safe keeping of the royal roads between

Carlow and Kilkenny'. Carlow, indeed, illustrates very well the plight of this area and the difficulty of keeping lines of communication open. When later in the century a newly elected Provost of Kilkenny was ordered to appear before the barons of the exchequer at Carlow, he wrote to the council explaining that he could not get to Carlow from Kilkenny 'for danger of his life on account of the enemies' wars on the perilous roads between the towns'. Lionel of Clarence, during the course of his expedition to Ireland, shifted much of the administration from Dublin to Carlow, making it virtually the capital of the lordship. But by the time Richard II led his expedition to Ireland in 1394, Carlow had become a frontier town, isolated and dangerous, and no fit place for the exchequer or any other department of state. And so the king made Dublin once again the centre of the administration. This abandoning of Carlow is highly significant and symbolises the Gaelic recovery in Leinster. It is clear that the king had little choice. Exchequer officials, forced to live in this highly dangerous situation, had frequently complained of their plight. And not without reason. For not only was food expensive and life uncomfortable, but sometimes their very lives were in danger. On one occasion, for example, the exchequer was destroyed when Carlow was laid waste by Leinster Irish. So serious was the situation that the government had to pay the officials extra fees, or what we would call 'danger money'. There were many appeals from the town itself, as in 1393 when the townsmen related that lately the town and crops had been 'burnt, wasted and destroyed' by the Irish and that most of the inhabitants 'have gone from the town to divers other parts . . . those who tarry there have it in mind to go and better themselves'. And so they appeal for help to rebuild their town and its houses, 'considering that the said town is the head and comfort of Leinster'. The government made a grant of money available, to be divided among 'those who are willing to re-inhabit the town there, each in proportion to his building'. But it was already too late and in the 1430s the Irish council, reporting to the king, said that 'the county Carlow was within those thirty years one of the keys of the land between Dublin and the outer parts; it is now inhabited with enemies and rebels; of 140 castles defensible therein only two now are left (in loyal hands), namely Carlow and Tullow'.

There were other river systems in a similar plight and many other towns equally isolated. The river Nore, or further east the river Suir, were both vulnerable. In 1393 a son of the late earl of Ormond petitioned for a grant of all lands in the cantred of Offagh in county Tipperary along the west side of the Suir, which had been neglected by the owners and overrun and laid waste by Irish enemies and English rebels, 'so that the passage of merchants and other lieges . . . and their road into these parts are stopped and by that means an entry given to the Irish enemies and to felons into the peaceable neighbouring lands, whereby they are greatly destroyed and laid waste'. And like Carlow, other towns were often isolated by the expansion of Gaelic Ireland into the feudalised parts and by the growing number of English rebels. A typical example was Waterford, which as early as 1331 petitioned that the mayor should be allowed to take his oath of office in the city instead of going to Dublin as was obligatory, 'on account of the distance and the perils of the way'. They added that Cork had already, for a similar reason, been granted this privilege. The request was granted and was re-affirmed at regular intervals thereafter. In 1400 the reason given was that 'seeing that by reason of the distance and because of the king's Irish enemies they may not without a costly power and peril of their life and property repair thither'. By 1447 there was 'nothing but rebellion, murder, robbery and war around'. By then, of course, conditions were really bad. The Drogheda parliament of 1450 was told that the town of Carrickmagriffin in county Tipperary was constantly in danger from English rebels: 'in those last fourteen years the town was twice entirely burned' and 'for the greatest part all the people (were) taken prisoners, and afterwards a great pillage of them made four times, and all this was done by English rebels'. The parliament decided that the town should be fortified with new walls 'for all men that go from Waterford to Clonmel, Cashel or Fethard, who can have no resting place or lodging in twenty miles of road except only at the said town of Carrick'. Travelling in and out of Waterford by land meant moving rapidly through open country from the protection of one walled town to another.

Further north the town of Trim illustrates the same contraction of the area in which law and order was maintained by the government and shows Gaelic Ireland, often in alliance with rebel English, gaining control. In the great days of the lordship of Meath, its capital Trim had been surrounded by the land of peace. But with the Gaelic revival the land of peace contracted and before very long Trim became a frontier town, its great castle one of the key border fortresses on the outskirts of the area which subsequently became the Pale. During Poynings' famous parliament in 1495 it was listed, next after Dublin, as one of the seven 'chief castles of the land'.

Some towns were engulfed by expanding Gaelic Ireland, especially in the more distant places; others survived, little islands in a Gaelic sea, difficult of access and sometimes cut off altogether. Many of these were, naturally enough, on the coast and were normally accessible by sea even if the land routes were closed. The inland towns found it much more difficult to survive and sometimes could only do so by buying off the local Gaelic chieftain by means of what became known as a black rent.

The plight of these towns was in part the result of the activities of the rebel English; but it was mainly occasioned by the success of the Gaelic revival. And this, as we saw, began in the thirteenth century in many parts of Ireland. One of the best illustrations of the breakdown of the frontier of feudal Ireland and of the pressure exercised by the resurgent Gaelic chieftains is provided by the roll of 'expenses of journies to divers parts of Ireland' of John of Sandford, head of the Irish government, in 1288–90. This account gives a very vivid picture of how serious the Gaelic breakthrough had already become by then. On many days he is depicted as parleying with Gaelic chieftains, making provision for guarding marches in many parts of the settled area, and mounting expeditions against local chieftains. On 9 September 1288, for example, he journied to Kildare and reviewed a muster of the feudal levies of Leinster. The record tells us that after Sandford had finished his review he sent the forces, under the seneschals of Kildare, Wexford, Carlow and Kilkenny, to guard huge areas deep in the heart of one of the most heavily settled parts of Ireland, 'which was then very hostile'. Again and again during his perambulations Sandford was told how hostile the local chieftains had become. Details are given of wars which have broken out in many parts, some of which the local communities found it difficult to support. Sandford compiled a special memorandum on the Irish of Leix and Offaly, 'rebels and enemies of the king', and said that they 'remained so hostile that no peace could be established in the marches of Leinster, but the king's lieges were daily killed, their houses burned and intolerable depredations were made'. Despite all his attempts, he said, he 'could not draw them to the king's peace'. Small wonder that a few years later the archbishops of Tuam and Cashel, and the bishop of Kildare, were able to reply to a request of Pope Nicholas IV for a subsidy that they and their clergy were so reduced by war, rebellion and depredation as to be in extremes of poverty.

Part of the area travelled by Sandford was Geraldine land, and the inquisition taken on the lands of John fitz Thomas in 1282 shows large tracts in Kildare and Kilkenny lying 'waste by the war of the Irish' or 'uncultivated owing to the war of the Irish'. Other inquisitions taken later in the midlands would show the same signs of destruction by the Irish enemies. The constant complaints of the settlers, particularly near the frontier of the land of peace, of 'losses, depredations, burnings', almost becomes a refrain through repetition. Much of this was the result of raids in search of booty, rather in the manner of the old style Gaelic cattle-raid of pre-Norman times and not at all connected with wars waged by resurgent chieftains. But a lot more was the result of the wars occasioned by the Gaelic revival. And as we move into the fourteenth century this becomes the case more frequently. Friar Clyn of Kilkenny, the Anglo-Irish chronicler, describes how in 1325 O Carrol of Ely, in north Tipperary, 'scarcely left a house, castle, or town in Eli O Carrol, among the English and lovers of peace, that he did not destroy by fire' and banished the settlers and occupied their lands and castles. Again in 1342 O More of Leix 'stirred up to war all the Irish of Munster and Leinster and expelled nearly all the English from their lands by force'.

Such examples could be multiplied, showing how successful the Gaelic revival was in most parts of Ireland by the fourteenth century. But it is worth emphasising again that it was in the thirteenth century that it enjoyed its first triumphs, a fact to which the parliament of 1297 attested when it devoted so much of its time to the problem of defence in the localities and how best to contain the Irish enemy. But when the government fell back on treachery by way of an answer, it only aggravated the already burning sense of oppression which Gaelic Ireland felt. One of the most notorious acts of treachery was one which was produced in evidence against the English in the famous appeal to Pope John XXII. It occurred on 13 June 1305. Piers Bermingham invited O Connor of Offaly and many of his relatives to celebrate the feast on Trinity Sunday at his castle of Carrick. But in the course of the celebration his unarmed guests were murdered. The heads of O Connor and of about thirty of his family were sent to Dublin. From the sequel it is clear that the government approved of what Bermingham had done, for a meeting of the Irish council agreed that Piers should have £100 for the decapitation of the O Connors. The Anglo-Irish community also approved. A contemporary ballad eulogised Piers for his deeds against the Irish, this one in particular:

> Another thing also,
> To Irishmen he was foe,
> That well wide whare[12]
> Ever he rode about
> With strength to hunt them out
> As hunter doth the hare.

But Gaelic Ireland naturally took a different view of the murder, which is well illustrated by what is said in the *Annals of Inisfallen*:

And woe to the Gael who puts trust in a king's peace or in foreigners after that. For, although they had their king's peace, their heads were brought to Áth Cliath, and much wealth was obtained for them from the foreigners. And when Piers was reproached with that, he said that he was not aware that there was a foreigner in Ireland who had not undertaken to slay his Gaelic neighbour, and he knew that they would slay, as he had slain; and that it was no wonder the foreigners harboured that evil resolution concerning them, for they (the Gaeil) had avenged themselves thoroughly before they were slain.

The strength of this Gaelic revival can be ascertained in many ways. Quite apart from the successes gained locally, which can only be appreciated through being examined in some detail, there are other signs which indicate the power of the local chieftain. Some of these we have already seen, such as the plight of certain towns. The impact on a local community can also be brought home when we discover that survival might depend on the

[12]That is 'everywhere'.

payment of black rent. At the end of the fifteenth century county Limerick was paying £40 to O Brien, Louth £40 to O Neill, Meath and Kildare £80 to O Connor Faly, and Kilkenny and Tipperary £40 to O Carroll. Mac Murrough was paid £40 from Wexford. He was also in receipt of an annual fee from the government, which was really another form of black rent, and so too was O Connor Faly. Indeed the number of Gaelic chieftains receiving fees during the fourteenth century is in itself significant of the government's failure to cope with the Gaelic revival. And it is ironical that sometimes the government employed the services of some of those in war, such as O More of Leix who in 1345 was paid £66 for leading a force of six men at arms, 178 mounted archers and 100 foot archers under the command of the justiciar, de Ufford. The employment of Gaelic chieftains in this way had the further disadvantage that it brought them into direct contact with the latest techniques of war, which later they could turn against their erstwhile employers. That the Irish were good at learning is apparent from Primate Swayne's description of the army which was captained by Mac Murrough in the war of 1429, arrayed in eight battles of 200 each 'in the guise of this country, that is every man an acton, habirchon, pischane and basnete' (body-armour, sleeveless coat of plate or chain mail, gorget, and light helmet). This is a far cry indeed from Giraldus' description of the Irish riding 'naked' (that is, without armour) into battle.

There was another way, much more subtle, perhaps, in which this Gaelic revival made a tremendous impact on the settlers. Putting it crudely, in a trite phrase which has become threadbare through overuse, many of the settlers became 'more Irish than the Irish themselves'. They were assimilated in some degree to Gaelic culture, and this too was in part the result of the growth in self-confidence of Gaelic Ireland as the political revival met with success. For there is no doubt that the Gaelic revival had its cultural manifestation which was of great importance. At its lowest, this found expression in the restoration of the Gaelic way of life to lands which had been feudalised and therefore either Anglicised or, more likely, Normanised. Traditional institutions were re-established. In Leinster, where kingship had been reinstituted in 1327 with the election of Donal Mac Morrough, the revival was symbolised in 1375 by the solemn inauguration of

12

Art Mac Murrough Kavanagh as king, and by the bardic poem which was composed to celebrate the occasion. This inauguration ode was the first bardic poem composed in Leinster from the time of the conquest, and it therefore represents a cultural as well as a political restoration. National bardic festivals were another way in which the revival was commemorated. In Uí Maine, for example, Willaim O Kelly gave a great feast in 1351 for all the poets of Ireland to celebrate his triumph. One of the poets commemorated the occasion in a famous poem which describes how O Kelly accommodated his guests in streets of specially built booths, all laid out in rows like the letters in lines of manuscript, and his own castle 'as it were a capital letter of beauteous stone . . . its outer smoothness like vellum'. So many poets accepted the invitation ('a mighty company') that the rest of Ireland was robbed of her poets for the festival, so that 'throughout this day in Leinster or in Meath of the gentle rivers, no note of music is heard, save the voice of the sweet bird from the trees'. But the most memorable celebration was that held by Margaret, wife of Galvach O Connor Faly, and daughter of O Carrol of Ely. In 1433, a terrible year which was remembered as 'the summer of slight acquaintance' because, it was said, 'no one used to recognise friend or relative', she invited all the poets, musicians and scholars of Ireland, Irish and Scots, to 'two general feasts of bestowing both meat and moneys with all manner of gifts'. This was a great national assembly of people who were preserving the cultural heritage of Ireland, enriching it by translating foreign books or by studying abroad and bringing back to their people the best they could find in foreign scholarship. The great concourse which attended the first festival on the local feast day of 26 March, 2,700 according to the number of names which is supposed to have been listed in the roll compiled on that day, represented the whole tribe of the 'men of learning' who formed, as it were, the cultural wing of the Gaelic revival in the thirteenth and fourteenth centuries. It was for men such as these that Niall O Neill in 1381 built 'a house for the entertainment of the *literati* of Erin' near Armagh. It was sited at Emain Macha, once the capital of the northern kings, with an ancient tradition which gave it a special place in the mind of all men of letters. So this, too, was symbolic of the revival of Gaelic power in Ulster and associated with it a renewal of Gaelic culture. Other symbols of this renewal are the great compilations of Gaelic literature, history and law which were made in the fourteenth and fifteenth centuries, anthologies of the traditional learning handed down by the Gaelic schools. Such a book was the *Book of Balymote,* which was put together for a Connacht chieftain, Macdermot, at the end of the four- teenth century (c. 1390). Like other compilations, such as the *Yellow Book of Lecan* (c. 1390) or the *Great Book of Lecan* (c. 1417), this great codex is the product of the intense scribal activity which marks the fourteenth and fifteenth centuries. Indeed, just as the period of national recovery after the Scandinavian attacks is symbolised by such earlier anthologies as the *Book of Leinster,* so too this period of Gaelic revival is marked by the production of more great codices.

With Gaelic culture thus invigorated, it was bound to make an impression on the settlers who came into close contact with it. Indeed from early on the settlers were already ripe for assimila- tion, since they were well on their way to becoming the 'middle nation' of the Remonstrance of 1318. Giraldus Cambrensis makes one of the participants at the siege of Dublin exclaim: 'What are we waiting for? Do we look for aid from our own people? No, for such is our position now that to the Irish we are English, and to the English we are Irish'. For some of them the result was complete assimilation to the Gaelic way of life. They changed their names to a Gaelic form and became indistinguishable from their Gaelic neighbours. A very early example was the Norman Gilbert de Angulo who was enfeoffed by the king of Connacht in the late twelfth century. The Irish called him Mac Goisdelbh ('son of Jocelin') and the name stuck, to be anglicised later as Costello. In the north the de Mandevilles became Mac Quillan. The Berminghams became Mac Pheorais ('son of Piers'), the Stauntons, Mac Evillys. Others added 'Mac' to their own names, and became Mac Philbin or Mac Hubert. The most famous example of all were the Burkes of Connacht, descendants of those de Burghs who had refused to acquiesce in the passing of the great lordship into the hands of an heiress. But the Burkes never became fully assimilated and in this they represent the more normal pattern of partial assimilation. Like them, many other families were to conform to what has often been called, rather inaccurately, the 'clan system' of Gaelic Ireland. Writing in the first half of the fourteenth century Friar Clyn of Kilkenny can refer to the 'nations and families' (*naciones et cognomina*) of the 'Geraldini', 'Poerini' and 'Rupenses'. Even in the official language of the time, this kind of terminology, reflecting the influence of the Gaelic social structure, found a place. An Irish exchequer account describes the justiciar Rokeby as going to Munster 'to pacify divers English nations'. The famous statutes of Kilkenny speak of 'any of the lineage, or of the adherents or retainers of any chieftain of English lineage' (*Chieftayne de linadge Engleis*) and this is only one of many echoes of the same thing. Another reflection of it is the official recognition given by the government to the chieftaincies of Anglo-Irish families, such as the Harolds of south county Dublin, by accepting them as 'captains of their nations' in precisely the same way as the Gaelic chieftains were recognised. Of course, some of these families were numbered among the 'rebel English', who were to become such a problem in the later middle ages. So much was made clear by the message from the Irish council in 1399, which said that 'the English nations (*les nacions Engleis*) who are rebels in all parts of the country, such as the Butlers, Poers, Geraldines, Berminghams, Daltons, Baretts, and Dillons, are not amenable to the law, and though they wish to be called gentlemen are in truth nothing but sturdy robbers'.

Many of these 'rebels' were aggrieved that they had lost estates through the operation of feudal law, when the Brehon law of Ireland, which debarred women from inheriting property, would have safeguarded their interests. And so they adopted the Gaelic law of inheritance and occupied lands illegally. The classic example is provided by the Burkes of Connacht, though many more could be cited—de Lacys, de Verdons, or those Berminghams who refused to accept the operation of feudal law in 1350 and took the Irish name of Mac Pheorais ('son of Piers'). There are some extraordinary instances of the determination of settler families, faced with the danger of estates being partitioned, to keep women from inheriting. For example, in 1299 an attempt was made to ensure that the de Rocheford barony of Ikeathy, county Kildare, would not be partitioned in default of male heirs in the main line, but would go to

the most noble, worthy, strong and praiseworthy of the pure blood and name of Rochefordeyns, issued from the blood of Sir Walter de Rupeforti and lady Eva de Hereford his wife . . . unless the four nearest of our blood and name choose to elect one better and more worthy of the Rochefordeyns to whom so elected the whole barony of Okethy with all appurtenances indivisible shall remain: so that the inheritance shall never pass to daughters.

And the Blakes of Athenry made sure that no woman could inherit in their family. As late as 1527 a Blake deed could say that 'a woman ought not and cannot be heir according to the custom and ordinance of the Blake nation'.

One of the greatest forces working for some sort of assimilation would have been intermarriage, and it is clear that from the start the colonists married into Gaelic families. This is not altogether surprising, for apart from any other consideration so many of the invaders were as much Welsh as Norman and so were susceptible to the women of Ireland. Strongbow married the daughter of the king of Leinster and Hugh de Lacy married the daughter of the high king. That was the start of a tradition which was to last as long as the lordship itself. It is usually the more important people we hear of in this context; but it is plain that many of the colonists followed the example of their lords and contracted marriages of this kind. One of the more charming stories told by Froissart was related to him by Henry Christede and tells how he found an Irish wife. While on a campaign with the earl of Ormond, Christede was captured by an Irishman and held to ransom. Eventually he married the daughter of his captor, 'Brin Costerec', and lived with him for seven years. Then his father-in-law was captured and promised release in exchange for Christede. But at first he would not agree to free Christede, 'for he loved me well and my wife his daughter and our children', the Englishman tells us. He finally agreed,

but he retained my eldest daughter still with him. So I and my wife and our second daughter returned to England, and so I went and dwelt beside Bristol on the river Severn. My two daughters are married: she in Ireland, has three sons and two daughters, and she that I brought with me has four sons and two daughters. And the Irish language comes as readily to me and the English tongue, for I have always spoken it with my wife and taught it to my grandchildren.

With marriage came the adoption of the Irish language and of Gaelic customs—fosterage, for example, which was always regarded as a particularly dangerous abuse and was roundly condemned by successive governments down to the time of Sir John Davies in the seventeenth century. For fosterage, perhaps more than anything else, led to the Irishising of generations of settlers. In his *Topography* Giraldus Cambrensis remarked how the Irish spent all their 'feeling of love or attachement . . . on their foster-children or foster-brothers' and he emphasised how quickly strangers to Ireland succumb to this habit: 'even strangers who land here from other countries become generally imbued with this national crime, which seems to be innate and very contagious'. No wonder it was picked out as the most pernicious custom of all by Spenser, the famous sixteenth century poet, in his *View of the State of Ireland*: ' . . . for first the child that sucketh the milk of the nurse, must of necessity learn his first speech of her, the which being the first inured to his tongue, is ever the most pleasing unto him, insomuch as though he afterwards be taught English, yet the smack of the first will always abide with him, and not only of the speech, but also of the manners and customs'. An Irish writer, in a famous fourteenth-century tract, takes a rather different view when he praises those feudal lords for the manner in which they had cast off much of their foreign ways. Referring to the momentous events of the Bruce invasion in 1315 he has this to say: 'For the old chieftains of Erin prospered under these princely lords, who were our chief rulers, and who had given up their foreignness for a pure mind, their surliness for good manner, and their stubbornness for sweet mildness, and who had given up their perverseness for hospitality'.

It is certain that the greatest of these feudal lords succeeded in claiming some of the rights exercised by their Gaelic predecessors in the kingdoms which they overran. Strongbow, for example, seems to have been able to procure the military service which tradition granted to the king of Leinster, and many lesser lords were also able to demand a variety of traditional services which can be summed up in the custom of *coign and livery*, the great scourge of the later middle ages. This is the sort of thing which Giraldus probably had in mind when early in the reign of King John he reports a rumour that some of the new settlers were already taking to themselves the rights of Gaelic lords: 'for, if report speaks true, their folly is risen to such a pitch of arrogance and presumption that they even aspire to usurp in their own persons all the rights of dominion belonging to the princes of that kingdom'.

First the language and then the literature and arts of Gaelic Ireland captured many of the settlers. When the earl of Louth was murdered in 1329, with him fell his bard, O Carrol, described by Clyn as a 'famous tympanist and harpist, in his art a phoenix . . . who if he was not the first inventor of the art of string music, was of all who preceded him and of all his contemporaries teacher, master, and director'. Twenty of O Carrol's pupils were also killed on that occasion, all in the company of the earl. Three years before that, in 1326, an earl of Ulster died and an elegy in Irish was composed to mark the occasion. He had been a great patron of Gaelic poets and he represents a process of Gaelicisation which had been going on since the first invaders landed. It was to an ancestor of this earl that a famous Gaelic court poet fled in the early thirteenth century when he was looking for refuge from an irate O Donnell. This was Muiredach O Dálaigh and clearly he expected that Richard de Burgh of Connacht would give him asylum. He paid for his sanctuary by means of a typical praise-poem, of the kind in which the Gaelic nobility delighted, in which he said: 'The king of Assaroe has unfairly threatened me: I will turn my mouth to the Saxon hawks because of their promises to me'. The poet may have been as cynical in this service as was a more famous descendant of his, Godfraigh Fionn O Dálaigh, who addressed a poem to an earl of Desmond in which he said: 'A sovranty they never get we promise to the Gaels in our odes; you need not take any notice of this, it is our custom'. And later: 'There are two kindreds for whom poetry is composed in Ireland of the cool springs—the Gaels, known to fame, and the English of Britain's dewy isle. In poetry for the English we promise that the Gaels will be banished from Ireland; in poetry for the Gaels we promise that the English will be routed across the sea'. As Professor David Greene has pointed out, 'the foreigners would not have bought these poems unless they had been thoroughly integrated both linguistically and culturally. Those who had been found this praise poetry heady stuff'.[13] One might see in the career of the rebellious first earl of Desmond, with his grandiose schemes for a revival of

[13]David Green, 'The professional poets' in Brian Ó Cuív (ed.), *Seven Centuries of Irish Learning*, Dublin, 1961, 47–8.

the high kingship in his own person, how far such flattery could lead an attentive and gullible person. Certainly the poets were prepared to pander to the aspirations of their Anglo-Irish patrons and to say the sort of thing the nobility liked to hear. In a panegyric hailing a Richard Burke of Connacht in the fifteenth century his poet exclaims: 'The charter of the sword—what better one is there?—is Richard's charter to Rath Raoileann (i.e. Ireland)'. On the other hand, the poets were often condemned for the dangerous flattery they purveyed. The Franciscan, Friar Michael of Limerick, writing c. 1286, denounced them as one of the poisons which endangered Ireland, 'by whose accursed promises the robber chiefs are so puffed up with pride that they cannot be converted to any good'.

In many other ways we can see how the settlers were at least partially assimilated to the Gaelic Ireland which they found all around them as the Gaelic revival continued. We have already noticed, for example, the influence of Brehon law in relation to inheritance; other parts of that law were also influential, that dealing with homicide, for example, and being adopted by settlers in many areas produced that particular amalgam of Brehon and English law known as march law. When an earl of Desmond's seneschal was hanged, drawn and quartered in 1345, he was accused, according to Friar Clyn, of 'exercising, maintaining and inventing many foreign, oppressive and intolerable laws'. In the careers of many of the great magnates one can trace the same process of assimilation. Perhaps the outstanding example in the fourteenth century is the third earl of Desmond, of whom a Gaelic writer had this to say: 'A nobleman of wonderful bounty, mirth and cheerfulness in conversation, charitable in his deeds, easy of access, a witty and ingenious composer of Irish poetry and a learned and profound chronicler; and, in fine, one of the English nobility that had Irish learning and professors thereof in greatest reverence of all the English of Ireland'. His poems demonstrate in a very vivid way how thorough his cultural assimilation had been. Indeed it is astonishing that a fourteenth century earl of Desmond should be able to compose Irish poetry at all, much less such excellent poetry. Here was a man who was so Gaelicised that he was one of the finest Gaelic poets of his generation. But he was also a man who was deeply involved in the government of Ireland at the time, attending parliaments and councils of the king in Ireland, regularly accepting office, in one capacity or another, in the south-west, and even once acting as justiciar and head of the Irish government. At the same time he was trying to live on good terms with his Gaelic neighbours, with whom he had strong ties of friendship and, with some, the even stronger ties of fosterage. He spoke their language, he adopted their customs, he was assimilated to their traditions. But he was in an impossible position, occasionally forced through his English connection to make war on these same neighbours and friends— forced, as it were, to forswear the Gaelic part of him. This clash between his two personalities is vividly illustrated by his poetry, throwing into relief the cruel dilemma in which Desmond and others like him often found themselves. One poem, written to his great friend Mac Carthy, tries to explain how it was that fear of the king of England made him make war on his friend: 'I made the decision, through which I was overcome, to turn against my real friends because I feared the anger of the Saxon king. I preferred to go against my brothers, no matter what they thought of me, than to be held under duress by the Saxon king in London'.

To the king and his government in Ireland, people like Desmond demonstrated the dangers of cultural assimilation. He could not be trusted all the time. In his Irish guise he, and very many others in the same position, patronised Gaelic poets and travelling minstrels who very often were thus able to penetrate the land of peace and to act as spies for chieftains in their raids on the settled areas. Even wandering friars, and especially the Franciscans, who found a welcome in many an Anglo-Irish friary or manor, could and did spy the land and carry back information to Gaelic leaders. There was real danger here: the more the Anglo-Irish 'degenerated' (as the government put it) into Gaelic habit, speech and custom, the greater the danger that incursions by 'Irish enemies' would follow. Indeed later Tudor commentators, like Spenser or Gerrard or Campion, were convinced that one of the main reasons for the failure of the English settlement in medieval Ireland was, as Gerrard expressed it, that 'the quiete estate of the land began to decay (because) the English degeneratinge become Irishe'. There were other dangers which this degeneracy occasioned, so that the so-called 'degenerate' English became all too often the 'rebel' English, defying the authority of the king and Dublin government alike and riding roughshod over the rights of the local communities everywhere.

In official eyes contact with Gaelic culture was a contamination. It was because the Irish people were degraded that any assimilation to them was degeneracy. They were uncivilised, as their way of life showed. Here the official attitude was no more than what was the common attitude of visitors to Ireland from England. Giraldus Cambrensis did not mince words in describing how barbarous the Irish were, even if they did have some qualities which provoked his admiration. Nearly half a century later another visitor, the Cistercian Stephen of Lexington, was equally scathing in his condemnations and went even further in his description of them as 'bestial'—by which he meant that emotion rather than reason ruled them. Their only hope of salvation, that is of becoming civilised, was to be absorbed into the civilisation and culture of Anglo-Norman society. No wonder, then, that official reaction to the assimilation of so many of the settlers was shock—which makes it all the more ironical that in 1414 at the Council of Constance, in order to justify their acceptance as a voting 'nation', the English delegation fell back on an historical argument in which Ireland figured as one of the four ancient kingdoms of Europe. In addition, there was the further unpalatable fact that the process of Gaelicisation was full of danger to the English interest in Ireland, as the Burkes of Connacht or the Powers of Waterford demonstrate so well. Contemporaries were well aware of the danger. A poem from the time of Edward III, written into the *White Book* of the Dublin exchequer by a clerk who was tired of the official jargon which he was copying, tried to explain how 'this land shall be much undone' and added:

> But gossipred[14] and alterage,[15]
> And losing of our language
> Have mickly holp thereto.

It is hardly surprising, therefore, that a policy of separating the races and driving a cultural barrier between them was instituted.

[14]'gossipred' was the custom of standing sponsor at baptism.
[15]'alterage' was the placing of children with foster-parents.

This policy is best expressed in the Statutes of Kilkenny of 1366. But the legislation of 1366 had been anticipated by a host of earlier enactments from 1297 onwards: bans on Irish dress, language, games, and so on, on marriage with the Irish enemy, on making treaties with them, on keeping rhymers or brehons, on trading with the Gaelic areas—none of this was new in the mid-fourteenth century. It was however given a new form and a new life at Kilkenny. Certainly later generations, to judge from the frequent confirmations of these statutes or references to them in the records of the later medieval period, regarded the Statutes of Kilkenny as the best and most authoritative summary of the so-called 'anti-Irish' legislation of the medieval Irish parliament.

This legislation and the policy underlying it was on the whole a failure. Frequent breaches of the statutes are mentioned and there seemed to be little difficulty in procuring a licence exempting one from the penalties involved in contravening even the most serious of them. So strong an attraction did the custom of fosterage retain for the Anglo-Irish that licences of exemption were frequently issued, such as that which the earl of Desmond procured in December 1388, permitting him to send his son to O Brien of Thomond 'to be brought up and educated and there to remain as long as he should think fit, notwithstanding any Statutes made to the contrary'. The Butlers continued to keep their brehons and court poets; the Geraldines still married and fostered with Gaelic families. Two great fifteenth-century Gaelic compilations, the *Book of Fermoy* and the *Saltair of Mac Richard,* were assembled for Anglo-Irish families, and indeed the latter one was so highly valued that it formed part of the ransom handed over by Butler to the earl of Desmond after the battle of Pilltown in 1464. It was a copy of, among other things, the ancient Psalter of Cashel, made for Edmund Butler, and it was dedicated 'with a blessing on the soul of the archbishop of Cashel, Richard O Hedigan, for it was by him that the owner was educated'. Some of the marginal entries vividly bring home to us the impatience with which Butler urged on the work, almost as if he could hardly bear to wait for the book to be completed. The scribes complain especially of having to work on Sundays ('May God forgive Edmund for colouring this book on a Sunday night') or in miserable, cold conditions, until the hand or the wrist gets sore with the copying. The library of the eighth earl of Kildare contained a large number of Gaelic books, side by side with volumes in English, Latin and French. Despite everything, then, legislation failed to prevent some degree of assimilation from taking place. Gaelic names in town oligarchies show that in these most English parts of Ireland not much attention was paid to the official policy of excluding the Gaelic race. Traffic with Gaelic Ireland continued and cultural assimilation went on virtually unchecked. By the sixteenth century, when the medieval lordship was nearing the end of its days, a chief justice could write: 'all the king's subjects of the four shires be near hand Irish and wear their habits and use their tongue'—the area referred to being that of the so-called four 'obedient' shires of Dublin, Kildare, Meath and Louth. In 1536 the deputy wrote to Henry VIII: 'Your highness must understand that the English blood of the English conquest is in manner worn out of this land, and at all seasons in manner, without any restoration, is diminished and enfeebled . . . . And, contrary-wise, the Irish blood ever more and more, without such decay, encreaseth'. And the chancellor, Gerrard, pointed out in 1577 that Irish was the common speech within the Pale.

The only real cure, and that was a drastic one, was the introduction of new settlers from England in sufficiently large numbers to prevent their being swamped. There were, indeed, some proposals for establishing new colonies: one of the stipulations made by the duke of Surrey in 1398, when he was made lieutenant of the king in Ireland, was that he should have out of every parish, or every two parishes in England a man and his wife for Ireland 'to inhabit the said land where it is wasted on the marches'. But schemes like this came to nothing and it was not until the sixteenth century that new colonisation, or plantation, was seriously undertaken. Meantime, legislation, if largely ineffective, remained upon the statute book and could always be invoked if the opportunity arose. So it was in 1468 against the two earls of Kildare and Desmond, the latter being executed as a result. During the fourteenth century, however, the problem of the Gaelic revival remained largely a military one which the government made every effort to solve. The final answer would have been conquest, but it was beyond the resources of a medieval government to attempt that. Certainly no Irish government in the later middle ages ever had anything like the necessary financial or human resources at its disposal to attempt a re-conquest of lost territories, even with the backing of England. Indeed as the fourteenth century was to show it was not within its competence to contain the Gaelic revival in most parts of the country, much less to push it back.

VIII The Fourteenth Century:
The Problem of Decline

IN July 1331 an English embassy arrived at the papal court in Avignon and during the subsequent sessions with Pope John XXII the affairs of Ireland were discussed. At one stage the pope was asked if he would recommend King Edward III to go to Ireland in person in order to promote peace there, a proposition which was not favoured. It may well be that when a year later King Edward cancelled a great expedition to Ireland, the advice of the pope was in his mind. But it is certain, too, that the chance of winning glory in Scotland made a greater appeal to him and it was to this purpose that he diverted the men and supplies gathered for Ireland. Whatever the reason, this change of plan was disastrous for the English interest in Ireland, where conditions were worsening with each year that passed. Intervention at this stage by a young king, at the head of a great army, would have at least halted the process of disintegration which was destroying the English colony.

It was probably on the occasion of this same embassy in 1331 that a letter was presented to the pope, from the justiciar and the Irish council, invoking the grant of Ireland by Pope Adrian IV as an excuse for seeking papal help in remedying the state of the lordship. An appeal to the papacy such as this is a good indication of how bad was the situation in Ireland. It paints a dismal picture of the violence, disorder and lawlessness of the times, of heresy and immorality, blasphemy and sacrilege, and of the persecution of the Church. It castigates the Irish, who are held to be responsible for all this, as 'an ungovernable people, enemies of God and man, sacreligious, burners of churches', and denounces them because they assert that the king of England holds Ireland in dominion by means of false bulls, being heretics besides. If the pope does not intervene, others will be infected by the perverse doctrines which are spreading. Neither the prelates nor the royal officials, who should be responsible for seeing that justice is done, dare to discharge their duties for fear of death.

As the fourteenth century progressed, the condition of the feudal lordship deteriorated and for this decline there is no simple explanation. There are, however, a number of facts which seem to have been of particular importance in the process of disintegration. Of these, the inability of the Dublin government to draw on adequate financial resources was of special significance. One result of the Gaelic revival and the loss of land that went with it was a decline in the revenues of the Irish government. In the thirteenth century, as we have seen, the Irish lordship had been sufficiently affluent to provide a large surplus of cash which was made available to the English king. In the fourteenth century, however, the position was reversed. Now it was the English government which had to subsidise the Irish lordship. At first the outlay was small; but as the century wore on and the financial position of the Irish government deteriorated, the king found himself committed to a growing expenditure on Ireland which reached a climax at the end of the century with the two great expeditions of Richard II. This financial involvement in Ireland was to become of crucial importance in the history of Anglo-Irish relations.

The serious nature of the decline of Irish revenues might be briefly illustrated. Under Edward I, except for a few years when the annual revenue was inflated by taxation and reached something over £9,000, the yearly average came to about £6,300. By the end of Edward I's reign it had fallen to just over £5,700. Under Edward II the decline continued: 2 Edward II—just short of £3,500; 3 Edward II—£2,500; 4 Edward II—£3,000; 5 Edward II—£2,800. A vigorous attempt at financial reform by the government of Edward II in Ireland did nothing to arrest this decline. In the years after 1315, the year of the Bruce invasion, the average annual revenue fell to something over £2,300 and thereafter for the rest of the century it hovered at the £2,000 level, except for periods of brief recovery.

One must not, of course, attach too much importance to these figures as an accurate index of exchequer revenue during the period in question; but they do illustrate in general terms a broad financial trend which is reasonably accurate. In other words they show that during the fourteenth century the revenues at the disposal of the Dublin government fell first, in the early part of the century, to approximately half what they had been in the heyday of the colony under Edward I, and later to almost one third. Such a decline was little short of catastrophic. The available revenues barely sufficed to meet the normal expenses of government, but were hopelessly inadequate for coping with the sort of situation which existed in Ireland throughout most of this century. In particular the Dublin government found it impossible to finance an adequate defence of the settled area, much less attempt a large-scale recovery of lands lost to Gaelic chieftains.

The basic fact in Anglo-Irish relations throughout this century was therefore a simple one: the Irish government was not financially self-sufficient and therefore required subsidisation by England. But for most of this period the king was involved in war with France and Scotland, a costly business which strained to the limit all the resources which he could employ. It was difficult, and occasionally impossible, to find anything to spare for Ireland. The alternative was to try to make the lordship pay its own way again. This could be done by means of increased taxation, a policy which was tried in a spectacular way in the 1370s under William of Windsor, who attempted to force the magnates and communities of Ireland into shouldering the burden of a regular series of parliamentary subsidies. His failure, and in the end his ruin, demonstrated once and for all the impossibility of carrying through a successful programme of taxation on a large enough scale to make the effort worthwhile. Apart from the natural resistance of all to a heavy incidence of taxation, which was enough to make Edward III withdraw support from his governor at a crucial moment, there was another fact which explains why a fiscal policy like that of Windsor was difficult to sustain. The yield from taxation was small, because the area in which it could be levied was small. The success of the Gaelic revival and the growing number of English rebels meant that as the years passed less land was subject to control, in any but the vaguest form, by the Dublin government. The part of Ireland, then, in which a subsidy granted by parliament could be levied tended to decrease all the time. If the government wished to increase the yield from taxation, without increasing its incidence too much, it would have to try to enlarge the area which was taxable, and at the very least prevent that area from declining further. This meant accepting heavy military commitments, which was expensive. There were, of course, other more important reasons why it was necessary to mount a regular series of military expeditions in Ireland right through this century, and there were also other ways in which governments and magnates tried to maintain the 'land of peace' from contracting further, such as making absentee landlords assume a responsibility for the defence of their estates. But heavy expenditure on military operations, which is a feature of the exchequer accounts of the period, has an important bearing on the whole question of taxation and must not be overlooked. When William of Windsor was first appointed lieutenant of the king in Ireland in 1369, his main function was clearly to make Ireland pay her own way. Edward III had already made it plain that he was no longer prepared to accept the heavy burden of paying for the wars in Ireland. Ten years before this he had written a letter to his chief ministers in Dublin informing them of his expedition to France and explaining his anxiety for the safety of Ireland during his absence abroad. But what is more significant, he also said that he was taking with him 'chiefs, magnates and others in no small numbers from England and also the money which he could conveniently collect, leaving the realm empty of armed power and destitute of lords, whereby there is no room to send men or money to Ireland at present, although it is said that they are needed there'. Within two years, however, the king sent his own son Lionel to Ireland, with a large army and at a huge cost to the English taxpayer. He was nevertheless still anxious about the financial burden of Ireland, especially during the period when William of Windsor held office there, and on more than one occasion in support of Windsor he emphasised that neither he nor his subjects of England could any longer support the expenses of the wars in Ireland. So it was Windsor's task to make the lordship support the cost of its own wars, which could only really be done by means of increased taxation. Yet it was clearly realised that to do this he had to be financed in the first place by England, so that the wars against the Gaelic chieftains might be successfully concluded. To maintain this strong military policy his first contract with the king specified that he should have £20,000 for himself and his retinue, while during his second period of service he was given more than £11,000 for the first year, fantastic sums in an Irish context and big even by English standards. All of this money was rapidly eaten away by the expenses of his military operations in Ireland, as was the money which he managed to raise through parliamentary subsidies. Indeed enormous as his outlay was, it proved to the totally inadequate for the task in hand.

Recourse to heavy taxation, then, was no answer to the problem in Ireland because to be effective it, too, involved the king and the English exchequer in heavy expenditure on the lordship—the very thing he was most anxious to avoid. What, then, was he to do if he could not afford, or was unwilling to accept, a heavy financial outlay on Ireland? One can argue—and it has been suggested that this is what the famous Statutes of Kilkenny of 1366 represent—that one alternative was to let a large part of Ireland go and to concentrate on retaining a firm grip on the most Anglicised areas in the eastern half of the country. In fact this was the chosen alternative at the end of the middle ages, when a Pale was created around Dublin. But not even an Edward III, dazzled as he was by the attractions of France and blind seemingly to the potential of Ireland, could conceive of deliberately abandoning any part of his patrimony. There is no evidence that at any time he ever entertained the idea of cutting his losses in Ireland and relinquishing any part of his lordship there. Quite the reverse, in fact, if one is to judge by the amount of money which from time to time he poured into the defence of Ireland. The interest might not always be sustained and the subsidisation might not always be continuous, but there is no doubt that throughout the century as a whole, far from abandoning any part of Ireland, a regular series of attempts was made at recovering what had been lost, of which the personal interventions of Richard II were the greatest and the natural climax.

There was one way in which the king, to some extent, could reduce his financial liabilities in Ireland without trying to improve the finances of the Dublin government and that was by throwing as much as possible of the burden of defence on the Anglo-Irish magnates. It was an accepted principle in Ireland that local defence was a matter for the local community and this was exemplified in the local subsidies which were common throughout the whole medieval period. The local magnates were expected to accept their share of this load as something other than the military service which those of them who were tenants in chief owed to the king for their lands. But quite apart from this it can be argued that the king tried to make the great magnates assume a greater responsibility by fostering their self-reliance. In particular the three great earldoms of Desmond, Kildare and Ormond were regarded as buttresses of Anglo-Ireland.

Even before the end of the thirteenth century the Irish government had to some extent begun to rely on the great magnates for preserving the peace in their localities. In 1299 both Peter de Bermingham on one side of Offaly and John fitz Thomas on the other were each granted an aid to make war on the Irish. But even more than that, it seems that a price had been put on the heads of leading Irish enemies, such as Mac Murrough in Leinster, or O Donnell in the north-west, early in the 1280s or O Connor Faley in the midlands. Later still £100 was offered for the head of Edward Bruce. Head money was a bounty which encouraged the hunting out of Irishmen and led to such notorious incidents as the mass murder of O Connors by Peter de Bermingham in 1305. Perhaps the greatest single instance of this kind of reliance on the great local magnate is Richard de Burgh, earl of Ulster. We have already noted the message from King Edward I which said that he relied on the earl 'more than any other man in the land'. In 1305 a jury at Castledermot advised that the land of Sil Murray in Connacht, which was held by O Connor, should be given to the earl because among other reasons, 'the earl has his lands in Connacht and Ulster, and a great force of English and Irish adjoining that land, by which he would be better able than another to chastise the Irish of that land'.

It would be dangerous to assume that any king deliberately chose this as an alternative 'policy' to free him from financial responsibilities in Ireland. Medieval policy was usually a matter of expediency, and certainly so far as Anglo-Irish relations are concerned it is difficult to escape the conclusion that the king and his council in England made decisions on a purely *ad hoc* basis, with little regard for the future. Nevertheless patterns of behaviour do appear and one can discern in the growth of the power and independence of the great magnates, in which the government at times seemed to concur, a half-conscious attempt to solve the problem posed by the Gaelic revival. This was full of danger and too frequently the local magnate, with his retinue of indentured retainers and his assumption of ancient customary exactions to which he had no right, struck out on his own quite independently of any restrictions placed on him by the king and his law. Despite repeated assertions by the government that parleying with the Irish, negotiating treaties, making peace or making war was no business of the local magnate, we find local lords everywhere doing just this and worse, forming alliances with Gaelic chieftains who were technically 'Irish enemies'. They could argue, if they ever bothered, that only in this way could the king's interest be maintained, however nebulously, in the localities and that this kind of independent action was the price which had to be paid.

Maurice fitz Thomas, the first earl of Desmond, is a good, if perhaps extreme, example of the independent attitudes which many of the magnates of Ireland were striking. Using Gaelic custom which entitled him to certain exactions, he was able to build up a body of retainers which quickly became the terror of the countryside. Soon his reputation spread. It was later stated during an investigation into his rebellion, that 'when other wrongdoers realised that they could have a man like Maurice as their lord, who was willing to aid them in this way in their wickedness, many came, English as well as Irish, to him from Connacht and Thomond, from Leinster and Desmond'. Known as 'Mac Thomas's Rout', this small army ravaged widely through Limerick, Cork and Waterford. Success went to Maurice's head and in 1326 he held a meeting with the earl of Kildare, the earl of Louth, James Butler, later earl of Ormond, the bishop of Ossory and a number of others (including Brian O Brien of Thomond). It was a formidable assembly of the greatest magnates in Ireland and it agreed that not only should they rebel against the king and assume control of Ireland, but that they should crown Maurice as king, share out the land of Ireland among those who joined the rebellion and destroy utterly all who resisted. It is hard to take this fantastic proposal seriously, though there seems to be no doubt that Maurice was ambitious to make himself king and now, with civil war looming in England, seemed a propitious time. In any event, the conspiracy came to nothing and Maurice became involved in a vicious quarrel with the Powers and Burkes, causing enormous damage to property and loss of life all over the south of Ireland. In 1331 he was hatching yet another plot to make himself king of Ireland and restore the ancient provincial kingdoms with Walter de Burgh ruling Connacht, William Bermingham ruling Leinster, Henry de Mandeville ruling Ulster and Maurice himself ruling Munster and Meath. He is said to have tried to involve Gaelic Ireland in a general uprising by saying 'to some of the Irish that it is ordained that the Irish shall drive all the English out of Ireland and, if the Irish will make him their king, he will help them to the utmost of his power. And he said that, even though the king of England, the king of France and other two kings should enter Ireland to attack them, he would resist those kings with all his strength'. The government could ignore him no longer and he was arrested, as were some of his chief supporters; one of them, William Bermingham, brother of the earl of Louth, was hanged for his treason. This was a shock. An Anglo-Irish chronicler in recording the execution burst out: 'He was a noble knight, the noblest and best of a thousand knights in the art of war. Alas and alas, who can refrain from tears in speaking of his death?' Does this reflect simple antagonism towards the justiciar responsible for the execution, Anthony Lucy, partisan good will towards the Berminghams, or something deeper altogether—hatred for chief governors from England which was strong enough to overlook the enormity of Bermingham's crimes? Not long afterwards Lucy was replaced and Desmond was released. By the summer of 1334 he had his lands restored to him!

Ten years later he was up to his old tricks and plotting to make himself king, or so it was alleged. He wrote to the kings of Scotland and France requesting aid in a conquest of Ireland. He also urged the whole of Gaelic Ireland to join in rebellion. Even more interesting was the report that he had sent messengers to the pope accusing the king of England of having violated the terms of the original grant of Pope Adrian IV and offering 3,000 marks annually for being his representative in Ireland. Once more he was in open rebellion, in league with 'Irish enemy' and 'English rebel', terrorising the countryside and causing havoc wherever he went. The government was forced to take action against him and sent an army in the summer of 1345. Lacking substantial support from either Gaelic or Anglo-Ireland, outlawed and unable to find the resources to lead a successful rebellion, Desmond met his match in a new justiciar from

England, Ralph of Ufford. A great army composed of men from Leinster, Munster and Connacht, marched against the earl. Some of his leading supporters were captured, hanged, drawn and quartered. Desmond himself escaped and found asylum among the Irish of Kerry. After the death of Ufford in April 1346, he agreed to surrender to the new justiciar, Roger Darcy, on condition that he be allowed to go to England under special protection so as to defend himself. There he succeeded in coming to some agreement with the king. He was pardoned in 1349 and was back in Ireland again the following year. Then in 1351 he succeeded in challenging the award of outlawrie against him and won his case on a technicality. There is no doubt, however, that political expediency rather than the claims of justice made Desmond a free man. Not only were his lands restored to him, but on 8 July 1355 he was actually appointed justiciar of Ireland by the king, an extraordinary ending to a sordid chapter of rebellion and crime. This, in fact, points to an important truth which we should always keep in mind: no king could afford to govern without the counsel and help of his great men, and in Ireland it was particularly obvious that the government had no alternative but to rely on the great magnates such as Desmond. A vigorous governor might take firm action, as did Ufford, but in the end the king had little choice but to fall back on men like Desmond. Without him, for instance, the whole of the south-west would have been lost— which in fact is what happened in the fifteenth century when a hotheaded descendant of the same earl virtually renounced his allegiance to the English king and that part of Ireland was forfeited by the English interest.

With the growth of independence among the feudatories and the increase in military resources which they commanded through the operation of so-called 'bastard feudalism', went the increase in the number of 'rebel English' all over the island. These were as much a menace to the rule of law as were the criminals of the age and the 'Irish enemies' themselves. They also provided a steady supply of 'idlemen', well-to-do young men with prospects in life other than the rewards which might be gleaned from joining the household of some magnate as an armed retainer. It was inevitable, under the circumstances, that fierce faction fights should break out and fourteenth-century

Ireland witnessed many. In some of these the greatest names in the lordship were involved. One of the most serious, shortly after the accession of Edward III, concerned the Geraldines, Butlers, Berminghams, Walls, Tobins, and others who fought the Powers and Burkes in what almost amounted to a civil war. The supposed reason for the outbreak of this struggle was the insult which Arnold Power offered Maurice fitz Thomas when he called him a 'rymour' or Gaelic bard, though in reality this faction fight was a reflection of the great political division in contemporary England. This caused terrific destruction. In Tipperary and Waterford, for example, the damage was assessed at £100,000! Royal commands that under pain of forfeiting their lands the opposing factions should cease to muster soldiers or make war on each other, to the terror and destruction of the liege people, were simply ignored. To such an extent did faction fights develop that towns were obliged to provide for their own defence, not against the Irish army, but against the English rebels. Royal writs from England ordered the Powers and Geraldines to resist from levying troops for the purpose of attacking each other, and the sheriffs of Cork, Limerick, Tipperary and Waterford were ordered to proclaim that no one should join those magnates 'who had sworn and confederated for the purpose of assailing the subjects of the crown'. But it was to little avail and a report on the state of Ireland in 1346 had to state melancholily: 'There are serious disturbances in various parts of Ireland and between the English, which are more harmful to the king's fortunes than the wars with the Irish'. Small wonder that a bishop of Cloyne, driven to distraction, should in 1380 rage against such tormentors. He was accused of slander and the court record describes how one day in celebrating mass in the royal chapel in Dublin castle, before the king's lieutenant and his household, he 'did after beginning the accustomed preface introduce these words, "Eternal God", and then omitted the divine words following but with a high voice said and sang these damnable words, viz.: "there are two in Munster who destroy us and our goods, namely the earl of Ormond and the earl of Desmond with their followers, whom in the end the lord will destroy through Jesus Christ our Lord, Amen" with many other such words'. He refused to 'desist from these shocking words but like a heretic persisted in defending them, and on following days in high and private masses he openly used them in place of the true preface, altering and omitting the divine words'.

It is against this background of faction fights that two famous murders, following in rapid succession, should be seen. The first came in June 1329 at Braganstown in county Louth, where the earl of Louth, together with two brothers, nine close relatives, and about 160 others, were murdered by some of the leading settler families in that country. It seems certain that Bermingham was terrorising the country in the manner of Desmond in the south and so his own tenants turned on him, being unwilling, as a chronicler put it, 'that he should rule over them'. Serious as were the repercussions of this assassination, the results of the murder of the last earl of Ulster in 1333 were much more damaging to the English interest in Ireland. Earl William, who was still only twenty-one, was heir to a double lordship in Connacht and Ulster where already there were signs that feudatories were chafing under the restrictions of the allegiance they owed their lord. The immediate cause of the murder seems to have been personal, namely revenge for the death of Walter de Burgh who had been imprisoned by the earl in his castle of Northburgh, where he died in 1332. But it is clear that as in the case of the Bermingham murder the real motive went deeper and involved the denial of feudal lordship. Within a matter of months most of the earldom was lost to the earl's heiress while within a few years a large part of the lordship of Connacht was seized by relatives of the murdered earl, who were to strike out on their own in defiance of feudal custom and common law alike, the complete examples of rebel, degenerate English. No wonder the murder came as such a shock, exposing as it did the power of the independent feudatories and their complete disregard for a feudal code of behaviour which now clearly belonged to a dying world.

There were other, less important murders which involved a similar breach of feudal ethics and many more which resulted from the growth of faction and the increase in the number of rebel English. These are all symptomatic of the general malaise of that age, of the growth of lawlessness and the government's inability to cope adequately. But they are also a reflection of the kind of danger which resulted from the policy of fostering the power of the magnates in the localities.

Yet given the situation, the king and his government had little choice but to accept the potential danger and place as much as possible of the burden of defence on the local lords. And not only defence, but peace-keeping operations generally were increasingly made the responsibility of the lords. It is a remarkable development in Anglo-Irish society that at a time when the government was becoming ever more alarmed at the 'degeneracy' of so many of the settlers, it should actively encourage what later became known as the 'clan system' in order to help to maintain the rule of law. Examples of this in its most extreme form saw the chief governor virtually inaugurating an Anglo-Irish lord as 'captain of his nation' in the Gaelic fashion. But a more moderate form was expressed in the legislation of the Kilkenny parliament of 1310, which made the heads of great families ('every chieftain of great lineage') responsible for those of his name who broke the peace. Here the resemblance to the Irish custom whereby responsibility lay with the kin, especially the father and close relatives, and ultimately with the chieftain, is obvious. Indeed long before this, in 1278, in what now remains the oldest piece of Irish parliamentary legislation extant, it was enacted that the heads of Gaelic family groups were to be responsible for their people. In 1324 the earls, barons, 'and the other grandees of lineage' entered into a solemn compact to seize all 'the felons, robbers and thieves of their family and sirname'. Later still, in 1351, at a time when conditions were chaotic, a great council ordained that when the heads of families were unwilling to seize lawbreakers in the family 'then the bodies of the said chieftains be taken for them and detained in prison'. It was clearly impossible to make this legislation work and by the mid-fifteenth century it was modified so that 'every man should answer for his sons and hired men', which had a more reasonable chance of success.

As a way of dealing with the problem of lawlessness, this was less than satisfactory. Furthermore, it did nothing to help solve the even more pressing problem of defence in the localities and the continuing fight against the Gaelic revival. The main burden was still resting on the local communities. It was aggravated by another problem, which to most contemporaries was mainly responsible for the continuing loss of land to resurgent Gaelic chieftaincies. That was the problem of absentees, which as early as 1297 was sufficiently acute to receive the attention of parliament when it met to devise a solution to the question of defence and peace-keeping in the localities. The parliament decreed that

the magnates and others who reside in England or elsewhere out of this land, who cause the profits of their land to be transmitted to them from this land, leaving nothing here to protect their tenaments or the tenants thereof, shall at once from now on allow a reasonable portion to remain in the hands of their bailiffs, whereby their lands may be efficiently defended and saved, if it happen that war or disturbance of the peace should be aroused there by any persons.

But the problem worsened in the fourteenth century and gradually a new formula was worked out which, it was hoped, would cope with the dangers which resulted from absenteeism. An English ordinance of 1331 provided that all who had lands in Ireland were either to reside on them or else 'place sufficient guard for the preservation of the peace in the same', the lands of defaulters being seized into the king's hands. On 15 October of that year Edward III wrote to the earl of Norfolk and the other great absentees, conveying the terms of the ordinance, warning them that he proposed to go to Ireland himself and that if he recovered any lands he would retain them 'as being of his own conquest'. In an earlier letter the king had complained that 'the Irish enemies and rebels have wasted and do waste his land and the lands of divers magnates who have lands in Ireland and dwell in England, because sufficient resistance against them is not ordained by the said magnates'. A petition from Ireland, which in 1342 was placed before the king and his council, complained that the lands of absentees which are not properly looked after, 'by default of not spending money in improving and keeping well the said lands', are easily destroyed, and with them neighbouring lands as well. At the meeting of the great council at Kilkenny in 1351, which issued a series of sweeping ordinances designed to cope with the most urgent problems in the public life of the colony, landlords resident in England were once again condemned and ordered to contribute to the defence of the lordship and to look after the safety of their lands on pain of forfeiture.

But the most important statement yet on the whole question

of the effects of absenteeism was made in 1368. A report had been sent to the king and his council in England which described how the Irish and other enemies were 'riding in hostile array through every part of the land', looting and destroying as they went, 'so that the land is at the point of being lost'. In seeking a remedy King Edward decided that a parliament should be specially summoned in Ireland to discuss the problem and advise him on what to do. The parliament met in Dublin and, as the record tells us

at length it appeared to them in particular and in general that the said mischiefs could not in any wise be redressed and ammended, nor the said land succoured, except by the coming and continuing residence of the earls, nobles and others of his realm of England, who have inheritance in the said land of Ireland, in their own person or by their strong men, sufficient and well equipped for war upon their lordships, lands, possessions, and inheritances within the said lordship of Ireland, for recovering their inheritances there lost, opposing the said mischiefs, and for the preservation of the estate of our lord the king, and of the rights of his crown, and the aid of the lands aforesaid.

Indeed the parliament suggested that 'each of them might and ought to be driven and compelled to do this quickly and within short space' and pointed out that during the first conquest of Ireland lands were granted in inheritance by the king 'to many noble persons and others of his realm of England, in order that they should continually reside and dwell in their own persons with their families upon the said conquest, to defend and maintain it for ever thereafter against all men who should attempt to rise or rebel against the said conquest'; but instead, these lords now for the most part live in England or elsewhere, taking all the revenues from their lands in Ireland without defending them, 'and without doing their duty in this case, whereby the said evils and mischief without any opposition have occured'.

Allowing for exaggeration, there can be no doubt that as far as the Anglo-Irish were concerned absenteeism was the greatest source of weakness in the colony and therefore required harsh methods of compulsion if it were to be successfully coped with: hence their emphasis on treating defaulters harshly. The king agreed and by way of answer published an important ordinance which prescribed that all those in England who possessed lands in Ireland should go and reside continuously there, with their families, men at arms and retainers. Those who for urgent reasons, which were acceptable to the king and his council, found it impossible to obey this injunction were to send a force of men, equipped and paid for at their own expense, to defend and maintain their Irish lands. Anyone who defaulted, 'of whatever estate, degree or condition they be', would be immediately deprived of all lands and possessions in Ireland.

Measures of this kind, however much they might demonstrate the serious nature of the problem they were designed to cure, were completely impractical and had no hope of ever becoming really effective. Many of the great absentees were persons of high estate in England, well connected with the centre of government and impossible to force in the manner specified by the ordinance. Five years after this, for example, a request had to be sent to the king that the earl of March should be compelled to come to Ireland and defend his vast estates there in Ulster, Meath and Connacht. But although the earl was duly instructed to proceed to Ireland as soon as possible, he did not in fact arrive until seven years later, 1380, when he came as lieutenant of the king and not in obedience to the earlier mandate. No government could ever hope to force people of this standing to abandon, even temporarily, their interests in England. So that as an attempt to surmount the growing problem created by absentees, legislation of the kind was by and large totally ineffective.

By far the most effective answer was provided by the so-called Statute of Absentees, promulgated by Richard II in 1380. This was much wider in its application than earlier legislation had been and was designed not merely to cope with great magnates like the earl of March, but with the lesser folk as well who held 'rents, benefices and offices' apart from lands. Once again in rehearsing the reasons for the statute it was emphasised that neglect of their lands by absentees had allowed castles and fortresses to go to ruin and left areas 'without guard, rule and government', so that the Irish enemies 'are increased and increasing and prevailing from day to day'. The remedy, as usual, was an order for all absentees to return to Ireland. But this time there was a sting in an additional proviso which is most important: in case of absence for reasonable cause, the absentee was to find enough men to defend his land, benefice or other source of profit—failing to do this, the Irish government was authorised to levy two-thirds of the profits or rents and apply them to meet the cost of defence. This was aimed at people who were normally resident in Ireland and who presumably therefore had a source of income which was readily tapped. The landlords who were normally non-resident, many of whose ancestors had already been absentees for generations past, were rarely in possession of an assessible income from Ireland; and so the earlier legislation had been useless, for how was the government to derive a profit from lands which, as was so frequently emphasised, were already overrun by Irish enemies or English rebels? Indeed this very point had been made in the petition from Ireland on which the same statute was based: 'In some cases it seems hard to dispose of all the profits of the said lands and benefices for the carrying on of the wars there'.

It seems clear, then, that it was tacitly recognised that the part of legislation which related to chronic absentees would be largely a dead letter, as had been the case heretofore; but in the case of holders of beneficies in particular it was hoped to reap a profit which could be applied to defence in general. And this seems to be borne out by the swift reaction which came when the statute was promulgated in Ireland. The Irish prelates and clergy protested to the king, arguing that they should not be bound by legislation to which they had not given their assent, thus raising an interesting constitutional issue concerning the application of English statutes to Ireland. The protest fell on deaf ears, however. The statute had provided that benefices held by those leaving Ireland in the king's service, or to study at the universities, or for any other reasonable cause should be taxed at only one-third (instead of two-thirds) their value. This hit the clergy hard because many of them had to go abroad to study, to visit Rome or other eccles- iastical centres on business, to make a pilgrimage, or for many other reasons. No wonder they protested so vehemently. But the statute was confirmed by Henry IV in 1399 almost immediately after his accession in England and seems to have been rigorously enforced in Ireland.

Naturally enough resident magnates in Ireland tried to invoke the legislation against absentees in the hope of augmenting their estates. In 1393 Thomas Butler petitioned the Irish council for a grant of all lands in the cantred of Offagh in county Tipperary, along the west side of the river Suir, which had been overrun by the Irish through neglect of the owners. His petition was successful, though it is doubtful if he managed to make passage along the Suir any safer.

There were other absentees who never left Ireland, people who abandoned lands in dangerous march areas and lived in greater safety in the land of peace. For example, the parliament of 1297 referred to this when it spoke of those who 'remain and dwell in their manors in a land of peace, their lands in the marches being left waste and uncultivated and without a guard'. The ordinances of 1351 ordained that 'all those who have lands in the march and are resident in the land of peace, make their residence in their lands in the march'. There was a flight of settlers before resurgent Gaelic chieftains and it became more marked as the Gaelic revival gained momentum.

This flight from the land caused emigration on a large scale. The Statutes of Kilkenny of 1366 legislated on the problem of the 'distress caused by want of servants . . . by reason that the common labourers are for a great part absent and fly out of the said land'. Most English towns of any size had immigrants from Ireland and by the mid-fourteenth century the expanding cloth industry, especially in the midlands and the west country, employed a surprisingly large number of skilled Irish artisans. When Richard II, preparatory to his expedition to Ireland in 1395, ordered all Irish living in England to return home, he flushed out a surprisingly large number of craftsmen, artisans and labourers, together with the expected clerks and students. Licences to remain in England were issued to no fewer than 521, which must have been a fraction of the total, including one man 'in consideration of his blindness and old age' and another 'in consideration of his poverty and feebleness'.

Emigration continued into the fifteenth century and remained a source of weakness in the lordship. A petition from the commons in the Irish parliament of 1421 pointed out that 'day to day (we are) burdened with divers intolerable charges and wars, so that ter-tenants, the artificers and labourers of the said land daily depart in great numbers from your said land to your kingdom of England and remain there, whereby the husbandry of your said land is greatly injured and disused and your said lieges greatly weakened in their power of resisting the malice of your said enemies'. Depopulation became so serious before the end of the fourteenth century that it was proposed to introduce new colonists from England: one of the stipulations made by the duke of Surrey in 1398, when he was appointed lieutenant in Ireland, was that he should have out of every parish, or every two parishes, in England a man and his wife for Ireland 'to inhabit the said land where it is wasted on the marches'. But schemes like this came to nothing and it was not until the sixteenth century that new colonisation, or plantation, was undertaken.

This exodus from the countryside to the towns and to England was mainly the result of pressure from resurgent Gaelic Ireland or even the lawless activity of rebel English, which at times produced a near-hysterical reaction among the settlers. But it was also a side effect of the great plague—the Black Death—which struck Ireland, in common with the rest of Europe, in the middle of the fourteenth century and exacerbated the long-standing effects of absenteeism. In 1360 a meeting of the great council at Kilkenny sent a message to the king complaining of absentees who failed to protect their lands and adding that there was a lack of great lords who, in the absence of the justiciar, used to defend the marches, and that this was partly because of the plague, 'which was so great and hideous among the English lieges and not among the Irish'.

This terrible plague was to destroy so many people in Ireland that it was commonly feared that the end of the world was come. Far away in Avignon, the Italian poet Petrarch, having witnessed its ravages, wrote: 'Will posterity, if there is one, believe without anyone's having seen, either coming down from the sky or up out of the earth, a devouring fire; without war; without any visible cause of destruction, the world was almost completely depopulated?' Here in Ireland, the Franciscan friar John Clyn of Kilkenny, writing his chronicle at the height of the plague, wrote at the end that he was leaving 'parchment to continue the work, if perchance any man survive, or any of the race of Adam may escape this pestilence and continue the work so begun'. Clyn himself died of the plague, as did a great many other friars. In the Dublin convent twenty-three of the friars died, and twenty-five at Drogheda, before Christmas 1348—almost the whole convent in both places. In Kilkenny eight Dominicans died on the one day in their convent there. From the time it appeared in August 1348, at Dublin and Drogheda, the plague spread like wildfire. Naturally the towns and other centres of population were hardest hit, and those were mainly Anglo-Irish. Cork, for example, petitioned for relief in 1351, 1354 and 1356 because of damage sustained by fire and 'by the late mortal pestilence'. Many a manor suffered gradual depopulation; some must have been wiped out almost overnight. Altogether the plague, which was endemic (it broke out frequently in the years that followed), reduced the population by at least a third and perhaps even as much as a half. Such a loss was catastrophic. Although the Gaelic areas did not altogether escape, it is clear that it was the more densely populated Anglo-Irish parts which suffered most. Richard fitz Ralph, archbishop of Armagh, remarked in a sermon that the people of Ireland were likely to be deprived of the indulgences of the Holy Year in 1350 because of the plague which had destroyed more than two-thirds of the English nation in Ireland. It had not killed many in Gaelic Ireland and therefore, he argued, the council in Ireland would never permit many of the Anglo-Irish to go abroad on pilgrimage for fear that this would allow an attack to be made on the settlement.

This depopulation had crushing economic consequences, for the resultant scarcity of labour caused prices to spiral upwards and brought about a decline in the general prosperity of the lordship. It was probably for this reason that the second half of the fourteenth century saw few new buildings going up, in marked contrast to the earlier period which was one of almost feverish building activity, or the fifteenth century when an economic recovery provided the basis for an architectural rennaissance.

More thinly spread than ever before, the settlers were the more easily engulfed by Gaelic Ireland. Always numerically inferior, many had long since been assimilated in some degree. But the decline in population, resulting from emigration and greatly accelerated by the ravage of the plague, quickened the process of assimilation. To the government this was degeneracy and was yet another problem which had to be faced in the fourteenth century. We have already quoted the sixteenth century Irish chancellor Gerrard who saw in this degeneracy the root cause of the decline of the medieval colony: 'the quiete estate of the land began to decay (because) the English degeneratinge become Irishe'. This process had gone so far by his own time, 1577, that Gerrard could write about the Pale: 'If Irish speache, habit and conditions made the man Irishe, the moste parte of the Englishe were Irishe'. No legislation prohibiting the adoption of the Irish language, customs or habits by the settlers, of which the statutes of the Kilkenny parliament of 1366 are the most complete expression, was able to prevent the Hibernicisation of the Anglo-Irish from continuing. It remained a problem which defeated the government to the end of the middle ages.

All of these problems were interlocked and every government had to try to cope with them as best they could, each in its own way. Most frequently, however, the problem which was given greatest emphasis was the military one. This was most acute in the localities, where the local communities were expected to bear the greater part of the burden. The government helped when it could, that is when financial resources were adequate. Large-scale military activity was, of course, government business and was usually possible only with English help. The norm, however, was an outbreak of local violence. Such outbreaks were often not connected at all with militant Gaelic chieftains, but were the result of traditional-style cattle raids (probably necessary to keep life in a population which for the most part lived very near subsistence level), feuds among the Anglo-Irish magnates and lesser folk, or the gangster-like activities of the rebel English who were increasingly becoming a nuisance. It is impossible to see any kind of real pattern of development in all this military activity. But there were occasions when the English government found it necessary to intervene directly, often at the request of an Irish parliament or council, and send a chief governor who would pursue a strong, military policy. It must be someone who was not too deeply involved in Ireland on a personal level, who could command sufficient resources to mount the necessary expeditions, who might have powers not normally given to a justiciar and be required to carry out a programme of reform fashioned in England. Many of these, too, found that measures too strong for the Anglo-Irish produced an angry backlash which forced the English government to recall them and restore a local magnate to power. Self-interest was here the guiding principle, sufficient to cause the magnates to bristle at a threat implicit in such strong measures as the refusal of Edward III after his assumption of power to extend the Great Charter to Ireland, or in the act of

14

resumption enacted in the Westminster parliament of 1331 and sent to Ireland, or the really horrific resumption of all grants made since the death of Edward I, ordered in 1341. One need not postulate at this time any kind of 'home rule' aspirations (of the kind imagined by Curtis) to account for Anglo-Irish reaction to strong rule, though, as we shall see, there is plenty of evidence to suggest that a growing resentment of rule by English-born chief governors, allied to a consciousness of Irish affiliations, was breeding a self-consciousness among the Anglo-Irish which was to make of them, as they were scornfully described in the Gaelic appeal of 1317 to Pope John XXII, a 'middle nation'.

The primary duty of these chief governors was to maintain the king's peace and this often meant going to war against the enemies of that peace. It is characteristic that they came from England supplied with some of the resources necessary for making war—'stocked and strengthened with men and treasure', as a petition from an Irish council so trenchantly put it in 1360. Indeed this was made a condition of service by John Darcy when he was reappointed justiciar in 1328. Since assuming the office of justiciar was mandatory, it is remarkable that Darcy should put forward conditions. Even more remarkable, however, is what he demanded: that certain named people should be appointed to office under him; that he have the right to pardon for felony and to inspect the treasury twice or three times a year; that he be consulted by the king before any grant of land or office was made, and many more conditions besides. Of particular interest was his insistence that English law should be extended to all the Irish of Ireland, by a statute to be made 'by common consent in his (the king's) parliament of Ireland'. But most interesting of all was his demand that because he 'cannot live on his fee in the state in which the land is now', he must have money for all expenses incurred beyond that fee of £500 a year. He also insisted that he should be paid in advance by the quarter and have £1,000 from England for the war in Ireland, 'for there is nothing there in the treasury, according to what he has heard'.

Most of Darcy's demands were met. They clearly formed a part of the hard bargaining which normally went on before a new chief governor was appointed, though rarely do we catch more than a fleeting glimpse of this. The agreed conditions would then be incorporated in an indenture between the king and his new official, such indentures becoming more normal in the later fourteenth century, when the king virtually contracted out of the government of Ireland. In 1344, for example, the king contracted to supply Ralph of Ufford with 40 men at arms and 300 archers, to be paid for by the English exchequer; in 1349, Thomas de Rokeby was to have (in addition to the 20 men at arms which every justiciar was expected to maintain out of his fee) 20 men at arms and 40 mounted archers; in 1373 William of Windsor was to have 200 men at arms and 400 archers; and in 1389 John Stanley was to have 300 mounted and 100 foot archers. The last quarter of the century saw the development of a more advanced contract system, involving full control over Irish revenues as well as continued subsidisation from England, and more freedom of action for the chief governors who were now appointed for a fixed term of office.

Military intervention from England became a characteristic of Anglo-Irish relations in the fourteenth century. What was most frequently hoped for, however, was the presence of the king himself. No king came after King John left Ireland in 1210, and though promises were made and preparations undertaken for a royal expedition, none ever materialised. In the autumn of 1331 the young Edward III announced his intention of leading an expedition to Ireland. He had long since made up his mind to come almost certainly as early as February, when a new chief governor was appointed to Ireland. This came shortly after the execution of Roger Mortimer in England and the assumption of power by the young king. The new justiciar was Anthony Lucy and it is possible to see his appointment as the prelude to royal intervention in Ireland. He brought with him a series of ordinances, made, said the king, 'for the improvement of the state of our land of Ireland and the quiet and tranquility of our people there'. Lucy arrived in June in the middle of Desmond's rebellion and he proved his mettle by not only meeting the earl, but arresting him and conveying him to Dublin castle as a prisoner. Then in the winter of 1331-2 he arrested the leading followers of Desmond and on 11 July hanged one of them, William Bermingham, as an object lesson to the others. He would have gone further, too, but that in August the king ordered all proceedings to cease until he himself arrived in Ireland. By then Edward had set a date, 1 August 1332, though this was later postponed to

29 September. Massive preparations were made, which intensified during the summer. On 24 July, for example, 2,000 archers were ordered to be arrayed in twenty counties and on 29 July 1,000 were raised in Wales. Edward obviously intended leading a major expedition to Ireland. But it was not to be. The parliament which met in September 1332 at Westminster decided that it would be too dangerous for the king to leave England because of the possibility of an invasion from Scotland. Men and money should be sent to Ireland, but the king should stay at home. In reality this cloaked the true reason for the change of plan, which was to make use of the chance given by the defeat of the Scots at Dupplin Moor in August. Edward saw the opportunity of winning glory in Scotland and he seized it. It was a decision which was disastrous for Ireland, ending the first effort at direct intervention from England on a massive scale at a time when it was badly needed.

The new justiciar, John Darcy, far from bringing the help promised by the Westminster parliament, was soon busy raising troops in Ireland to join the siege of Berwick! It was the murder of the earl of Ulster in June 1333 which diverted these troops from Scotland to Ulster to put down the disorders there which followed the murder. But two years later, after months of preparatory activity, finding men, supplies and shipping, Darcy led his expedition to Scotland. The king had been widely optimistic when he ordered the justiciar to raise 600 men at arms, 1,500 hobelars and 6,000 foot, though this is a measure of the reliance placed on Irish held for this campaign in the west of Scotland. The whole enterprise assumed a slightly unrealistic air when fourteen Gaelic 'princes' received letters from the king which affectionately required their attendance in Scotland with horses and arms—these included O Neill, O Connor of Connacht, O Connor of Offaly, O More of Leix, O Brien and Mac Murrough. The dangerous practice of issuing pardons in return for service was employed, though the murder of the earl of Ulster was excepted. None of this produced the large army Edward hoped for, but by Irish standards the expedition which eventually sailed was impressive enough: 2 earls, 14 bannerets (a superior grade of knight, receiving more pay and usually leading a large contingent), 472 men at arms (knights and squires), 291 hobelars (or light cavalry) and 805 foot (mainly archers)—altogether nearly 1,600 men, of whom half were mounted.

Expenditure came to nearly £2,300 and of this only 500 marks (or £333 6s 8d) came from the English exchequer. In fact the expedition cost the Irish exchequer half of its revenue for that year, at a time when the available money was already grossly inadequate for the military needs of the Irish government. Nothing could more clearly indicate the real indifference of the government of Edward III to the problems of Ireland at this time.

It was not until the appointment of John Morice in 1344 that there was a firm intervention again from England. He was made responsible for a programme of reform in the Irish administration which was to be revolutionary. It placed the control of Ireland in the hands of English officials who had lands in England and it involved a resumption by the king of all grants made since the death of Edward I. Such a wholesale clearance of the administration is hardly surprising for the English government had long since been given good reason to suppose that the Irish administration was not only inefficient but corrupt as well. In June 1336, for example, the king wrote to the chancellor and treasurer in Dublin, saying that it

has been shown to the king by honest men of those parts and public fame proclaims that the justiciar, chancellor and treasurer and the other ministers and officers of the king there are respectors of persons and do not treat the powerful, middle and simple men of that land by an equal law, but show too great favour to the powerful, permitting them to oppress the poor, to invade the king's rights, to usurp the royal power, to detain the king's debts, to institute novelities and perpetrate various crimes.

Firm action was called for and tardy as it may have been, the reform programme of 1341 was, on paper at least, a beginning.

Predictably, it brought a fierce Anglo-Irish reaction. The great magnates saw their position of power and favour threatened by direct control from England. For this reform marked the first, tentative steps on the part of the king to free himself from reliance on the Anglo-Irish magnates whose vested interests and invovement with Ireland was the least satisfactory kind of guarantee for his rights in the lordship. A strong king with some real interest in Ireland might have persisted. Edward III did not. He bowed to the storm of criticism, expressed most notably in a long petition of April 1342, from an Irish parliament, which denounced the new officials and complained bitterly of their oppressions and their total inadequacy. Not least did the 'prelates, earls, barons and community of Ireland', who sent the petition, complain of the effects of the recent act of resumption which had deprived the 'loyal English of Ireland' of much land, franchises and rights granted to them in the past and this, they say, despite the fact that they have 'all the time . . . conducted themselves well and loyally towards their liege lord' in comparison with those of Scotland, Gascony and Wales who 'often in times past have levied war against their liege lord'. Anyone knowing of the rebellions of Desmond and others, not to mention the constant faction fights which threatened the peace, must have taken all that with a grain of salt. Nevertheless the order to resume grants had been enforced and it touched the Anglo-Irish on the raw. No wonder that they were bitterly resentful and that the partisan Dublin chronicler could report that 'never before had there been so marked a rift between the English of England and the English of Ireland'.

By 1342 the proposed reforms were withdrawn by the king and the bite was taken out of Morice's administration. He was succeeded by Ralph of Ufford in 1344, who pursued a strong policy against the rebellious earl of Desmond, whom he rendered powerless before he died in 1346. His ruthless drive and energy were not really seen again in Ireland until after Sir Thomas of Rokeby was appointed justiciar in the summer of 1349 and direct intervention from England was once again to stiffen the Irish government. Because the land was 'not in good plight or good peace', he brought a small force of men with him. In the summer of 1350 orders from England required him to conduct sweeping inquiries into some of the more pressing problems, for example absentees, the incompetence of many officials, the corruption of others, and other matters of this kind. The result was a long series of ordinances enacted by a great council which met at Kilkenny in November 1351. These ordinances are hardly any less important than the more famous statutes of Kilkenny of 1366, many of which repeat, word for word, the 1351 ordinances. They may be taken as reflecting the true condition of the lordship, the major problems facing the government and how it was proposed to deal with them. What the legislation makes clear, and this is what we might expect, is that the most pressing problem of all was that of defence and much space is taken up with ordinances prescribing a solution—how war is to be waged and peace is to be made and maintained. It is emphasised that this is the government's business, and that there shall be only one peace and one war throughout Ireland. Idle men shall have lands to farm, to keep them out of mischief. Wardens of peace are to be appointed in each county, to assess and muster armed men. English truce-breakers are to be imprisoned and the English are not to stir up war among themselves. They are to use the common law only and not to ally in any way with 'the English or Irish enemies', by 'marriage, fostering of their children or in any other manner'. A number of ordinances deal with the conduct of officials, fees, the duties of sheriffs and their accounts, the continuing problem of absentees, and the proclamation of the English statute of labourers.

Rokeby was very active during his term in office and enjoyed some remarkable successes. In the winter of 1350–51 he conducted a campaign in the south-west with 1,000 men, a large enough army by Irish standards. He was not completely successful here, but he rebuilt Bunratty castle and, most remarkably, introduced settlers to reoccupy lands which had been regained from the Irish. The following autumn he was in the field in Leinster against the O Byrnes, again with an army of 1,000, without achieving much success. A year later he was in Leinster again, this time with an army of 1,100, and met with complete disaster. Despite this, he made a very good impression on the Anglo-Irish: after he left Ireland the mayor and community of Cork wrote in tribute to him to the king and urged that he be restored to office. But looking back we can see that all his efforts were of no avail and that when he left Ireland the king had little alternative but to fall back on Anglo-Irish magnates once again. He gave Rokeby a second chance, reappointing him in July 1356, again with an enlarged retinue. In the spring of 1357 Rokeby went to Leinster again, once more with an army of over 1,000 men. But before he had the chance to achieve anything decisive, Rokeby died at Kilkea in county Kildare in April 1358.

A succession of chief governors did nothing to ease the situation in Ireland, which gradually grew worse with trouble in Leinster and Munster which demanded frequent expeditions and parleys. Connacht and Ulster seem by now to have been beyond redemption. Things were clearly getting out of hand. In July 1360 a council at Kilkenny elected messengers to go to

England and inform the king of 'the mischiefs, perils and the state' of his land of Ireland and of his lieges 'who are on the point of being lost' unless he succour them in all haste. Amongst many other matters the messengers informed the king of the desparate straits of the people, enfeebled by the plague, impoverished, deserted by magnates who failed to defend their lands. The treasury in Dublin was empty, so they requested the king to send of his charity, to the succour and relief of the land and people, 'a good and sufficient chieftain' out of England, with 'men and treasure'. This seems to have been the first time that the Anglo-Irish looked for a great English lord as chief governor, a demand which was to be more frequent in years to come when a definite policy of appointing a great English peer was adopted, and later still, in the fifteenth century, appointing lieutenants of royal blood.

It was in response to this appeal of 1360 that the king's son, Lionel, later duke of Clarence, was appointed lieutenant of the king in Ireland in July 1361. Here was a 'good and sufficient chieftain' with a vengeance. Moreover, he was married to Elizabeth de Burgh, the heiress of Ulster, and so was the greatest of the absentee lords of Ireland. His appointment, then, marked a renewal of interest in Ireland and an expression of determination to tackle the great problem of absenteeism. No less than 64 great absentees were summoned to meet with and give traditional counsel to the young Lionel and then were ordered to accompany him to Ireland with troops, in person or by proxy, and to resume their responsibilities there. But like all attempts to force absentees to help to keep the Gaelic revival in check, this one, too, failed. Of all the great absentees, only the earl of Stafford returned and not even a later order from the king, issued only five months after Clarence had arrived in Ireland, and containing the serious news that his 'dear son' and his people were 'in peril' because of the war going badly, was able to bring any response from the absentees, beyond the grant for two years of their revenues in Ireland—an empty token for most absentees, who had long since ceased to enjoy a profit from Irish lands. It is noteworthy, however, that Lionel made a vigorous attempt to impose sanctions in Ireland against absentees, confiscating lands and regranting them to persons he considered more worthy. For example, in 1365 he made a grant of lands in Carlow, 'which have long been wasted and destroyed by Irishmen of Leinster' and which had been 'recovered by great war made upon them' by the king's son. The new grant was specific about the reason for the seizure of the lands: 'it is directed by a certain proclamation made at our command that all those who have castles, fortresses, lands and tenements in the marches should occupy the same as gallantly as possible within a fortnight of St John the Baptist next following under pain of having the same forfeited to us and let by us to others at our will'.

Edward was not dependent on absentee support, however. The treaty of Bretigny, sealed in October 1360, established peace with France and freed the king from his massive military commitments there. He was thus able to support his son Lionel in Ireland to an extent not possible before. One of the earliest budgets ever prepared for an English government shows how sharply planned expenditure on Ireland had risen. The summary of expenses for 1359–62 shows only £556 16s 8d for wages of war in Ireland. But in the sheet of expenses for the year 20 February 1363–20 February 1363 wages of war in Ireland accounts for nearly £13,000 (far and away the biggest single item in the budget), while the wages of captains and mariners and the hire of ships for the voyage of Clarence to Ireland came to over £2,000. This, however, was for the duke's second army in Ireland. For his first expedition more money was made available.

The scale of the preparations was indicative of the effort involved in making sure that the king's son lacked for nothing. Ships were pressed into service in both English and Irish ports; soldiers were recruited; horses were found for troops (many in Ireland, which even then enjoyed a reputation for producing fast, light ponies) and specialist craftsmen, such as masons and carpenters, were engaged for military operations. John of Clifton was the officer responsible for finding ships in Chester and Liverpool and in the two ports he seized twenty-two ships, many of them Irish, such as the *Seintemarybot* of Howth. The ship set aside for Clarence was fitted out to meet the duke's personal requirements. Four special sconces were purchased and ten 'round lanterns' for his quarters on board, with different coloured worsteds as hangings and one carpet of blue for his cabin. Clifton also purchased, on Clarence's instructions, material to make a great star on the sail of his ship, and an image of St Christopher ('for safe voyage', the accounts tell us)—the twin signs under which the duke sailed to Ireland.

Lionel, apparently, liked his comfort and was not slow to provide for his pleasure. In Dublin the castle was not only renovated in anticipation of his arrival, but Lionel himself ordered special 'works agreeable to him, for sports and his other pleasures, as well within the castle of Dublin as elsewhere'. These works included the making of a castle of wood and a fence, probably for the holding of tournaments in the castle grounds. The gardens, too, were refurbished. But the serious side of the enterprise was not neglected. It is not possible to calculate the exact size of the army which he brought to Ireland, but it numbered around 900 and may have contained as many as 1,000 men. Clarence's own retinue, until he returned to England in the spring of 1364, remained constant at 140; the earl of Stafford had a larger troop of 200; William of Windsor had 120. However, the number of soldiers dropped alarmingly after the army had been a time in Ireland, probably the result of soldiers returning home. For example a large troop of mounted archers from Lancaster fell in numbers from 360 at the end of 1361 to 168 by 6 June 1362, and only six by 12 June following. A notable feature of the different retinues is that all the troops seem to have been mounted, suggesting that it was intended to augment the army greatly by recruiting foot in Ireland. The earl of Stafford, for example, recuited an O Kennedy, with 11 hobelars and 86 foot, who served for 156 days against the Irish of Leinster (though he took a short break for Christmas, between 22 and 31 December). The earl of Ormond likewise served. But if Clarence had hoped to build up his army locally with the help of the Anglo-Irish magnates, he was disappointed. There seems to have been much bad feeling, much of it long-standing, between Anglo-Irish and English, and this is reflected in a story told by an Anglo-Irish chronicler. Clarence ordered that no man born in Ireland should approach his camp and was later surprised to find that 100 of his men were missing, until he discovered that these were Irish born and that English soldiers, taking advantage of his orders, had massacred them! In June 1364 the king referred in a letter to 'divers dissensions and debates arisen between the English born in England and the

English born in Ireland, whereby in times past hurt and peril has happened in Ireland, and worse is feared unless the same be speedily appeased'. A famous statute of Clarence's Kilkenny parliament of 1366 ordered that no such distinction of birth was to be made in future—the one was not to call the other 'English hobbe or Irish dog'—but 'all shall be called by the one name, the English lieges of our lord the king'.

Even an army of 900 or so, composed as it was mainly of mounted men, was very expensive to maintain and the English exchequer had to pay out large sums to finance the expedition. By August 1364 Walter of Dalby, the clerk of the wages, had paid more than £22,000 on wages and shipping. It was two and a half years more before Clarence left Ireland for good and by then expenses must have added many more thousands to the bill which the English taxpayer had to pay. Even then, as we shall see, there was to be no let-up in expenditure, for the next chief governor who came to Ireland cost even more per annum.

With such a heavy outlay of money positive results were expected and for a start Clarence seemed to be achieving the kind of success which had eluded his predecessors. In Leinster, for example, the king, Art Mac Murrough, and his son were taken prisoner. From the north Aedh O Neill and his son, Niall, submitted. In Munster lands were recovered which, an exchequer record tells us, 'were perambulated by the king's lieutenant (Lionel) with a great army and by great war acquired'. On the whole, however, Clarence was not very successful in war, possibly because he was unable to accommodate himself to Irish conditions. Despite the high hopes which marked his departure from England (he had been sent to Ireland 'for the salvation of the said land'), so little had been achieved that early in 1365 the king wrote of Ireland being 'sunk in the greatest wretchedness'. The previous year, on 25 April, Clarence had sailed for England, leaving behind him only the rump of his army—6 knights, 60 squires, and 69 archers. It was intended that massive support should be supplied. Not only were the entire revenues of Ireland to be devoted to the raising of troops, but preparations were made in England for a new army to be sent to Ireland. Ships were arrested in a huge circle of ports from Southampton to Bristol to Chester and to Furness. Unfortunately there is no indication of how large this new army was. But it enabled Clarence to conduct new campaigns in Leinster and Munster, recovering much lands and procuring submissions, most notably that of O Brien. He finally left Ireland for good on 7 November 1366.

It is likely that Clarence was thoroughly sick of Ireland by the time he left. His wife, his only real link with the country, had died in 1363. When we ask ourselves what his achievement was, we can only conclude that it was very little. A parliament of 1367 complained to the king that 'the land was at point to be lost, if remedy and help were not immediately supplied', and a year later a message from the Irish magnates said that the land of Ireland was 'for the most part destroyed and lost'. For all the massive financial and military support, then, little had really been done to prevent the situation in the lordship from further deterioration. A more positive result of Clarence's visit was the shifting of the centre of government from Dublin to Carlow in 1361. This was a sensible move, since Dublin was too isolated from most of the country to be really effective as a centre; Carlow was on the Barrow, one of the great highways of Ireland, running through the most densely settled areas, and more immediately accessible. But even this move was eventually a failure, since the continuing Gaelic recovery in Leinster was soon to threaten to engulf Carlow, so that at the end of the century Richard II had to make Dublin once more the capital of the lordship.

By far the most important legacy which Clarence left to Ireland were the statutes of his Kilkenny parliament of 1366, with which his name is always linked. This is the most famous piece of legislation in the history of medieval Ireland and has long been notorious for the anti-Irish and racial bias of many of the enactments. It is true that some of the statutes were designed to prevent the spread of Gaelic habit and custom, and to check the further degeneracy of the settlers: there was to be no alliance by marriage, fosterage or concubinage with the Irish; the English language only was to be used by the settlers, with the English mode of riding and dress; no Irish minstrel or entertainers of that kind were to be received in the English areas; no religious house in these areas was to receive Irishmen, and none were to be presented to cathedral or collegiate churches. The most famous statute of all (or at least the one most frequently quoted), which forbade 'the games which men call hurlings with great clubs at ball upon the ground, from which great evils and mains have arisen to the weakening and defence of the said land', was intended to make compulsory the practice of archery, throwing lances and 'other gentle games which appertain to arms', so as to keep men fit for defence— as the statute says, 'a land which is at war requires that every person do render himself able to defend himself'. Far from being anti-Irish, this kind of legislation can be matched exactly in contemporary England. It is probable that 'hurlings' was in fact a game popular among the Anglo-Irish and not, as is commonly imagined, the modern Irish game of the same name. The point about this legislation is that it is defensive in tone, designed to highlight the necessary precautions that must be taken to defend the feudal areas from further encroachment, cultural or military, by Gaelic Ireland. Some statutes deal with the right way to make war against, or truces with, the Irish. Many others are concerned with the maintenance of order in the lordship. Some, as was common with this kind of legislation, dealt with the rights of the Church. No less than ten legislated on the conduct of officials, the fees they were to have, the criminal law and its administration. Two important, and neglected, statutes dealt with the fixing of reasonable prices on merchandise entering the country, and with labour problems, especially the crisis caused by the continued emigration of labour.

The content of these statutes was not substantially new. The problems dealt with were old ones and the remedies suggested had, for the most part, long since been applied without success. Many statutes were copied directly from the 1351 Ordinances of Kilkenny, and others from earlier legislation. Why then did these statutes achieve such importance subsequently? Mainly because of their comprehensive nature, unusual in medieval Ireland. They were the most complete attempt to deal with the outstanding problems besetting the colony and as such they were regularly appealed to by later generations. For us they are important for the same reason. The weight they attach to the success of the Gaelic revival and the resultant threat to the English lordship, the inadequacies of the administration, the problems of local peace-keeping operations—altogether the statutes reflect in a very vivid way the state of Ireland in 1366.

The wording of the first part of the preamble to the statutes, with its stress on degeneracy through the use of Irish 'manners, fashion and language', has led many astray into thinking that the statutes represent an attack on all things Irish. But a later part of the same preamble gives us a much better clue to the purpose of the statutes, where they are said to be for 'the good government of the said land and quiet of the people and for the better observance of the laws and punishment of evil doers'. For this reason, the prohibitory statutes are directed against the inhabitants of the feudal area and the marchlands bordering on the Gaelic lands. One statute, for example, states that 'beneficed persons of Holy Church living *amongst the English* shall use the English language'. Another provides that 'no house of religion which is situated *among the English* . . . shall henceforth receive any Irishman (to their) profession'. This exclusive character of the legislation, the limitation of the area in which many of its prohibitions were to operate, suggests that the government was now facing up to the realities of the Gaelic revival and concentrating its efforts on those parts of Ireland which were still within effective reach of its administration. This was a policy which was to find a more complete expression later, especially in the fifteenth century, when the area of concern was limited to the four so-called loyal counties in the east, Dublin, Kildare, Louth and Meath, and later still, in a more extreme form, to the Pale, the small heavily-fortified area around Dublin. But it would be absurd to see in the statutes of Kilkenny a deliberate policy of cutting losses in Ireland, so as to hold on to what could be saved. This was the view of Edmund Curtis: 'The evident purpose of the Kilkenny statutes was not to declare war upon the Irish race as such, but, at the cost of abandoning a large part of the 'English land' to the Irish and to the 'chieftains of English lineage', to preserve the remainder for the English speech, race and law'.[16] But no English king could even contemplate letting part of his partrimony go—witness the energy devoted to France at this very time by Edward III. And to judge by what he was prepared to spend on Ireland, the king was certainly determined to recover what he could. Despite his constant complaints that he cannot afford to maintain a heavy burden of

[16]E. Curtis, *A history of medieval Ireland*, 2nd edition, 233.

expensive wars in Ireland—in one letter he says that he 'had incurred great cost and expenses upon the upkeep of the war in Ireland without taking any revenues or profits therefrom, and neither the king nor his subjects of England can comfortably bear these expenses in the same way as they bore those formerly occasioned by the wars with France and Spain'—he nevertheless continued the expensive policy of direct intervention, aimed at not merely retaining what he still held, but at recovering part at least of what had been lost. In this way the lordship would be able to shoulder the burden of its own defence once more. Surprising as it may seem, this was in the king's mind when he sent Clarence to Ireland in 1361. Years later, in the English parliament of 1366, in relation to the expedition, he admitted what his hope had been when he said 'which place (Ireland) had been profitable and in hope that it should be so again in the future'. It was too optimistic to hope that Ireland would become a source of profit again, but it was still possible to make her affluent enough to bear the costs of her own wars and to pay her own way.

This was the kind of thinking which lay behind the decision to maintain the heavy expenditure of the Clarence expeditions in the years after. When Lionel left Ireland at the end of 1366, it did not mean the end of English intervention. After a short interval, during which the king fell back on the customary use of a great Anglo-Irish magnate (in this case the earl of Desmond), the decision was taken to send William of Windsor to Ireland and this meant a continuation of the policy behind the Clarence expeditions, involving continued subsidisation of Ireland. Windsor was chosen because of his military experience and his knowledge of Ireland. He had served with Clarence in 1363 and the years following, with his own retinue of 60 men at arms and 66 archers. It was as a soldier, then, that he returned to Ireland as chief governor—a *miles strenuus in armis et animosus* ('a vigorous and spirited knight in arms') as an Anglo-Irish chronicler calls him—with an army, and his primary task was to restore law and order in Ireland by means of that army and whatever armed forces he could raise in Ireland. In his indenture with the king, completed on 1 February 1369, Windsor contracted to serve for three years, with an army of 200 men at arms and 300 archers for the first year, 120 and 200 for the second, and 80 and 150 for the third. For this he was to receive £20,000 altogether: £10,000 the first year, £6,000 the second and £4,000 the third. In fact, he brought an extra 50 men at arms and 60 archers and had to be paid an addition of nearly £2,300. His mission, therefore, was to be expensive (he was paid £22,300) and to justify it he had to pursue a strong military policy in Ireland. The evidence suggests that he tried to conduct a regular series of campaigns in Leinster and Munster, in an effort to impose peace. Whatever success he had, however, was vitiated by the bitter opposition of the Anglo-Irish to his harsh efforts to squeeze as much as possible out of them in taxation. Mounting complaints reached Edward III and in the end he capitulated and recalled Windsor in the spring of 1372. After his departure his army melted away and this absence of English levies soon undid the work of Windsor and left the situation no better than before he came. His recall, however, did not mean a departure from the familiar policy of investment. His successor, Robert of Ashton, contracted to bring 60 men at arms and 100 archers from England and to find 80 hobelars and 200 kerns in Ireland. But he lacked the ability shown by Windsor and despite the insistence of the Anglo-Irish that he should not be appointed to Ireland again (they asked for Mortimer, earl of March), William was under contract again by September 1373 and back in Ireland by 18 April following when he landed in Waterford with his full retinue. This numbered, as set out in his indenture and as verified in a muster held after he landed, 200 men at arms and 400 archers and cost the king £11,213 6s 8d a year. Once more he concentrated his attentions on Leinster, leaving Munster in the main to others. An expedition to Ulster met with disaster. All the time Windsor was hamstrung by lack of any adequate support in Ireland. Living off the country in the traditional Irish fashion only aroused the bitter enmity of the local communities. Desperate for money, he resorted to excessive taxation and this tactic met with fierce opposition. The war inevitably ran against him, giving his enemies further ammunition to use against him. As before, complaints began to reach England and Windsor's enemies made it their business to see that these reached the ears of the king, now in his dotage. Serious charges were formulated against the Irish government. William was summoned home and eventually he surrendered himself to stand his trial.

However, late in 1376 all proceedings against him were dropped. But the chief royal officials were dismissed and a new justiciar was appointed.

In many ways Windsor was the victim of circumstances. He was given an impossible task, without adequate resources to support him. His fiscal policy in Ireland was inevitable, given what the king was trying to do there. There was no escaping a heavy incidence of taxation if Ireland was to be made to pay her own way again. Yet twice the king yielded to pressure and at critical times let down his chief governor. English politics, too, played a part, for William's wife, Alice Perrers, a favourite of the ageing king, was the centre of a court party which had aroused fierce opposition. Naturally this opposition jumped at the the chance of hitting at Alice through her husband. The unfortunate William soon found that his opponents in Ireland were always assured of a ready hearing in England and their most extravagant condemnations of him were given a credence they would never otherwise have possessed. In the end, then, his efforts in Ireland, and the huge cost to the English taxpayer, brought no spectacular results.

This is not to say, however, that Windsor achieved nothing in Ireland. Taking the Clarence and Windsor interventions together, as part of a continuing movement, we can see that a positive advance had been made in restoring order in Ireland, even though it may not be immediately apparent. While engaging in the traditional kind of campaign against the Irish enemies, and winning only modest success, both governments concentrated more attention on warding (or protecting with strongly garrisoned positions) important or dangerous areas. This method of keeping hostile chieftains in check was effective, but expensive. Lack of sufficient money ruined all hope of success, just as was to happen later with Richard II, since permanent garrisons became too expensive for the government to maintain. But the military activity of both governments did produce some results, however short-lived. For a time the exchequer was regularly receiving money from Dublin, Meath, Louth, Kildare, Kilkenny, Limerick, Waterford, Wexford, and less regularly from Carlow, Cork and Tipperary.

It is hard to blame the English government for not adequately supporting Windsor. More than once Edward III made it plain

15

that if he were to continue a heavy subsidisation of Ireland, the Irish taxpayer would have to play his part by assuming a greater share of the burden. This was the nub of the matter, for Windsor's attempts to raise taxes only brought a storm of protest on his head. He came into headlong conflict with the taxpayers of Ireland in parliament and the controversy which followed brought into prominence the whole question of the parliamentary subsidy and, more important, the powers of the representatives elected by the local communities. For this reason alone his period in office was momentous in the history of the development of parliament as a representative institution in medieval Ireland.

During his first term in Ireland Windsor summoned four parliaments and four councils, and on his second visit three parliaments and one great council. In every one of these twelve assemblies, held in the short space of less than five years, he requested a subsidy of some kind. Resistance to his demands grew and the representatives of the local communities (the commons) refused to give their assent in parliament to more taxation. They accepted the important principle that assent by elected representatives in parliament bound the community. But they insisted that such consent must be freely given. Pressures of one kind or another by Windsor sometimes forced the commons to give consent. For example, the commons of county Meath complained that on 8 June 1371 a parliament was held at Bally-duagh, a 'waste place' where no provision had been made for feeding them. At the parliament Windsor requested a subsidy, but the representatives refused their consent. After three days resistance, however, worn out by their stay in that place and by the tedium of the debate, they capitulated and gave their consent. But it was not, they later said, freely given. At another parliament, it was claimed, the representatives of county Louth were thrown into prison by an angry Windsor when they refused to agree to a subsidy. In 1376 matters came to a head when two proctors from each diocese, two knights from each county, and two citizens or burgesses from each city or borough were to be elected to come to a special meeting in England to consult with the king about granting him an aid. The communities eventually agreed to elect representatives (though they were careful to point out that they were under no obligation to answer summonses to parliament or councils in England), but they refused to give them power to grant a subsidy. Windsor brought great pressure to bear in an effort to force the communities to give their elected representatives the necessary power, ordering new elections in some places and in Dublin having the elections supervised by two royal officials who were to see to it that the requisite power was given. If the electors persisted in their refusal, William said, they were to be 'distrained by all their lands and chattels' to give their consent.

It was this kind of high-handed attitude on the part of the lieutenant which brought the storms of protest which led to his final recall and the charges against him in 1376. But his disgrace had little effect in the long run. The policy of underwriting all major military operations in Ireland was still maintained by the English government. The new lieutenants continued to contract to serve in Ireland with large retinues (or small armies) in return for fixed payments of sums far in excess of the annual income of the Irish exchequer. Windsor's immediate successor, the earl of Ormond, had a retinue of 120 men at arms and 200 archers and received more than £5,000 from the English exchequer. Mortimer, appointed in 1379, was to receive 20,000 marks over three years; Stanley, in 1389, received 8,000 marks a year; Gloucester, in 1392, was to receive 34,000 marks for the three years following; Surrey, in 1398, was promised 11,000 marks a year. The purpose behind this injection of money and armed men into Ireland was still the same: to make the lordship able to pay its own way again, so that it would cease to be a burden on the English taxpayer. It was still remembered in England that in the past Ireland had been a source of profit to the English Crown and Richard II, when he made Ireland virtually a palatinate for his favourite de Vere in 1385, made it a condition that once the land was conquered he would receive 5,000 marks a year from it. This was wishful thinking, however, and not even the king could have hoped for a return to the palmy days of the thirteenth century. But in a more realistic mood in 1392, in his indenture with Gloucester, it was agreed that after three years the lieutenant should receive no more money from England because by then the government of Ireland should be self-supporting.

All of this was designed to free the king from the burden of governing Ireland and a further tentative step was taken in the same direction in October 1379, when Edmund Mortimer, earl of March, was appointed lieutenant of the king on the sort of financial and military terms now usual. But his contract contained one new condition which was vital: he was to receive all the revenues of Ireland without being accountable for them. Such financial independence was unprecedented and it was taken even further in 1385 when Robert de Vere was granted the land and lordship of Ireland in a manner which more or less made it an independent palatinate: not only were all writs to run in his name and not the king's, but even his arms were to replace those of the king in Ireland. De Vere had been created Marquis of Dublin and then duke of Ireland, and to help him conquer his new acquisition he was granted lands in England and other perquisites, such as the ransom of John of Blois, which would have brought him a substantial profit. But he never came to Ireland and in the maelstrom of English politics his grant lapsed when he himself suffered exile and forfeiture. There was a return to the old policy of appointing soldier lieutenants when Sir John Stanley took office in July 1389, with a retinue of 100 men at arms and 400 archers and a stipend of 8,000 marks a year.

All the time the situation in Ireland had been going from bad to worse. The financial position was desperate at the beginning of Richard II's reign and a further menace was added by the new Gaelic alliances, not only among the Leinster chieftains, but between them and those of Munster as well. In 1378, for example, O Brien arrived in Leinster with many from Munster, allied himself with Mac Murrough and others, and went on the rampage. In 1384 O Brien made an even grander alliance, joining many from Munster, Connacht and Leinster. It is indicative of the weakness of the government that the only solution they could provide to the threat of O Brien was the ignominious one of buying him off. Even then, the government found it difficult to raise the meagre 100 marks required. The buying off of Gaelic chieftains in this way was becoming increasingly frequent, especially through the notorious 'black rents' by which local communities bought protection from local chieftains. Even the government had to resort to the same expedient, often retaining chieftains by the payment of 'fees' or 'gifts'. In 1377, Mac Murrough, who claimed an annual fee of 80 marks, assembled his army and because the fee hadn't been paid, committed 'divers slaughters, devastations and burnings' in Wexford, Kilkenny, Carlow and Kildare. The fee was hurriedly paid and to add insult to injury, in the following year Mac Murrough claimed, and was paid, £40 compensation, fixed according to Irish law, for the slaying in county Carlow of Donald Kavanagh, one of the chieftains under him, an event which very likely occurred during the hosting of 1377. In 1379 the same Art was retained to keep safe the roads between Carlow (still the virtual capital of the lordship) and Kilkenny, the very area which was regularly under pressure from either himself or his allies!

All the time the government was in financial difficulties. In 1378 the earl of Ormond had to lend himself money as justiciar to employ armed men against the confederation of Leinster and Munster chieftains, which included some rebel English as well; and in 1379, shortly after his appointment as lieutenant, Mortimer had to lend the king £1,000 to help defray the cost of his expedition to Ireland. The situation was so bad that in that same year, 1379, first Ormond and then Kildare refused to take office in Ireland. Ormond's fee was in arrears. He was owed nearly £1,000 and he finally had to accept 1,000 marks in settlement. The accumulation of such debts was by now an occupational hazard in the Irish administration and the office of chief governor had become a financial liability. Almost inevitably the end of a term in office saw fees in arrears and money owing. Two years after he was appointed lieutenant in 1379, the earl of March was owed 10,000 marks. This situation not only had the effect of making it difficult to recruit suitable governors, but an even more serious result was that those appointed were often reluctant to involve themselves in really expensive military operations in Ireland, which might mean risking an accumulation of debts. A lieutenant's army, too, might begin to vanish when arrears of pay began to mount, as happened with Windsor and others. When Sir Philip Courtenay was dismissed from office in 1386, his soldiers were owed more than £400 in back wages.

The reluctance of great men to take office was made apparent to all when Mortimer died suddenly on the night after Christmas in 1381, an event which naturally caused much confusion. The earls of Desmond and Ormond were requested by the hurriedly assembled Irish council to take charge of the Irish government, but both refused, offering as excuse the war on their marches. Eventually, after a great deal of debate and discussion, which lasted into the next day, the chancellor, John Colton, was compelled to take office, though he imposed a condition that he should be allowed to give it up in the next parliament. The final blow came when it was learnt that the king had appointed as lieutenant the new earl of March, Roger Mortimer, who was only seven years old. This unsatisfactory solution, which produced at least one angry comment from an Irish parliament, did not last long and in July 1383 Sir Philip Courtenay was appointed lieutenant.

Courtenay could hardly have been very acceptable to the Anglo-Irish, coming as he did from a modest background and having no landed or other connections with Ireland. He was a good soldier, however, and it was hoped that he might be able to put his military experience to good use in Ireland. But he ran foul of the Anglo-Irish magnates, made little headway in war, and had to fall back on a policy of buying off Irish enemies. A great council in Dublin in October 1385 petitioned the king to come in person to Ireland, where his lordship was in imminent danger, not only from the Irish enemies and English rebels, but from 'other enemies of Scotland and Spain'. The magnates asserted that within the year 'there will be made a conquest of the greater part of the land of Ireland', a fear which was wildly exaggerated. But it was not entirely groundless, however, since Scottish raids were intensifying and piratical activity in the seas around Ireland was frequent.

It was now that Richard II took the decisive step of handing over Ireland to his favourite, de Vere. This would have been a complete answer to the problem of Ireland, had it worked. But de Vere was acceptable neither in England, where Richard temporarily lost power in 1387, nor in Ireland, and the scheme came to nothing in the end. There was therefore a return to the traditional soldier-governor. But the presence of the king, or at least a royal chief governor, was now considered an urgent necessity. In May 1392 the duke of Gloucester was appointed lieutenant and promised the huge sum of 34,000 marks, in addition to all the revenues of Ireland. This was to be intervention on a massive scale; but the progress of peace negotiations with France meant that Gloucester's appointment had to be cancelled. By then he had already made great headway with his preparations to lead an army to Ireland, contracting for the service of many leading English magnates and extensively purveying supplies: he spent £225 on the purchase of artillery alone.

The young Mortimer, now aged nineteen, was appointed to fill the vacancy. But meantime a stopgap justiciar had to be found. Once again Ormond was told to fill this unwelcome role, and again he refused, pleading that he was not capable of taking on the governance of Ireland in the state in which the land was at present: 'nor do we know how we can sustain it without great dishonour and destruction of our poor and simple estate'. But this time the Irish council would accept no excuse and made him assume an office which, unfortunately for him, lasted for two years before Mortimer at last came to Ireland. By then the king had made up his mind to come to Ireland in person and to deal at first hand with the Irish problem, as he hoped, once and for all.

Richard's great expedition to Ireland was in many ways a continuation of the kind of policy which lay behind the expeditions of Clarence, Windsor and the rest. The presence of the king, of course, was unprecedented: not since 1210 had the absentee lord of Ireland visited his lordship. It was only natural, too, that a royal expedition should be bigger and better in every way than any which had come before. But when we look at the size of the army which Richard brought with him and the scale of the preparations for the expedition (the chronicler Froissart tells us that it numbered 4,000 men at arms and 30,000 archers, and that 'it is not in memory that ever any king of England made such apparel and provision for any journey to make war against the Irishmen, nor such a number of men at arms nor archers'), it is obvious that the king's purpose involved conquest and a recovery of lost lordship. As events in Ireland were to show, Richard was determined to expel Mac Murrough and the other Gaelic chieftains from Leinster, thus ending the permanent threat they represented to the colony, and to force or persuade the other chieftains (including the rebel English) to submit and acknowledge his lordship, which would thus be re-established throughout the island. This is why the army he brought to Ireland was so large, why preparations were so extensive, and why so many absentees had been ordered to return. It had been a feature of earlier expeditions that the preliminaries included an attempt to get the great absentees involved. Richard, too, tried to round them up and some of the greatest came to Ireland with him, men like the earls of March (lord of Trim, Ulster and Connacht) and Nottingham (lord of Carlow). But here again we notice a difference with Richard's expedition. More tenants were required, small men who would inhabit newly-conquered or depopulated lands. A conquest without settlement to back it would be useless. So in June 1394, not long before he set out for Ireland, the king ordered all Irishmen living in England to return home before 15 August, under the harsh penalty of forfeiting all that they possessed. That a vigorous attempt was made to give effect to this extraordinary ordinance is evidenced by the number of licences exempting individuals from the penalty, though imposing stiff fines in lieu. Well over 500 such licences were issued in the weeks following.

The English council had recommended the king to use 'harsh measures' in dealing with the Gaelic chieftains (or 'Irish rebels', as Richard called them), and it was therefore prepared to back him financially to the limit. So much is clear from correspondence with Richard after he landed in Ireland. A remarkable letter written by the king on 1 February 1395 to his council in England contained his famous tripartite division of the people of Ireland into 'wild Irish, our enemy; Irish rebels; and obedient English' and expounded his proposals for dealing with the rebels, who constituted the main element in the Irish problem. He is candid in admitting that they had been driven to rebellion: 'the said Irish rebels are rebels only because of grievances and wrongs done to them on one side and default of remedy on the other'. He suggests, therefore, that a wise policy would be to give them redress by a grant of a general pardon to each of them and to receive them into the king's peace: 'if they are not wisely treated and put in good hope of grace they will probably join our enemies'. In its reply, the council agreed that despite having previously counselled the king to use harsh measures in dealing with these rebels, it was now convinced that it would be expedient to deal with them as the king suggests.

When exactly and why Richard changed his mind is not known, though it was probably as a result of advice he received from people like the archbishop of Armagh, who was trying to persuade O Neill to submit to the king. The change was wise. A letter which he received from Niall Óg O Neill shows us that Richard had communicated with Irish kings, probably exhorting them to return to the king's peace: 'I received your majesty's letters stating that part cause of your coming to Ireland was that you would do justice to every man'. Other Gaelic chieftains wrote expressing sentiments of loyalty and explaining that lack of justice had led them into rebellion. Their attitude was best summed up by O Connor of Offaly in a letter he wrote in January: 'I know that I have transgressed against your excellency before these times, mainly because I found no one to do justice between the English and me'. The king's recognition of their just grievances, and his avowed intention of 'doing justice to every man', seems to have been largely responsible for bringing many Gaelic chieftains back into his allegiance. There is no reason why we should suspect them all of being cynical. When King John came to Ireland in 1210 very many of them showed their readiness to do homage to him as their liege lord. Now that the king was here in person, it was natural for them to seek his protection if he were willing to offer it. It was not mere diplomacy which made O Neill write that 'when I heard of your joyful coming to the land of Ireland I greatly rejoiced and now rejoice, hoping to obtain justice for many injuries done by the English marchers to me and mine'. As events were to show, Richard's protection was not worth much; but they were not to know that in 1394-95.

At the same time it seems certain that Richard's show of force in Leinster and Munster and his easy victory over Mac Murrough were a help in spurring on Gaelic chieftains to submission. Indeed Froissart was convinced that the mere presence of the king at the head of a great army was sufficient to bring the Irishmen in: 'But when the Irishmen saw the great number of men at war that king Richard had in Ireland this last journey, the Irishmen advised themselves and came to obeissance'.

Richard landed at Waterford on 2 October 1394. Since June elaborate preparations had been made in England for his passage to Ireland. A fleet of about 500 ships was assembled at Milford Haven to carry the army, its horses, heavy artillery, supplies and equipment of all kind. Of particular interest are the arrangements made to ship an adequate supply of arms and artillery to Ireland. Some were sent ahead during the summer, to be stored in Dublin castle. Later, with the king, came the bulk of the arms normally stored in the Tower of London, together with an unknown quantity of artillery. There is no evidence that the artillery was ever used in Ireland. But its presence there, and the quantity of arms shipped, show more than anything else how determined the king was that his Irish expeditionary force was going to be as well equipped as possible. He was equally determined that it was going to be as large as possible and in the end he brought with him between 6,000 and 7,000 troops, certainly the largest army brought to Ireland during the middle ages and the equal of many an English army which fought in France during the Hundred Year's War (that which fought at Poitiers numbered about 7,000). Its numbers were augmented by recruiting in Ireland, so that as many as 8,000 troops may have been at the disposal of the king in Ireland.

Not only was the army large, it was well and regularly paid (a fact remarked on by Froissart), well fed, and immediately under the control of the king. He was thus able to deploy it as he wished and by the time he moved out of Waterford against Mac Murrough on 21 October he had evolved his plan of campaign. He would harass the Leinster Irish into surrender, using his mounted archers whenever possible in sudden attacks in rough country and leaving the heavy cavalry to work in the open. A letter sent to England by someone serving in Leinster describes the engagements of one such raiding party,

in one of which he (the Marshal) slew many people of the said Mac Murrough, and burned around Idrone nine villages and preyed of his cattle up to the number of 8,000. And on another journey he broke in upon him, and, if he had not been foreseen, he would have found the said Mac Murrough and his wife in their beds. But they, being told of the affray, escaped with great difficulty and at such short warning that they were very nearly taken. And among other things was found a coffer belonging to the said Mac Murrough's wife, in which were certain articles of feminine use, but of no great value. And among other things was found the seal of the said Mac Murrough with the inscription around it 'Sigillum Arthurii MacMurgh Dei Gracia Regis Lagenie' ('The seal of Arthur MacMurgh by the grace of God king of Leinster'). And when the said Earl Marshal failed to take Mac Murrough, he was sorely vexed thereat, and determined to punish him, and had his house burned, which was in the said wood of Leverough, as also some fourteen villages round about the said wood, and had 400 cattle driven away with him.

The harrassing was successful. By the end of October Mac Murrough and the leading Leinster chieftains submitted and Richard moved on to Dublin. He placed a ring of garrisons around Leinster to hold it down while he put the next stage of his plan into effect. This was nothing less than the evacuation of Leinster by Mac Murrough, O Byrne, O More, O Nolan and all the chieftains. On 7 January 1395, 'in a certain field between Tullow and Newcastle', Mac Murrough promised not only to restore 'all lands, tenements, castles, fortresses, woods, and pastuers with all their appurtenances, which have been of late occupied by the said Art or his allies, men or adherents with the land of Leinster', but he also swore that by the first Sunday of Lent (28 February)

he will leave the whole country of Leinster to the true obedience use, and disposition of the king . . . and that all the armed men, warriors, or fighting men of the following, household, or nation of the said Art shall quit the whole land of Leinster and shall go with him and shall have fitting wages from the king, for the time being, to go and conquer other parts occupied by rebels of the said lord king, and that Art and all his men aforesaid shall have all his lands which they may thus acquire and hold them of the said lord king, his heirs and successors as above, and as his true lieges and obedient and subject to his laws, by liege homage and befitting duty done therefore as above to the king, his heirs, and successors, and that they shall enjoy them in perpetuity and by hereditary descent.

The other chieftains likewise swore to

deliver all their possessions in Leinster to the said lord king . . . and quit that country, saving however their moveable goods always to themselves. And when that is done the lord king shall maintain these captains at expense of his household at good and fitting wages, fees, or salaries, payable yearly from the king's treasury to all and sundry these captains for the term of their lives, and that the lord king will give to them and their fighting men aforesaid fitting wages to go, attack and conquer other parts occupied by rebels of the king. And he will give them all lands which they shall so acquire and they shall hold them of our lord, his heirs and successors, by liege homage and befitting duty, as his true lieges, obedient and subject to his laws.

It was also agreed that Mac Murrough and his heirs were to have 80 marks a year and the barony of Norragh was to be restored to him—this latter was a sore point with Mac Murrough: it was the inheritance of his wife, Elizabeth Calf, but in 1391 it had been seized by the government because of her marriage.

On the face of it, this proposed settlement of Leinster seems preposterous. But there was logic in what Richard was doing, given that he seemed determined on the conquest of Leinster as the only real answer to the military problem it posed to Irish governments throughout the fourteenth century. By setting up wards around it and introducing new tenants, he could anglicise the area. Nor was it intended that there should be a general clearance of the Gaelic population. Only the chieftains (or 'captains') and their fighting men and immediate dependants were involved: the remainder could stay. Mac Murrough, O Byrne and the rest would be treated like the great gallowglass families, such as the Mac Donnells, and retained as mercenaries at a guaranteed fee. This might easily have been an attractive proposition for chieftains long accustomed to rely on the receipt of 'fees' of one kind or another from the government and local communities, and with a precarious hold on land, apart from the largely unproductive lands of the Leinster highlands. At any rate they accepted the plans. We can only speculate on what made them do so; but it is probable that they were persuaded in the long interval between their surrender on 30 October (after which some of them, though not Mac Murrough, were brought to Dublin) and 7 January when the agreement was made.

Richard's proposals for Leinster came to nothing in the end. For one thing, after he had received the submissions of most of the other Gaelic chieftains, there was little land left for the Leinster chieftains to acquire by conquest and inhabit (though some at least of them were paid the promised fees for a time). Relations with Mac Murrough broke down when he got neither his wife's inheritance in Norragh nor his promised fee of 80 marks. And the ring of steel around Leinster had to be withdrawn for the reason which always defeated the plans of Irish governments, inadequate financial resources. There was no way of compelling the chieftains to vacate Leinster when they chose not to go.

Meantime others were active on behalf of the king elsewhere. The earl of Rutland was busy in the south-east and the archbishop of Armagh was working in the north. In January 1395 the father of Niall Óg O Neill did homage and fealty to the king at Drogheda, though the son did not make his submission until 16 March. The problem here was the presence of the earl of March, who was insisting on reasserting his rights as earl of

Ulster, demanding traditional service which had long since been usurped by O Neill. Niall Óg was naturally worried lest the restoration of mesne lords like Mortimer would mean further encroachments on his own lordship in the future, a fear which, as we shall see, was well founded. He was not alone in this fear, for the presence of great absentee lords with Richard, men like the earl of Nottingham, and their obvious intention of restoring lost lordships, threatened many a Gaelic chieftain with the loss of lands and services. O Neill of course occupied a position of pre-eminence in Ireland and at the height of the delicate negotiations with him Niall Óg wrote to the archbishop of Armagh telling him that he had received envoys from O Brien, O Connor, Mac Carthy, 'and many others from the south urging me strongly not to go to the king'. In the end he did go, as did O Brien, Mac Carthy and the rest, because he was promised justice and the guarantee of the king's law. Throughout the spring of 1395 a formidable list of Gaelic chieftains made their submissions and did homage and fealty. The important ones submitted on behalf of their sub-chieftains too; but so painstaking was Richard in his operations that he procured the personal submissions of the lesser chieftains as well whenever possible. By the time the king left Ireland on 15 May, the vast majority of the chieftains had accepted him as their liege lord and had made their peace.

The one class with which the king may have had little success were the rebel English. Burkes, Berminghams and others had submitted, but we lack information on just how many were persuaded or forced to come in. It is hard to believe that the king would have sailed for England without dealing with them as thoroughly as he dealt with the Gaelic chieftains. On the other hand, it could be argued that Richard did not see them as a pressing problem: he made no mention of them in his letter of February 1395, when he informed his council how he proposed to deal with the 'rebel Irish'.

Richard had every reason to be pleased with himself. He had enjoyed a spectacular success in Ireland, won a notable victory in Leinster, had put his armed might to the test, and was able to return to England confident in the belief that he had solved the main Irish problem which had caused such trouble in the past. Within four years, however, he was back with another great army, his earlier settlement in ruins. What had gone wrong?

The king had left too many loose ends. He had removed the centre of government from Carlow back to Dublin and he took some steps subsequently to improve the quality of the Irish administration. But he did not initiate the necessary revolution. He left no machinery for implementing his Leinster project. Worst of all, he left no safeguards for people like O Neill against the magnates who were now reviving old grants and asserting old claims. In many ways the situation he created was a throw-back to the early years of the Anglo-Norman conquest, when speculative grants brought chaos to some parts of the island. Mortimer, Ormond and others now began to push their newly resurrected claims and fierce disturbances naturally followed. The climax came on 20 July 1398 when Mortimer, now lieutenant and heir to the English throne, was killed in a skirmish with the O Byrnes near Carlow. By then, however, the king had already made up his mind to come to Ireland again, announcing this in 1397. His settlement of 1394–95 was now destroyed.

Richard had preoccupations in England which prevented him from organising another expedition to Ireland until 1399, when he landed at Waterford on 1 June. His army this time was much smaller and he found it impossible to compel Mac Murrough to submit as he had five years previously. Instead his own troops were harassed and harried, and a stubborn Mac Murrough claimed to be rightful king of Ireland! It is doubtful if Richard would have achieved anything on this occasion. Apart from evidence of mental instability which impaired the military skill he had displayed in 1394, and the smaller army which accompanied him, the king had to put up with treachery in his own camp. Suddenly in July came the grim news from England that Henry of Lancaster had landed and was taking possession of the country. Richard had to hurry home, sailing on 27 July. By then he had lost the initiative in England and not only was he shortly a prisoner of Bolingbroke's, but he had lost his throne as well. It was an unexpected achievement for Art Mac Murrough that, as Curtis put it, 'by delaying Richard in the wilds of Leinster, (he) let in usurping Bolingbroke and wrecked the unity of England for a hundred years'.[17]

Perhaps the most fitting commentary on Richard II's achieve-

---

[17]E. Curtis, *A history of medieval Ireland,* 2nd edition, 277.

ment in Ireland is the message which was sent by the Irish council in 1399 to the newly crowned Henry IV. This was the first official message of the reign and with almost unseemly haste the royal officials in Dublin despatched a most dismal report on the state of Ireland. Not only is Mac Murrough again at war, says the report, he is 'now gone to Desmond to aid the earl of Desmond to destroy the earl of Ormond, if they can; and afterwards to return, with all the power they can get from the parts of Munster, to destroy the country'. O Neill, too, has threatened war. There is no army to send against the rebels, and 'no money in hand to pay any soldiers . . . and thus the land is in danger of final destruction if it be not quickly relieved and succoured'. The dismal picture continues: 'the Irish enemies are strong and arrogant and of great power, and there is neither rule nor power to resist them, for the English marchers are not able, nor are they willing to ride against them without stronger paramount power'. The rebel English 'destroy the poor liege people of the land'. Revenues are down, mainly because so many sources of revenue have been alienated. The condition of the exchequer is as bad as can be, the officers ignorant and incompetent.

It is almost as if the two great expeditions had never occurred. For this Richard must accept a share of the blame. He had been too hasty in his arrangements, maybe even devious in his treatment of the Gaelic chieftains, and too ambitious in his concept of an English Leinster. But the fault lay with the situation in Ireland, over which no one could exercise real control. These two expeditions were a natural climax to the policy of armed intervention from England and the final attempt to solve the Irish problem by methods which had become traditional. Major expeditions financed by England, with the possibility of reconquest in the background, and the warding of danger spots (such as had been done by Clarence, Windsor and Richard II), retaining some Gaelic chieftains for particular services—measures of this kind were far too expensive and could never be sustained. Richard II's reign saw these methods given their final chance, and on a most ambitious scale, and saw their failure. In the fifteenth century it was the Anglo-Irish magnates who were to come to terms with the Irish situation, each in his own lordship, compromising where necessary, bending with the Gaelic wind and all the time growing in power and self-reliance. It was through the network of lordships, Anglo-Irish and Gaelic, that an equilibrium was maintained in Ireland, and the government's role became more restricted and much less important than it had been in the fourteenth century.

IX Anglo-Irish Ascendancy and the End of the Medieval Lordship of Ireland

THE collapse of King Richard's settlement of Ireland and the Lancastrian usurpation in England meant that the early years of the fifteenth century witnessed a new phase in the development of Ireland. The forces of separatism, already at work since the early days of the colony, now took over and everywhere independent lords pursued their own ways. Even the towns, later to be called 'the sheet anchors of the state', became more autonomous in this new age. In most of Leinster, where the king had intended creating a new land of peace, English and loyal, the Gaelic lords took over completely. An O Byrne promised in 1401 to allow the king to enjoy the lands of Newcastle McKynegan! In 1419 the O Tooles raided Ballymore Eustace and carried off 400 cows. And the Mac Murroughs, despite a challege from the O Byrnes, succeeded in asserting their kingship of Leinster to the end of the century.

This fragmentation of the Irish policy and the growth of lordship did not mean a degeneration into anarchy. Local warfare of a kind persisted, as it did in every medieval state, and life remained as uncertain as it had been before. Indeed the conduct of war seems to have fallen into an exclusively Irish pattern, involving submissions in the traditional mode, with the giving of hostages and tribute, and the taking of great preys of cattle becoming a common activity. This was not new, being increasingly common in the fourteenth century so that even the great army of Richard II had been forced to fall in with Irish ways—we have seen how the marshal had taken huge preys during the campaign in Leinster. But now it became normal for Irish governments under Desmond, Ormond, Kildare and others, long accustomed to fighting wars on Irish terms, to resort to the native way. And this, on the whole, was an improvement since it tended to ameliorate the condition of war and regulated war-time practices such as coign and other exactions, however onerous they may have appeared to the populace forced to endure them.

Alliances, often based on family ties or the even stronger ties of fosterage, helped to create some degree of stability and order. The government could always profit from the local connections of the great magnates when they were in control, just as it suffered from these same connections when the Anglo-Irish were not in control, or when faction fights developed.

The greater stability of this new age, despite all superficial appearances to the contrary, is indicated by the extraordinary revival which took place in Ireland at this time, not least in areas in the west which were furthest removed from the law-enforcing authority of the central government. New buildings sprang up everywhere, evidence not only of a greater measure of peace, but of an increased prosperity as well. A native style of architecture emerged (late Irish Gothic) which, while borrowing from England, went back to an earlier period and reintroduced some pure Irish features (stressing again the pervasive influence of native modes at the time). This architecture is in many ways the highest point reached in post-Norman Ireland. The building activity associated with it necessarily depended on patronage, which in turn depended on wealth. There is abundant evidence that patrons were readily available, and this argues for more prosperous conditions that had hitherto prevailed. It seems, then, as if a great economic recovery took place and an expanding overseas trade gave a new lease of life to many of the smaller ports, particularly in the west. Trade with the Gaelic hinterland flourished and prosperity followed.

All of this argues for more settled conditions. It is as if the different warring elements in Irish society, urban and rural, Gaelic and Anglo-Irish, feudal and tribal, decided to settle down and tolerate each other in a new kind of relationship. A more constructive age followed. It is important to stress this, for too close a concentration on the confused politics of the age can easily give an impression of near-anarchy and disorder which is certainly erroneous.

The English standpoint, too, had changed. By now a growing national consciousness, reflected, for instance, in the war with France, which had become a war between two nations, sharpened concern for security, a concern which was vividly highlighted by the anonymous author of the *Libelle* (or 'little book') *of Englyshe Polycye*. He advocated that 'we be masters of the narrow sea', which he called 'the round wall' of England. This meant gaining control not only of the sea around Britain, but of that around Ireland as well. For, as he declaimed in one passage, 'Ireland is a butress and a post under England' and he therefore gave warning to the English council:

> Ye remember and with all your might take heed
> To keep Ireland that it be not lost.

Only this, he said, 'could set us all in rest', for otherwise the enemies of England will avail of the opportunity, should Ireland be lost. Then 'farewell Wales'. New alliances would mean that England would 'have enemies environ about'. At all costs, therefore, the loss of Ireland must be prevented. But he went even further in his argument: what money was wasted on the French wars in the course of one year would be sufficient if applied to Ireland to bring a conquest to a successful conclusion. He had been assured of this by the earl of Ormond, who had fought in France.

> The expenses of one year done in France . . . .
> Might win Ireland to a final conquest
> In one sole year, to set us all in rest.

Ireland, then, became a security problem and it was mainly as such that it impinged on English governments during that age. The Lancastrian, Yorkist and Tudor dynasties in turn were forced to recognise the risk and to solve it as best they could. As usual, strong military action was one answer and a war of conquest, if seriously undertaken, would have solved the problem once and for all. Not that any government ever seriously considered a full conquest as a solution. The author of the *Libelle* was wildly optimistic in supposing that the expenditure of one year on the war in France would have been sufficient to conquer Ireland, a fact which later Tudor governments were to discover to their cost. Far more money was required, beyond anything which any Lancastrian king could afford. For one reason or another these governments were often chronically short of money and this, as always, was the crucial fact in Anglo-Irish relations throughout the period. Little could be afforded for Ireland, which regularly came well down the list of priorities when the council came to deciding how to spend insufficient revenues. The desire to spend more on Ireland was often there, especially when security was at stake; but the means were not alway at hand and all too often the government defaulted in its obligations.

This became obvious right at the beginning of the fifteenth century, when Henry IV, a usurper facing a domestic crisis, could afford to take no risk in Ireland, especially after the outbreak of revolt in Wales. Everything alarmed him. Two months after his accession he was writing to the Irish chancellor telling him to stop using the seal of Richard II, as he had been doing. The chancellor claimed that it was not known in Ireland that Richard was no longer king, which was very unlikely. Henry's letter certainly implies that he thought otherwise. He applied the traditional policy which he had inherited from the fourteenth century, which was heavy subsidisation of Ireland by England and the contract system of providing for its government through lieutenants. The full measure of his support can be seen in the summer of 1401, for in June of that year he appointed his second son, Thomas of Lancaster, lieutenant of Ireland for six years. What is more, he insisted that Thomas, young as he was (he was only thirteen at the time), should go to Ireland to govern in person—a significant move, for not since Lionel of Clarence in 1361 had a son of the king been given charge of the government of Ireland. No less important, Thomas was granted a stipend of 12,000 marks per annum. There could be no clearer indication than this that Henry IV was unwilling to run any risk in Ireland. It was his reply to the message of 1399 from the Irish council, which painted the most gloomy picture of the state of affairs in the lordship.

But quite apart from the recurrence of the problem posed by the Gaelic Irish, and particularly Art Mac Murrough, Henry had another reason for watching the lordship carefully, for there was a real prospect that Ireland might yet offer a threat to the security of his dynasty on the English throne. He must have wondered if the infant earl of March, who had a rightful claim to the throne, might win some support in Ireland where the Mortimer family had long enjoyed enormous prestige. It was from Scotland and Wales, however, that he feared the main danger would come. But when Owen Glyndyr of Wales tried to bring Ireland into a confederation of enemies of the Lancastrian dynasty, he was giving point to a new factor in Anglo-Irish relations, the danger that Ireland might become a link in a chain of enemies surrounding England. This danger had existed in the past, when on two occasions, before 1315 and in 1327, Robert Bruce had tried to bring Welsh, Scots and Irish together by an emotional appeal to their common antipathy towards the English and their common Celtic ancestry. This was exactly the kind of appeal which Glyndyr made in November 1401, when he wrote letters to some Irish kings, claiming common kinship with them and looking for help against the oppression and tyranny of their common enemy, the Saxons. He alleged that although he was personally unknown to them, he put his trust in them, and referred to a prophecy which foretold 'that before we can have the upper hand in this behalf, you and yours, our well-beloved cousins in Ireland, must stretch forth hereto a helping hand'. But he shrewdly balanced this by saying that 'so long as we shall be able to wage manfully this war in our borders, as doubtless is clear unto you, you and all the other chieftains of your parts of Ireland will in the meantime have welcome peace and calm repose'.

We don't know to whom in Ireland these letters were addressed, though it is likely that Mac Murrough was one of those contacted, and very possibly on the advice of the uncle of the earl of March, Edmund Mortimer, who knew Ireland well and who joined the rebel Glyndyr in 1402. What matters to us here, though, is that Henry IV certainly knew of this attempt by Glyndyr to involve Ireland in his rebellion, for the messengers carrying the letters to Ireland were captured and beheaded and the letters came into the king's hands. As it happened, the appeal from Wales came to nothing. But it is interesting because it illustrates the sort of danger the author of the *Libelle* was to warn against in the next generation. .

King Henry had therefore every reason to safeguard Ireland by sending his son there. Through Lancaster a heavy investment was to be made in the defence of Ireland. But already, at the very beginning of the reign, Henry had overreached himself financially and before long it was obvious that whatever he may have wished, his financial resources were too limited to permit a heavy financial outlay on his son's government in Ireland. Sir John Stanley, who had been appointed lieutenant in December 1399, was reporting a year later that 'a great part of the payments due to him are in arrears', with the result, the king was told, 'that he has not been able to do so much for resisting our rebel Irish as he could wish'. And by February 1401 the head of the Irish government was reduced to the ignominious position of having to receive letters of protection from the king so that he could not be pursued for debt. It was therefore foolish to promise Thomas of Lancaster 12,000 marks per annum when he was appointed to succeed Stanley; and sure enough, within a short time, the royal lieutenant was in grave financial difficulties in Ireland because of his father's failure to pay him the stipend agreed on in his indenture. In fact, having run out of ready cash, his troops began to desert him for want of pay, and even his personal attendants in his household threatened to leave him unless they were paid what they were owed. In desperation Thomas had to pawn nearly all his jewels and plate, in an effort to prevent complete ruin in Ireland. On 20 August 1402 the archbishop of Dublin wrote that Thomas had 'not a penny in the world' and that poverty had virtually made him a prisoner in Naas. By June 1403 his arrears had amounted to £9,000 and the king decided to assign him the customs and the subsidy of the port of Kingston on Hull to provide his annual stipend in future and to make up his arrears. But this was hopeless. Thomas, in fact, had already been assigned money from customs and had failed to collect. For example, in May 1409 he failed to cash 27 tallies on the customs, worth 7,000 marks.[18]

[18]The system of *assignment* was a means of anticipating revenue when the government was short of ready cash. Normally a *tally* was cut at the exchequer as a receipt for cash received. In emergencies, however, the government often paid its way by issuing tallies for sums which had not actually reached the exchequer. It was up to the person who received the tallies to go to the source of revenue on which they were drawn and to cash them. Thomas of Lancaster, for example, would have to cash the tallies he received on the receipts of the wool custom at Hull through the local collector, who would eventually return the same tallies to the exchequer in lieu of cash when accounting for the receipts of the custom. The trouble was that there were too many demands to be met and the government issued too many tallies on the same source of revenue. In other words, it was over-drawn. In that case the tallies could not be cashed—they were bad tallies and had to be returned to the exchequer where they were replaced by new ones. There was no guarantee, however, that the same thing would not happen again and, as we shall see, many of the tallies issued to the Irish royal officials were bad ones and had to be returned to the exchequer in England not once but many times, sometimes over a period of

Nothing could be clearer. It was obviously quite impossible for the impoverished government of Henry IV to find 12,000 marks yearly to meet the stipend agreed on in the contract with Thomas of Lancaster. Yet what could be done? The contract was binding for six years. Fortunately for the king, Thomas lost his half of the indenture which he had sealed with his father in 1401, and this was made the excuse for drawing up a new contract in March 1406, when the opportunity was seized to reduce the stipend from the original 12,000 to 9,000 marks. But even this was found to be too high and impossible to meet, so when a new indenture was sealed in July 1408 the stipend was reduced still further to 7,000 marks. Once more this was found too high and the money owing to Lancaster began to mount up again. In 1411 his old tallies, which he found impossible to cash, were worth over £5,000. Not surprisingly, then, when Sir John Stanley was appointed lieutenant in 1413 the stipend agreed on was drastically reduced to the more realistic figure of 3,000 marks a year (with an additional 1,000 marks for the first year). Stanley was appointed for six years, but he died three months after arriving in Ireland (the result, according to the annals, of being fiercely satirised by the Irish poets whom he had persecuted). His replacement was the famous soldier John Talbot, who was to receive 5,000 marks a year. But as had now become customary in the case of Ireland, Talbot found it impossible to procure satisfactory payment of this stipend, low as it was, and in 1417 he had to leave Ireland and go to England to try to procure payment in person.

I have gone into this rather dreary business of the stipends of lieutenants in some detail because it illustrates clearly an important change in Anglo-Irish relations after the accession of Henry IV. Under the Lancastrians, though the 'contract system' for the government of Ireland was maintained, and with it the practice of subsidising the defence of Ireland, the amount of the subsidy was drastically reduced from what it had been in the fourteenth century and was constantly in arrears. Tallies cut for the king's son fell short to the staggering extent of £18,000. The simple fact was that the Lancastrians could not afford

---

years, before the unfortunate recipient could get some, rarely complete, satisfaction. Payment in cash became increasingly rare in the case of Ireland.

Ireland. Lancastrian government, as has been well said, was 'a pauper government ruling by the consent of its wealthier subjects'. What limited resources it controlled left little to spare for Ireland. Just how limited those financial resources were is well illustrated by a letter which the treasurer of England, Laurence Allerthorpe, wrote to Henry IV at the end of 1401, in which he explains that he had done his best to carry out royal instructions regarding expenditure on Ireland and Guienne, but emphasises that there just wasn't enough money available to him:

Wherefore, revered and gracious lord, because the revenues of your kingdom are burdened so outrageously that there can be no relief, and also because the major part of the fifteenth and tenth was assigned before I took over office, as I have often told you before this, will your gracious highness abstain now from charging me beyond my power to pay or else hold me excused for not accomplishing your said letters and commandment? For truly, revered lord, there is not in your Treasury at the moment enough to pay the messengers who are to bear the letters which you have ordained to be sent to the lords, knights and esquires to be of your council.[19]

There was little money, then, which could be diverted to Irish needs. Money could always be found for really important business. For example, when Constantinople was under pressure from the Turks, the Emperor Manuel II visited the west and came to London looking for help. In September 1399 £2,000 was paid to the emperor via a Genoese merchant and two years later a further £2,000 was sent. But Irish needs were rarely seen to be pressing. Indeed, there is little doubt that successive Lancastrian governments did not consider the Irish lordship of much importance, except when it became a security risk. If we are to judge from the infrequency with which Irish affairs were discussed at the English council, very little time was devoted to the problems of Ireland. But a more important yardstick with which to measure the importance of Ireland is finance: the real measure of the English government's interest in, or worry over, the Irish lordship is the amount of money which it was prepared to spend on it (never mind what it actually did spend). And it must be admitted that on the scale of priorities which the council

[19]E. F. Jacob, *The fifteenth century*, Oxford, 1961, 76.

employed, Ireland came well down on the list. It was a good way behind Scotland and Wales, and nowhere compared with France and above all Calais. For example, when John earl of Huntingdon was appointed lieutenant of Guienne for six years in May 1439, his indenture specified that he was to have a retinue of 300 men at arms and 2,000 archers, at a stipend of nearly £36,000 a year. Compare this with the appointment of the earl of Ormond as lieutenant of Ireland in 1442, with a retinue of 300 archers and an annual stipend of 3,000 marks or £2,000. Even the keeper and governor of the two small islands of Jersey and Guernsey at this time had a retinue of 130 archers and a stipend of nearly £1,200 a year. When the duke of York was made lieutenant-general and governor of France and Normandy in 1440, his stipend was £20,000 per annum; seven years later when he was appointed lieutenant of Ireland, he was given 4,000 marks for the first year and only 2,000 marks for the remaining nine years in office.

It is even more instructive to compare expenditure on Ireland throughout this period with what was spent on Calais. In his account for the period 1399–1403, Nicholas Usk, the treasurer, showed that he received a total of £47,000 from England (of which he spent £46,000 on wages of the garrison). In one year, 1410–11, Richard Thorley, treasurer of Calais, received £12,000 from England. It was during these same years that the English government defaulted so seriously on payment of much smaller sums to John Stanley and the king's son, Thomas of Lancaster. Clearly Calais came first on any list of commitments. For example, in Lord Cromwell's famous estimates of 1433, when he prepared a budget of income and expenditure for the following year, the cost of maintaining the English interest in Calais had now shot up to an estimated £45,000. By comparison with that, Ireland hardly counted. The minutes of a meeting of the English council on 19 March 1411 contain an account of a discussion of financial estimates for the coming year. The wool custom was expected to yield £30,000 and of this three-quarters, or more than £22,000 was already earmarked by parliament for the defence of Calais. Of the remaining quarter, the council agreed to set aside 4,000 marks for Ireland, though in the end even that small sum was found to be too large. That will give us some idea of the comparative value of Ireland and Calais to the Lancastrian government. In 1431 Lord Hungerford, the treasurer of England, petitioned the council that notwithstanding any warrant which had previously been issued to him for payments to Sir Thomas Stanley, lieutenant of Ireland, he should be allowed to give preference to other payments relating to the defence of France. In other words, in the queue for money Ireland had constantly to give way to the needs of other places. Three years later the treasurer put it even more bluntly: having been ordered to pay 5,000 marks owing to Stanley for the wages of his lieutenancy, he said to the council that he 'does not dare to pay or to assign the said wages' because of the pressing need for money elsewhere.

The fact, then, is that by comparison with what was spent on Calais the subsidisation of Ireland was minute, and it even came a long way behind expenditure on the Scottish or Welsh marches. Furthermore, when the occasion demanded Ireland had to give way altogether and had to yield a prior claim on a particular source of revenue in England, such as the wool custom at a particular port. In other words assignments which had already been made in favour of the chief governor of Ireland were sometimes cancelled abruptly when other pressing demands for money had to be met by the English treasurer. This is what Hungerford had in mind in his petition of 1431. Assignments which had been made in favour of Stanley would be cancelled and the same money could then be allocated to France. Stanley would therefore be left with bad tallies, which were worthless because they were not cashable. This sort of thing is yet another indication of how comparatively unimportant Ireland was to the Lancastrian government in normal times, for the chief governors of Ireland got far more than their fair share of bad tallies throughout this period. Indeed to get a true picture of the financial relations between the Lancastrians and Ireland, it is not enough merely to see how the stipends of the chief governors were drastically reduced; we must also be able to see how difficult it was, and often even impossible, for the lieutenants to collect even the reduced stipends. More often than not they were paid, not in cash but by means of tallies of assignment which too frequently were impossible to cash.

For various reasons the Lancastrians had to live beyond their means, with the result that not only did they rely on assignments far more than was normal, but that they also over-assigned sources of revenues and issued far more bad tallies than had, say, Richard II. And unfortunately Ireland received too high a proportion of these. This can be well illustrated by some examples from both ends of this period, first from the reign of Henry IV and then from that of Henry VI. On 17 December 1399 Stanley was given £2,000 in assignments, most of the tallies being drawn on the customs. But as late as 22 November 1400, having failed not only to get some of these tallies cashed but also to obtain others which had been cut to replace them in the meantime, he was returning tallies to the exchequer in exchange for new ones. But some of the new tallies were also bad and by 1 June 1403 he was back having those replaced. And so it went on. On 10 December 1403 he was back again in the exchequer with no fewer than twelve bad tallies, amounting to more than £2,000. Stanley, in fact, was never able to catch up on his bad tallies. In other words, he was never fully paid the stipends he had been guaranteed when he contracted to serve as lieutenant and later deputy of Lancaster in Ireland.

We have already seen that Thomas of Lancaster, notwithstanding that he was the king's son, was treated no better than other chief governors. One can easily illustrate from the English records a pathetic story of his attempts to cash his tallies and the mounting debts which he incurred because his father failed to pay his stipend. But one example will suffice. On 1 June 1405 his agent, Robert Ramesay, turned up at the English exchequer with bad tallies worth £9,741 5s 7½d, for which he was given new assignments. But three years later he was still trying to have some of these tallies cashed: for example, on 16 June 1410 twenty-two bad tallies, worth nearly £4,000, were returned to the exchequer.

Much later in the fifteenth century the situation was no better and bad tallies were still being foisted on the chief governors of Ireland. Richard Talbot had been appointed justiciar in November 1444. As justiciar his fee was the ludicrously low sum of £500 a year, as fixed by ancient usage going back to the thirteenth century. Conscious of how small this stipend was, the council agreed that 'unto the help and succour' of the king's wars he should maintain an additional retinue of twelve men at arms and sixty archers at the king's cost, which Richard did for a year and a half. But during that time, as he subsequently complained to the king, he had not had 'any penny of the revenues of the said land' either for his own fee or to pay for the additional retinue. Consequently he appealed to the king and on 17 July 1447 a warrant under the privy seal was issued to the treasurer of England ordering the arrears, which amounted to more than £2,000, to be paid. Eventually Richard received this sum from the exchequer—not in cash, of course, but in tallies of assignment. But most of the tallies turned out to be bad ones. So Richard had no choice but to return his bad tallies to the exchequer in exchange for new, and, as he hoped, more negotiable ones—we find his old tallies being exchanged for new ones on 14 November, 2 and 3 December 1447, 18 February 1448 (and some of those being exchanged on 2 July), 19 July (and again on that day he exchanged some of the 18 February ones) and 29 July. It was endless.

John Talbot, earl of Shrewsbury, for all his prestige and influence in England, had long and bitter experience of the difficulties of a lieutenant of Ireland in getting his tallies cashed. So when once again he was appointed lieutenant in 1445, he tried to protect himself by making sure that he would receive his stipend in cash. On 16 August 1446 a warrant under privy seal was issued to the treasurer ordering him to pay Talbot in cash and not in tallies. It was pointed out that by 'daily information' the king understands that the Irish enemies do all they can to 'raid and subdue' the lordship. To resist them, the king says, Talbot is prepared to go 'in all haste' to Ireland 'so he had money content for to war with all his retinue'. The king continues:

> Wherefore he has besought us lowly that he might restore unto our Receipt of our exchequer for us and to our use tallies received in the same Receipt and containing the sum of 2,000 mark, the which as he supposeth will be paid in ready money . . . and to have therefore 2,000 mark in ready money for to wage with all his said retinue.

The treasurer was therefore order to pay Talbot in cash, using money which Beaufort had loaned the king, giving Beaufort assignments for the money on the subsidy granted by the last parliament. But in fact the warrant was not obeyed and when Talbot turned up to exchange his tallies he had to be content with receiving new assignments and not cash.

A final illustration will demonstrate that considerable hardship might result from this sort of credit transaction if the person concerned was not, like John Talbot, a man of considerable wealth, or like Richard Talbot an archbishop with considerable resources to fall back on. Giles Thorndon, the ex-treasurer of Ireland, petitioned the king that he was owed £230, for which he had received tallies of assignment at the exchequer. The tallies were bad and could not be cashed. A warrant was therefore issued by the king on 15 December 1448 ordering the treasurer to pay off the debt in ready money:

And for as much as the said Giles for divers and great vexations which he hath long time suffered as well for the livelihood of his wife as in other wise manyfold, unto his importable cost and expenses, is at this time in so heinous poverty and indebted so greatly unto many creditors that he may not abide in any wise the payment of the said sum by the mean of the said tallies. We therefore having consideration unto the premises as how the said Giles for non-payment of the said debts unto his said creditors is like at this time to be perpetually hurt and shamed without some remedy to be had by us in his behalf, we therefore will and charge you that upon restitution made of the said tallies by the said Giles into the Receipt aforesaid you do pay and content the said sum unto him in ready money, any appointment, restraint or ordinance made by us or our council unto the contrary notwithstanding.

So far as can be discovered, no payment was ever made to Thorndon as a result of this warrant, so that presumably his hardship continued.

Regular failure to reimburse lieutenants of Ireland for their financial outlay on the wars there naturally had the effect of making it more difficult to attract suitable people to the office. More reliance had to be placed on the local magnates, who for the most part were only too anxious to have the office. We have seen that early in the reign of Richard II the earl of Ormond twice and Desmond on one occasion refused to accept the office, pleading the pressure of war on their own marches as an excuse. But near the end of the century Ormond made it quite plain what the real reason was, when he said that he was not capable of taking on the governance of Ireland in the state in which the land was at that time, and added: 'Nor do we know how we can sustain it without great dishonour and destruction of our poor and simple estate'. In the fifteenth century, however, though the office remained a financial risk, the degree of commitment was reduced so that before long the potential financial loss was not so great as to debar ambitious men from seeking office. It is clear, too, that the king was regularly forced to make concessions of a kind which he normally would not have tolerated. For example, he often had to allow the lieutenant to act through a deputy. More important, lieutenants were given the right to appoint and dismiss some important royal officers, which in effect gave them control over the king's council in Ireland and through it a fair measure of control over parliament. With the now customary right of enjoying all Irish revenues without being accountable for them, lieutenants were far too independent of control. It was undoubtedly this fact, allied to the rights of patronage enjoyed by the chief governor, which made the office so attractive to magnates like Ormond, Desmond or Kildare. The power of the lieutenant greatly augmented their position in Anglo-Irish society and made it easier to control their vast lordships and wide-ranging interests. This is well illustrated from the refusal of the Anglo-Irish of Meath in 1443 to denounce Ormond for his illegal exactions: it was said at the time that the reason for their refusal was because they feared the lieutenant, Ormond, and his power of reprisal. They did not fear him as earl and lord of Ormond: his position and power as lord of Ormond would not have debarred them from denouncing him. But his power as lieutenant frightened them.

The office, then, conveyed power. It enabled a great magnate to build up a network of support through the patronage he could dispense as chief governor. This made the office worthwhile for a magnate with sufficient resources to sustain the inevitable financial loss involved. This is why there sometimes was a struggle for power in Ireland, revolving around the holding of this office and finding expression in quarrels between opposing factions grouped around contending personalities. The best example of this is the long rivalry between the Talbot and Ormond factions in the first half of the fifteenth century, which produced bitter recriminations, charges and counter-charges, and even violence, until at last it was settled, in typical medieval fashion, by a marriage alliance between the two families. Butlers and Geraldines, too, had their struggles; and if these often became confused with the wider allegiances which involved the participants in English political strife (most notably during the Lancastrian-Yorkist struggle in England), the main issue always remained personal advancements through control of office in Ireland.

By the second half of the fifteenth century, however, the Geraldines had virtually secured a monopoly of the chief governorship and unashamedly used it to buttress their power within and without their lordships. Gerald, the 'Great' earl of Kildare, was so powerful that it was beyond the capacity of even the first of the Tudors to remove him permanently from office in Ireland—a fact which the citizens of Waterford made clear to the royal ambassador Edgecombe in 1489, when they told him that there was no good in his saying that Kildare would not be reappointed as deputy, when everyone knew that his power was so great that he would make the Anglo-Irish elect him as justiciar, whether or not the king appointed him. And for long afterwards it was remembered in Ireland that possession of the office made the earls of Kildare the virtual masters of Ireland; for who was to protect the people against the oppression of the earl, when any opposition to Kildare could be construed as opposition to the King's representative and therefore treason to the king? Hence the frequent (though futile) attempts to prevent the earl from being reappointed when he was temporarily out of office and the denunciations, such as that of O Donnell in 1520, that if the king gave office to Kildare again, then he might just as well hand Ireland over to him and his family for ever.

This was an exaggeration, of course, but it expresses well the fear of O Donnell and others like him of Kildare at the head of the Irish government. For it was this control of the government which augmented Kildare's power to the point when he was feared by all. Fear of the governor's power was frequently expressed in fifteenth century Ireland. It made the financial risks well worthwhile.

To some extent, too, the magnates who succeeded in gaining office tried to cut down the financial hazard by making war less expensive. Medieval soldiers valued regular pay less than the rewards of booty and in Ireland they were given plenty of scope through the operation of what to many was the greatest scourge of the age, the system of 'coign and livery'. The one, *coign*, was a method whereby the soldiers were quartered on the country and exacted regular payments from the people of either fixed sums of money or its equivalent in kind; *livery* allowed the requisitioning of supplies for the soldiers, which in theory had to be paid for at the current market rates, but in practice were either not paid for or else paid by means of tallies which might be uncashable in the end. A famous denunciation of the system by John Swayne, archbishop of Armagh, in 1428, shows what contemporary opinion was:

All the lietuenants that have been in this country, when they come thither, their soldiers live on the husbandmen, not paying for horse-meat nor man-meat, and the lieutenants' purveyors take up all manner of victuals, that is to say, corn, hay, beasts and poultry and all other things needful to their household, and pay nothing therefor to account but tallies, so far forth that, as it is told me, there is owing in this land by lieutenants and their soldiers within these few years £20,000. And, more also, at parliaments and great councils the lieutenants have great subsidies and tallages granted to them. And all this the poor husbandry beareth and payeth for, and the war on the other side destroyeth them.

These exactions were, of course, illegal and had frequently been condemned in parliament. But they could never be stamped out so long as they were employed by the head of the government. They were, too, a part of the way of life of Ireland, borrowed from similar exactions which had been customary in Gaelic Ireland from time immemorial and illustrating well the degree to which the two cultures had been assimilated to each other. Everywhere the Anglo-Irish lord imitated his Gaelic counterpart in imposing similar burdens on his unfortunate tenants. Such exactions were bewildering in their variety, including not only 'man meat' and 'horse meat' for the support of retainers, but also taxes and impositions designed to support and entertain the lord himself. Early in the fifteenth century a bishop of Cloyne tried to protect himself and his tenants from such illegal exactions by agreement with three of the leading magnates in his diocese, as well as with the earl of Ormond. What is most extraordinary about these agreements is that in each one of them there is a ready admission by the magnates that the impositions are illegal—they are *onera illicita* ('illicit burdens'). But this did not prevent the lords from levying them whenever they liked on their own people. So much, then, for the rule of law and the authority of the king.

These impositions undoubtedly contributed to the power of the great magnates and made them less amenable to control. But their power also rested in part on alliances of marriage or friendship with Gaelic lords, which enabled them to manipulate situations to their own advantages, and sometimes the advantage of the community at large. But it also meant that concessions had sometimes to be made to Gaelic lords which caused damage to some local communities. The fourth earl of Ormond, for example, was related by marriage with Donnchadh Mac Murrough and Henry O Neill and we can see how useful this was to him in the ready help which he got from the Irish in his campaigns. But he had to make concessions too: it was generally believed that he allowed O Connor Faley to cross his lands without interference to raid the English elsewhere.

What the growth in power and independence of the great Anglo-Irish magnates meant was that they became the arbitors of the age. For not only did they outstrip the king (except, of course, when one of them acted as his governor in Ireland), but they also left the Gaelic lords behind as well. It is a remarkable fact that the representatives of the old ruling dynasties, who had adopted a royal style in the thirteenth and fourteenth centuries, drop their titles in this age and become simply O Neill, O Brien, or Mac Murrough. It is also a sign of their dependence that they are all allied by marriage with the great Anglo-Irish, on whom they come to rely to a greater or lesser extent. This can best be seen in the case of the eighth earl of Kildare, Garret Mór (the great), as he was called, who epitomises (if in a somewhat exaggerated form) all that the great Anglo-Irish lords had become. He virtually controlled the government, monopolised office, spread his power widely throughout Gaelic and Anglo-Ireland through a network of personal relationships, arbitrated the quarreis of his peers, controlled vast resources which made him immensely wealthy, and generally behaved as if he were, which he was later called, the 'all-but-king of Ireland'. He was, in a very real sense, master of Ireland during most of his public life. And that was for long enough, for he became earl on the death of his father in 1477 and did not die until 1513. Thirty-six years is above average for those days and it helped to make the earl the formidable figure he was. But other great magnates had also very long innings. The 'white' earl of Ormond, the fourth

17

earl, acceded to the title in 1405 and held it for the best part of half a century before he died in 1452. James, the sixth earl of Desmond, held the title from 1420 to 1462, a period of more than forty years. Even some of the Gaelic lords ruled for long periods: Aedh Rua O Donnell, for example, from 1461 to 1505; Henry O Neill from 1456 to 1489; Conor O Brien from 1466 to 1496.

Such longevity must have contributed markedly to the growth of stability, making it all the easier for the great lords to establish themselves securely. They frequently showed scant respect for the king's law, a fact which was lamented by one of the greatest of the fifteenth-century poets, Tadhg Óg O Higgins, in verses addressed to one of his Burke patrons:

The law of the Saxon kings has often been broken; the Goill set no store by legal document; none of them obeying the King's law, each of them is an earl for himself.

About Éire the principle of them all is respect for the strong man; fearful their greed; all respect for law is gone.

But another O Higgins could say of an earlier Burke that 'the charter he contends by is of the sword'. This was true of many: the only charter they had was that of the sword—the lands which they illegally occupied were not very different from the 'sword land' of Gaelic tradition, or land usurped from the legal proprietors through conquest and occupation. Later generations were to pay the price when newcomers to Ireland, descendants of those who had received grants of Irish lands in a distant past, were to produce old charters and try to dispossess those in illegal possession.

The new alignments of lordships in Ireland, the blurring of distinction between Gael and Anglo-Irish, and the increased autonomy of the lords in the localities, made the government as a force in Irish politics less important than it had been in the fourteenth century. It was, in any case, less effective because it was financially starved and was in no condition to undertake ambitious schemes of renewal. For those who sought the chief governorship the substance of power was vested in the office and not so much in the financial resources available to the government. These were strictly limited, as the surviving financial records of the fifteenth century show, and they were earmarked for particular customary fees and wages, leaving little if anything for the chief governor. This made nonsense of the privilege extended to the lieutenant in his indenture that he was to enjoy all the revenues without being accountable for them. A minute of the proceedings of the English council of 28 August 1442 provided that a letter was to be sent to Ormond, lieutenant of Ireland, acknowledging that his indenture with the king allowed him to have 'all the revenues and profits' of Ireland, but saying that it was now the intention of the king that 'all ordinary charges and wages and rewards to the officers shall be borne and paid of the said revenues'; whatever is then left he is to have for himself from the treasurer. Normally there was nothing left. In 1441 the treasurer, Giles Thorndon, informed the English government that 'the charges of the justiciar of Ireland and his officers this year exceed the revenues by £1,456'. This may have been an exaggerated case; but certainly no chief governor could now rely on there being a balance available, which the treasurer would pay over to him.

Some figures are available from the fragmentary surviving treasurers' accounts which show that average annual receipts came to little more than £1,000. For example, Hugh Burgh accounted for a receipt of £385 in six months in 1420; William Tynbegh for £3,500 for 1421–4; Hugh Bavent for £2,300 for 1424–6; Nicholas Plunket for £1,630 for 1427–9; and he and the bishop of Ossory for only £790 for 1429–30; Giles Thorndon for £2,310 for September 1439 to January 1442; and Thorndon again for only £1,288 for the two years ending at Michaelmas 1446.

Under the circumstances, then, there was clearly no money available for emergencies. Indeed it is obvious that no government could even maintain a regular payment of fees and wages to its own officials. The surviving records support this. They show that even the fees of high officials were regularly in arrears. For example, the issue roll of the treasurer, Hugh Burgh, for the period 24 February–26 July 1420 records payments on 10 June of £26 13s 4d to Stephen Gray, chief justice of common pleas, whose arrears amounted to the staggering sum of £487 12s 2d; and £50 to the chancellor, Laurence Merbury, whose arrears came to £118 13s 2¼d.

The financial position was even worse than that reflected by these figures, for fees were normally paid by assignments and in its desperate plight the exchequer had to issue many bad (un-cashable) tallies, even to the chief governor and to great officials like the chancellor and treasurer. In the audited account of the treasurer Hugh Bavent, for example, we find that bad tallies had been issued to the justiciar, Richard Talbot, and six other royal officials; the account of the bishop of Ossory shows that the earl of Ormond, as justiciar, received two bad tallies worth £38, Edward Ferrers, constable of Wicklow castle, received two bad tallies worth 34s 8d in 1419. The list is endless. It re-inforces the suggestion already made, that in Lancastrian Ireland the holding of office was of some value, even if the risk of financial loss was great.

Even more important, however, is the failure of the govern-ment to benefit from the obviously increasing prosperity of the fifteenth century. At a time when signs of affluence appear everywhere, the exchequer remained slumped in poverty. The government did not have the means of cashing in on the new prosperity. Yield from taxation remained low because the area which was taxable was still small. In 1410 the parliamentary subsidy came to only 800 marks; in 1412 to 400; and in 1419 to only 300. These grants were never fully realised, since collection was never completed. And the money was slow to come in, with some collectors in arrears for years. Local subsidies, too, yielded only tiny sums: in 1423 the commons of Louth granted £40 and the clergy a mere nine marks. The breakdown of the courts deprived the exchequer of traditional revenues from the profits of justice. Even the royal demesne was no longer very productive. Customs brought in virtually nothing. There seemed to be an almost fatalistic acceptance of the situation and it was not until the end of the century, under the first of the Tudors, that an attempt was made to bring about the necessary revolution in government which would enlarge the sources of revenue available to the exchequer. By that time the Dublin government had long since learnt how to restrict severely its financial com-mitments, curtailing military operations and concentrating attention on the area most immediate to Dublin. The four 'obedient' shires of Dublin, Meath, Louth and Kildare emerged, from early in the century, as the area of concentration and gradually this was narrowed to a smaller area known as the Pale. In 1435 the Dublin parliament sent a message to the king that 'his land of Ireland is well-nigh destroyed and inhabited with his enemies and rebels, in so much that there is not left in the nether parts of the counties of Dublin, Meath, Louth and Kildare, that join together, out of the subjection of the said enemies and rebels, scarcely thirty miles in length and twenty miles in breadth there, as man may surely ride and go, in the said counties, to answer the king's writs and to his commandments'. This is approximately the area which was later ordered to be enclosed with great ditches and heavily defended, along a line which in 1515 ran from Dundalk via Ardee, Kells, Dangan, Kilcock, Clane, Naas, Ballymore-Eustace, Rathmore, Rathcoole, Tallaght, to Dalkey.

It is not known when exactly the idea of constructing a Pale emerged, though it was clearly inspired by the Pale of Calais which had proved so successful. The earliest mention of a Pale as such occurs in 1446, in the submission of Hugh Roe Mac Mahon, when he promised 'to carry nothing out of the English Pale contrary to the statutes'. By then it was a clearly defined area, though it can hardly have been the enclosed area which appears later in the century. Long before then the government had tried, successfully as it happened, to encourage the gentry to build castles, fortalices and towers and made grants available for the purpose. For example, in 1429 parliament agreed that anyone in county Louth who was willing to build a 'sufficient' castle or tower within the next five years, 'in length twenty feet, in breadth sixteen feet, in height forty feet', would be granted a subsidy of £10. The following year this offer was extended to counties Dublin, Meath and Kildare. Subsequent parliaments repeated the inducement and many small castles were built as a result, forming a chain of defence against the enemy. In 1472, for instance, the abbot of Baltinglas was granted a subsidy to build a tower on a rock near 'Windgates' in county Kildare.

Most chief governors also concentrated their attention on this same area. The retinues which they retained in service (mostly English or Welsh), according to the contracts, were enough to form the professional nucleus of an army when augmented by recruits in Ireland. Normal military operations were defensive in nature, since such small retinues could hardly have carried on offensives with any regularity. Efforts were mostly concentrated on protecting the borders of the area which became the Pale, either by forcing the Gaelic lords into some kind of submission through strong military action, or by agreements with them, or even by retaining them in service or paying the equivalent of black rent. The activities of John Talbot illustrate perfectly the policy of clearing and protecting the borders. A letter written on his behalf in 1417 testifies to his 'great labours, travels and endeavours' and the 'many great journies and hostings' he made against the Irish, such as O More of Leix, O Reilly, O Farrel, Mac Mahon, O Hanlon and O Connor, all on the perimeters of the Pale. His military successes frightened O Neill, O Donnel, Maguire and others from further afield, so that they sued for peace. Perhaps the most extraordinary attempt to protect the borders of the Pale was the proposal to settle the Mac Mahons as 'friendly Irish' in the district of Farney in the modern county of Monaghan. This was a position of great strategic importance. The Anglo-Irish of Louth complained bitterly of the presence of Mac Mahon, which they rightly regarded as an intrusion rather than a defence.

It was only to be expected that when strong personalities were sent over from England, such as John Talbot, they would clash with independently-minded Anglo-Irish who were determined to pursue their own interests at all times. The stress of political life and of living constantly in a frontier situation produced among many of the Anglo-Irish an attitude of independence which easily shaded into political separatism. Occasionally this sharpened into a self-consciousness, a sense of otherness, which led the great Irish historian Edmund Curtis to a belief in the existence of a Home Rule movement in fifteenth-century Ireland. It is hard to sustain such an extreme view of Anglo-Irish political life in that era. But there can be no doubt that Anglo-Irish resentment of governance from England was not always and solely the result of personal ambitions and selfish aggrandisement. The plot against Talbot which was uncovered in 1418, when one of those arrested was found to be carrying a copy of the English coronation oath and a famous tract proposing radical alterations in the powers and structure of Parliament (the *Modus Tenendi Parliamentum*, or 'How Parliament should be held'), the possession of which was enough to suggest subversive activity, cannot be explained away as the first shot in the Talbot-Ormond struggle which followed later. An almost routine request in the message from the Irish council to the king in the summer of 1441, that the Anglo-Irish (or 'Englishmen born in Ireland') should have the same rights in England as Englishmen, is a startling reminder that the old antagonism between the two was still very much alive and was a source of bitterness. It helped to buttress the determination of the Anglo-Irish to govern themselves, under the king, so that they would not be answerable to writs out of England (except for treason), would not be bound by the legislation of any parliament other than their own, and that all Irish pleas would be terminable in the courts here. This separatist tradition found its classic expression in the declaration of the Irish parliament in 1460:

> That whereas the land of Ireland is, and at all times has been, corporate of itself by the ancient laws and customs used in the same, freed of the burden of any special law of the realm of England save only such laws as by the lords spiritual and temporal and commons of the said land had been in great council or parliament there held, admitted, accepted, affirmed and proclaimed, according to sundry ancient statutes thereof made.

It has been argued that there is no historical foundation for this declaration, though as we shall see this is too simple a view of what even then was a highly contentious matter. But the important thing is that such an extraordinary declaration should have been made at all, and in such radical terminology, stressing the corporate nature of the Irish lordship. Nor can we suppose that it was solely the result of prompting by Richard, duke of York, who needed the protection of an independent Irish parliament. So long as he or his friends controlled Ireland he was safe: there was no need for him to take the dangerous step of spurring the Anglo-Irish into a declaration of independence. It is more likely that they used the occasion of York's dependence on them to formally enunciate what had for long been a principle.

The whole question of the application of English statutes in Ireland is highly complicated and extremely controversial. It is impossible to do justice to the subject in a short space. But certain elementary facts will demonstrate that by the time of the 1460 declaration there was at least a grave doubt in the minds of many lawyers on the matter. So far as the earlier period is concerned, there can be no doubt that English statutes were binding on Ireland. Common practice was for the king to send a writ to the Irish chancellor ordering the particular statute or statutes to be exemplified, enrolled and proclaimed. Usually proclamation was by the sheriffs, but during the fourteenth century there was a growing tendency for it to be through parliament. And in the fifteenth century, with the increase in the authority of parliament, it became normal for English statutes to be proclaimed by the Irish parliament. It was easy, therefore, to argue that such statutes were of force only because they had been proclaimed by an Irish parliament. It was that which gave them authority. This practice was turned into a principle in 1460. By then the theoretical position was far from clear.

A famous test case, concerning the appointment of John Pilkington to the office of escheator in Ireland, enabled no less a person than the famous English jurist Sir John Fortescue to give the following opinion:

And further, the territory of Ireland is separate from the kingdom of England, for if a tenth or a fifteenth be granted here, it shall not bind the people of Ireland, and if a statute be made here, it shall not bind those in Ireland unless they approve it in their own parliament, even though the king under his great seal shall send the same statute to Ireland.

Even though Fortescue's opinion was subsequently overruled, it does show that there was much to be said in favour of what was declared in 1460. The confusion that existed was once again illustrated in 1468, when the Irish parliament confirmed the English statutes of rapes because the lawyers were of different opinions as to whether the statutes would be valid without such confirmation. The fact that Tiptoft, who controlled the Irish parliament and whose mission was to check the separatist tendencies of the Anglo-Irish, took the trouble to confirm the statutes in an Irish parliament, shows that he believed that there might be substance to the doubts of the lawyers. Another famous case, the Waterford 'ship case', raised the same question again. In the exchequer chamber, where the case was heard, the justices gave the opinion that Ireland was not bound by English statutes because 'in Ireland they have a parliament among themselves and courts of all kinds as in England, and laws are made and laws are changed by the same parliament, and they are not bound by a statute made in England because they do not have knights in the parliament here'. This judgement was also overruled and the Waterford merchants lost their case. They appealed again and the chief justice gave his opinion 'that statutes made in England bound those in Ireland'. But significantly the record adds that 'each of them (i.e. the other justices) had a contrary opinion in the previous term in his absence'. Once again, therefore, in the highest English courts a majority of English justices ruled that Ireland was not bound by English statutes.

It was not until the 1494–95 parliament of Edward Poynings that the question was resolved. The thirty-ninth act ordained that 'all statutes late made within the realm of England, concerning or belonging to the common and public weal of the same, *shall from henceforth* be deemed good and effectual in law and be accepted, used and executed within this land of Ireland'. Only then were the many doubts allayed. It is significant that the king, who was leaving nothing to chance, had this important principle enacted by the authority of an Irish parliament. It is no less significant that while he went out of his way in the same parliament to denounce the 'pretensed prescription' of the 1460 parliament concerning writs out of England, he made no attempt to denounce the other declaration of that 1460 parliament that Ireland was 'corporate of itself'.

Clearly, then, there was some historical justification for the 1460 claim. Whatever about theory, practice seems to have supported what was then turned into a principle. It is no doubt true that the purpose of the declaration, and of the equally important assertion that no one could be summoned out of Ireland by English writs, was the protection of Anglo-Irish from attack from England. But it is hard to escape the conclusion that selfish motives of this kind, when they rise to a solemn declaration in a representative assembly, had at least the effect, if not the intent, of urging forward political separatism. This suited the great Anglo-Irish lords very well, since it enabled them to go their own way without too much interference. It also helped some of them to concentrate power in their own hands, most notably the ninth earl of Kildare who, as we shall see, was virtually the master of a good part of the lordship by the end of the fifteenth century. The ascendancy of Kildare was thus in part the result and in part the supreme expression of Anglo-Irish separatism. But it was also the natural outcome of the vast resources which he controlled, through inheritance and acquisition, and the great influence he exercised through farflung family connections. Luck, too, was on his side with the removal of the great rivals of his house and the virtual withdrawal from public life of the Desmond dynasty of Geraldines. Earlier in the fifteenth century the earls of Ormond had been the most powerful of the Anglo-Irish, so much so that the fourth earl's feud with Talbot had been enough, according to Primate Swayne of Armagh, to keep 'all this land severed'. It had disastrous results: 'and this debate betwixt these two lords is cause of the great harms that be done in this country'. Swayne later told the king that 'in good faith the enemies dreadeth them both more than they do all the world. I trow for if any of them were in this land all the enemies in Ireland would be right fain to have peace'. So great was the prestige of Ormond. But the Butlers became fatally involved in the politics of the Lancastrian court, opposed the bid of Richard duke of York for power, and were very nearly ruined for thus backing the wrong horse. The fifth earl was executed in 1461 and his removal left the way clear in Ireland for the old rivals, the Geraldines. They had supported York, provided him with refuge in Ireland at a vital moment in his career, and thereby earned the gratitude of his son after he became Edward IV of England. Their rise to power was thus closely linked with the ascendancy of the house of York.

Richard of York first became involved with Ireland when he was appointed lieutenant in 1447. English historians have seen this appointment as a form of banishment, 'an honourable exile'. But since he was allowed to act through a deputy and since in any case he did not come here until nearly two years after his appointment, there were obviously better reasons for sending him to Ireland. That there was a genuine need there for someone of ability there can be no doubt. The country at that time was greatly disturbed. In particular the earl of Desmond went on the rampage and caused widespread destruction, provoking a reply from the earl of Ormond that was hardly less damaging in its results. The community of county Kilkenny in a petition to the king complained that 'since the conquest of our said sovereign lord his land of Ireland to this day, the said country took no such rebuke of none of our said sovereign lord his Irish enemies as they did by the said earl of Desmond'. He and his Gaelic allies, it was said, 'with banners displayed came into the said country and overrode it, burnt, wasted, and destroyed sixty and sixteen of towns and burnt and broke sixteen churches and robbed them of their cattle and goods that may not be numbered and took divers prisoners and men slain, to the final destruction of our sovereign lord his liege people of the aforesaid county'. Someone like York was an obvious choice — indeed the Kilkenny petition alluded to the fact that York was one of the people whose property suffered from the destruction caused by Desmond. He was well fitted to take strong action in Ireland. A man of great standing, with much experience of government in England and France, and moreover with vast interests in Ireland as heir to the great Mortimer inheritance there, which also brought him enormous prestige among Anglo-Irish and Gaelic lords alike, he seemed an indeal choice. His enemies, however, can hardly have been anxious to send him off to Ireland to win glory and renown. More likely they hoped that he would ruin himself there, sustaining not only great financial losses, but also a military disaster which would destroy his prestige. York, of course, must have hoped for a resounding success that would add to his stature.

Like other chief governors before him, York was soon in financial difficulties and was in great fear that military failure would follow. He badly wanted success in Ireland and in a remarkable letter which he wrote in May 1450 to his brother-in-law, he complained how the failure of the king to pay him what was owing was leading him to disaster. In a moment of candour he wrote:

> For doubtless, but if my payment be had in all haste, for to have men of war in defence and safeguard of this land, my power cannot stretch to keep it in the king's obeisance: and very necessity will compel me to come into England to live there upon my poor livelihood. For I had liever be dead than any inconvenience should fall thereunto by my default: for it shall never be chronicled nor remain in scripture, by the grace of God, that Ireland was lost by my negligence.

In fact York enjoyed a marked success in Ireland. The magic of the Mortimer name worked in his favour and both Gaelic and Anglo-Ireland accepted him readily. His success meant that when later he made his bid for control in England he had in Ireland a power base which was to prove to be indispensible. After the disaster of Ludford Bridge in October in 1459, when he had to fly for his life, he and his second son came to Ireland, while the eldest son and the earl of Warwick fled to Calais. It was natural for Warwick to go to Calais, of which he was still captain. York was still lieutenant of Ireland, though we can hardly suppose that that was sufficient to bring him here. Just as Warwick was to raise men in Calais for another attempt to seize control in England, so we must suppose that York was going to try to cash in on the undoubted goodwill he enjoyed in Ireland. He must have known, too, that his friends were in control there and that they would protect him from rampant Lancastrians determined to finish him off.

He did not miscalculate. The Anglo-Irish gave him a great welcome and gave him a legal title, ignoring his attainder by the Coventry parliament which met in November. They protected him by the law of treason, safeguarded him from writs out of England (the unfortunate William Overy, who arrived from England with writs for the apprehension of York, was arrested, tried, and hanged, drawn and quartered) and secured him from the operation of English statutes, such as the acts of attainder of the Coventry parliament. York could not have been safer, so long as the Anglo-Irish, and especially Desmond and Kildare, supported him. He relied on them absolutely.

After the execution of Overy, the Lancastrian government knew that they could not get at York in Ireland. Nor could they prevent regular communication between him and Warwick in Calais. In March 1460 Warwick sailed to Ireland for a conference with York, during which the invasion of England was planned. In June the army from Calais landed and on 10 July routed the Lancastrians at the battle of Northampton. This did not settle the issue, however, and York later sailed from Ireland to help. In December he was killed at the battle of Wakefield and it was his son who was crowned king as Edward IV.

It is possible that York recruited men in Ireland, even if he did not actually employ them in England after his return. There can be no doubt that he enjoyed widespread support in Ireland, or that this largely rested on the goodwill of the Geraldines who now began that long attachment to the house of York which was to lead them to ascendancy in Ireland. On the other hand, the Lancastrians too enjoyed considerable support here, which was largely the result of Butler involvement in English politics, though it stemmed as well from local opposition to Geraldine (and by extension Yorkist) aggrandisement. Shortly before he was captured and beheaded the earl of Wiltshire, also fifth earl of Ormond, was reported to be raising an army for Queen Margaret (wife of the deposed Henry VI), which included Irishmen as well as French and Bretons. Ireland had become well and truly enmeshed in English politics. Queen Margaret intrigued in Scotland against the usurper, and through her agent Donald Ballagh she tried to stir up rebellion in Ireland. When Sir John Butler, brother of Wiltshire, landed in Ireland in 1462, a surprisingly large number of people declared for him and the Lancastrians. Butlers with their friends and allies in Kilkenny and Tipperary naturally rose in rebellion and some towns as well. What is more surprising, however, is the strength of support which came from Meath. According to the Irish parliament of 1463, 'the commons of the county of Meath to the number of five thousand made insurrection and rising'. According to the same parliament, Butler was defeated 'because of the great continual war had all the last summer by the said deputy (i.e. Desmond) and the said John of Ormond and his adherents' and because Desmond stayed at war as long as was necessary, 'at his own proper cost with his men to the number of twenty thousand'. The battle of Pilltown, near Carrick-on-Suir, saw the Butlers and their opponents completely routed, the end of Lancastrian hopes in Ireland, and the confirmation of Geraldine ascendancy. Subsequently Butler lands were confiscated and doled out to Desmond, Kildare, their friends and supporters.

Edward IV had good reason, therefore, to be grateful to the Geraldines. Not only had they given shelter, protection and support to his father in his time of need, but they had continued the support (albeit for more selfish reasons) during the new Irish crisis brought about by the invasion of Sir John Butler. Desmond was rewarded by being made deputy of Clarence, the nominal lieutenant of Ireland. In 1463 the Irish parliament sent an extraordinary message to the king, extolling the deputy and asking that he be suitably rewarded. He had done 'great services' to the duke of York 'at his coming last in to this land of Ireland'; he had defeated Sir John Butler, put down the rising in Meath and 'by his great labour and travail this land is in reasonable rest, peace and tranquility at this time'. They ask the king to have him 'in special rememberance and to have him in tenderness and special favour and him thereupon heartily thank and reward after his most wisdom and bounty'. Substantial gifts and favours were in fact bestowed on Desmond and others, so that Edward did not stint his gratitude.

But the king was soon anxious about his position in Ireland. Complaints against Desmond gave him reason to think that there was considerable opposition to the deputy and other Geraldines in Ireland. Being the man he was, always anxious to assert the rights of the Crown and make government more personal, he could not help being suspicious of the growing concentration of power in the hands of Desmond and his supporters. Throughout his reign he kept in closer touch with his lordship than his predecessors for generations, tried to assert his authority, and generally tried to restore a degree of supervision which had long since disappeared. That he did not succeed, and that his successor Richard III was no more successful, is a measure of the great strength of the position now held by the Geraldines in Ireland. But Edward had to try.

As soon as his situation in England permitted—and that was only after his diplomacy was successful enough to prevent Lacastrian plotters from procuring assistance abroad, and more especially after the capture at last of Henry VI in July 1465—he made his bid to free himself from reliance on the Geraldines. In 1467 John Tiptoft, earl of Worcester, arrived in Ireland as deputy. One of the first things he did was to summon a parliament to Dublin which met on 11 December. It was adjourned to Drogheda, a safer place in which to mount an attack on the Geraldines, and there both Desmond and Kildare were attained of 'horrible treasons and felonies contrived and done by them' Desmond had foolishly attended the session, trusting in his own inviolability. But to the horror of the lordship he was arrested and was executed on 15 February 1468. It was later put about that this was an act of revenge by the queen for some disparaging remarks supposedly made by the unfortunate Desmond. But it was in reality the first move in an attack on the Geraldines. That Edward was responsible is not to be doubted. But the reaction, when it came, showed him how he had miscalculated if he believed that leading Geraldines could be lightly thrust aside. Meath, (now held by the king as heir to the Mortimers) was burnt and laid waste by a huge army; Kildare was rescued from prison and joined the brother of the murdered earl; two great Gaelic lords also joined him, O Connor of Offaly and Donal Kavanagh. Widespread disorder followed and the attainder against Kildare had to be reversed. Worcester remained as deputy until the spring of 1470—he was executed later that year during the temporary Lancastrian restoration—and soon after the Irish council elected Kildare as justiciar.

From now on it was the Kildares who were to be the real masters of Ireland. When the eighth earl clashed with a newly appointed deputy, Lord Grey, in 1478, the king eventually had to uphold the earl and make him deputy. When Richard III set out to reassert royal control over Ireland, he soon found that Kildare was more than a match for him. Even the first of the Tudors, Henry VII, was able to do no more than barely clip the wings of Kildare, despite his leading role in the rebellion of Lambert Simnel and his probable collusion, or at the very least dangerous neutrality, during the Perkin Warbeck plot. What each of these kings discovered was that it was impossible for them to rule Ireland peaceably except through the house of Kildare. The famous story concerning the meeting of the earl with Henry VII in 1496 may be apocryphal, but it stated one truth worth recording. The story tells how after the bishop of Meath had levelled serious accusations against the earl, the king remarked that 'he is meet to rule all Ireland, seeing all Ireland cannot rule him'. Even as late as the 1530s Thomas Cromwell was told that the people of the Pale 'covet more to see a Geraldine to reign and triumph than to see God come amongst them'. From 1468 the Kildares controlled the government, with few interruptions, until 1534, when their power was destroyed by Henry VIII.

The basis of Kildare power was primarily the great landed wealth which they controlled, vast estates that stretched throughout the lordship. This helped them to build up an extensive network of family relationships, cemented by astute marriages or by the even stronger bonds of fosterage. And this in turn helped them to gain control of the government and the power of patronage that went with it. The most powerful single factor which more than anything enabled the eighth earl ('Garret More' or the 'Great Earl', as he is usually called) to retain the governance of Ireland in his hand for so long was probably his control over the Irish council. This all-important body, which should have been a check on the chief governor and a defence of royal interests, became an instrument in Kildare's hand which helped to keep him in power. The crucial element in his control was the right to appoint, or dismiss, certain royal officials who sat *ex officio* on the council. Naturally the king's interests demanded that he retain the right of appointment and dismissal over these and attempts were regularly made to withold this right from Kildare. Failure to do so permanently is a clear sign of how much the king had come to rely on Kildare.

Even after his treason in crowning Lambert Simnel, Kildare was in no way submissive in his attitude towards Henry VII. When he was pardoned in July 1490, it was made conditional on his coming to England the following summer. Not for ten months did Kildare answer the king, and then only to excuse himself from coming. When Perkin Warbeck landed in Ireland in November 1491, the king replaced Kildare in office and discharged his father-in-law, Roland fitz Eustace from the treasurership after a spell of forty years in office. What particularly outraged Kildare, however, was that Roland was replaced by James Ormond, a hated rival. Geraldines and Butlers fought in the streets of Dublin and in the winter of 1492 Kildare showed his contempt for the commander of the royal forces in Ireland, Thomas Garth, by throwing him into prison and by hanging his son. He could no longer be ignored and the king sent another small army, equipped with ordnance, to Ireland. In 1493 he spent nearly £3,000 on the army in Ireland, an indication that he was getting worried over the control exercised by Kildare. When he agreed to pardon the earl, it was only on condition that his son should be sent to England as a virtual hostage.

Henry's sterner attitude is also reflected in some of the acts of the 1493 parliament. Fitz Eustace was taken into custody until he had authenticated his accounts for the previous forty years, a clearly impossible task. More ominous was the general act of resumption of all grants and licences since 1422, a clear threat to Kildare and his supporters who had rewarded themselves over the years with grants of one kind or another. If one co-operated, a licence of exemption could be procured. If not, then the act was there, like the sword of Damocles, hanging over the Anglo-Irish.

Order was restored and by November 1493 Kildare was at last in England, 'to purge himself to the king of the crimes which were laid to his charge', according to the *Annals of Ulster*. He, and soon Desmond as well, made their peace with the king. Most of the army withdrew from Ireland. But the summer of 1494 saw widespread disturbances in Ireland, with Desmond in rebellion once again. O Donnell in the north was allied with the Scots. Worst of all, for the king, was the expected landing of Perkin Warbeck in Ireland and the possibility of a Yorkist takeover there. It was no time for half measures. The situation demanded not only the strongest military action, but a general overhaul of the Irish administration as well, so as, at the very least, to neutralise Kildare-Yorkist support there. In addition, Ireland had to be fitted into the web of English diplomacy, to prevent Yorkist help from arriving from abroad. In August 1494 Charles VII of France was told by Henry that he was going to subdue Ireland and put the 'Irish savages' into order so that they could live in peace and justice. He was sending a large army, with important officials. And so in September the young Prince Henry (the future Henry VIII) was made lieutenant and Edward Poynings was appointed his deputy.

The mission of Poynings marks a turning-point, not least because it witnessed the first real attempt since the fourteenth century to make the administration dependent on the English government and to improve the financial position of the Irish government. Two English officials, Henry Wyatt and William Hattecliffe, both highly experienced in the new administrative techniques of Henry VII's government, came to Ireland to lead the reform. Old sources of revenue, especially customs and subsidies, were carefully scrutinised and estimates were prepared of what they could be made to yield. An estimated balance of income over expenditure of nearly £500 was anticipated, after salaries had been paid. This was not much, but in the Irish context it was something which hadn't been seen for years. The efficiency of the team was vindicated when the expected surplus was realised. But this did not take into account military expendi-

18

ture, for which a much larger surplus would be required. This the reformers failed to procure. Nevertheless they had shown that the application of stricter controls, better book-keeping methods, and English expertise, could increase the Irish revenues.

Administrative reform, however, was not the primary purpose which brought Poynings to Ireland. He came, like so many before him, as a military chief governor, at the head of an army, to wage a campaign. The enemy were not the Gaelic lords, whatever Henry VII might say to the king of France, but rather the potentially dangerous Anglo-Irish lords in alliance with a Yorkist pretender to the English throne. By 1494 Perkin Warbeck was not only getting recognition in some parts of Europe as rightful king of England, but was preparing an invasion. King Henry was worried by all this, anxious to make sure that Perkin would get as little support as possible. He could take no chances so near home as Ireland. The army sent with Poynings was not large, around 700 in all. But it was well equipped (there were 90 gunners) and was augmented in Ireland. And it was costly. By the summer of 1496, when the army was paid off, it had cost Henry VII more than £18,000. Nothing could better show how worried he had been about the potential danger of a Yorkist rebellion in Ireland.

Poynings enjoyed great success in neutralising the threat. The proof lies not only in what his record in Ireland tells us, but in the fact that the king could return Kildare to office in 1496, with extensive powers and privileges, and feel secure that no Yorkist plot or continual intrigue would endanger him again in Ireland. He may have needed Kildare in Ireland, but that suited him well enough now that the real danger had been averted. There was a return to the old policy of reliance on Kildare, but with one difference. His wings were clipped in one important way which reassured the king: the independence of the Irish parliament was ended through the operation of what became known as 'Poynings' Law', which was the ninth act of the parliament summoned to Drogheda late in 1494. It declared that no parliament was to be held in future until the king's licence had been obtained, all the bills having been first approved by the king and his council in England. In the summer of 1496 Kildare, in the presence of the king and his council at Salisbury, swore (among other things) to uphold Poynings' Law. Never again, then, could an independent Irish parliament enact legislation which might endanger the

Tudor dynasty. Parliament might still be an instrument of Kildare policy, but only with the prior consent of the king and his council.

This famous act was but one of forty-nine which were passed by the Drogheda parliament of 1494–95. Many repeated long-familiar injunctions which had grown threadbare through repetition in the past two hundred years—freemen are to have arms suitable to their status; the use of Irish law is condemned; those having land in the marches are to dwell there and defend them; coign and livery is outlawed; the Statutes of Kilkenny are confirmed; no peace or war is to be made except by the government. Others were new and were designed to cope with immediate problems (such as the act ordering 'ditches to be made around the English Pale'). Most important were those designed to curtail the power of the Irish chief governor, so that the appointment of leading officials was reserved to the king, the 'Statute Fitzempress' was annulled, certain important military positions were reserved to men born in England, and the famous Poynings' Law which controlled parliament was enacted. A most sweeping act of resumption threatened all who did not toe the line. Two famous acts made all English statutes applicable to Ireland and annulled the 'pretensed prescription', solemnly proclaimed in the 1460 parliament, which made it treasonable to attach any person in Ireland under any writ of England. Henceforth the great seal of England, the privy seal and the signet were to be obeyed in Ireland.

The restoration of Kildare to power was almost inevitable, but it was certainly beneficial, in the short run at least, to the king. A letter written from Dublin in the autumn of 1496 made the point well: 'Now thanked be God the king hath peace in all the land without strake or any great charge or cost to him and all men be glad to submit themself to the king's grace of their own free will without compulsion'. Henry got security without any great cost to himself. The price was the renewed supremacy of Kildare. When Perkin Warbeck landed once again in Ireland in the summer of 1497, there was no real support forthcoming, not even from the earl of Desmond. He was captured soon after in England and executed.

From now on Kildare was to grow in strength. The 'Kildare Rental', commenced in 1518, contains a list of what are called

'Duties upon Irishmen' which certainly go back to the time of the eighth earl. These were payments, mainly in kind (such as horses, cattle, sheep, pigs, fish, butter, honey and all sorts of food), levied on an extraordinary number of Gaelic lords over a wide area, for protection. In fact, they are the equivalent of the famous black rent which Gaelic lords levied on many unfortunate Anglo-Irish communities. Great lords like Mac Murrough, O Hanlon, O Byrne, O Toole, O More, O Connor, O Reilly, Mac Mahon, to name but some of the more important, paid dearly to the earl to have his protection. What is more, similar payments were made by other lords to Anglo-Irish magnates, so that a system of defence was created which was wholly irregular, even though it was tolerated by the government. In this way the control exercised over Ireland by the English government reached its lowest point and a peace of sorts was maintained by reliance on the great lords. A fifteenth century poet expressed well the dangerous situation which had arisen: 'About Éire the principle of them all (i.e. the lords) is respect for the strong man; fearful their greed; all respect for law is gone'.

In 1500 the great battle of Knockdoe, in county Galway, showed the range of Kildare's power and interests. Not only had he with him the great lords of the Pale—men like Gormanstown, Slane, or Howth—but also Gaelic and Anglo-Irish lords from all over Ireland as well. Kildare had an impressive victory over Burke and O Brien and demonstrated once and for all how invincible he was. King Henry made him a Knight of the Garter and was seemingly quite content to watch the earl become, for all practical purposes, the real lord of Ireland. Secretely, however, he must have been worried by the great concentration of power in Kildare's hands. In the winter of 1506 he contemplated a great royal expedition to Ireland which would clearly have meant the end of Kildare's rule. Not only was an army of 6,000 to be sent (a thing unheard of since the time of Richard II), but much ordnance and 'handguns' as well. Whatever prompted this notion, it never materialised. But it indicates that even the phlegmatic Henry VII was occasionally stirred to worry at the Irish situation. Still, it was too easy to rely on Kildare and till his death in 1513 he continued to rule Ireland.

His son, the ninth earl, succeeded him in office and for a time managed to hold his father's place in Irish politics. Gradually, however, his position was weakened. The traditional Butler enmity had been appeased for a time with the rise to power of Piers Butler, to whom Kildare had astutely married his daughter when he learnt of the success of Henry VII. But the old rivalry was renewed during the ninth earl's lifetime and Butler influence at the English court was gradually to help erode the goodwill towards Kildare. More important, however, was the imperialism of Henry VIII, which naturally made him suspicious of Kildare and unwilling to be dependent on him. Inevitably he tried to intervene, as his father had done before him. The mission of Thomas Howard, earl of Surrey, marks a decisive shift. Appointed lieutenant in 1519, Surrey not only replaced Kildare but initiated a new policy of recovery at the personal insistence of the king. Henry was beginning to show the strong hand. But as others before him had found, direct intervention of this kind was a costly business and before long the king was withdrawing. He still tried to free himself from reliance on Kildare, however, by appointing the earl of Ormond to the office. But in the end, as always, Kildare had to be restored. The alternatives were too costly and not always as successful in maintaining peace.

Had Kildare played his cards adroitly, there is little doubt that his ascendancy would have been maintained. But as he grew older, he grew careless. He no longer succeeded in protecting the Pale from ever-increasing raids and no longer justified the power placed in his hands. He could not prevent the earls of Desmond in the 1520s and 1530s from dangerous communication with France and the emperor. Worst of all, he himself was implicated, at least by rumour, in this treasonable diplomatic activity. The situation of danger faced by Henry VII in the 1490s loomed again. Whatever the cost, King Henry could not afford to allow Ireland to become a danger to England. It became more essential than ever to replace Kildare, something that could only be done by a wholly new approach to the problem of Ireland. What was needed was a system, not a man, upon which the king could always rely. In supplying this system, even though he built upon medieval foundations, Henry VIII brought to an end the medieval lordship of Ireland and ushered in a new age. The transition, of course, was gradual and took many generations to accomplish. Its beginnings might really be seen in the experiments of the days of Wyatt and Hattecliffe, in Poynings' Law, in the 'new men' sent over in the early sixteenth century to reshape the administration. Experiment and change continued slowly and effectively to undermine the power of the great lords. The corollary was military intervention on a large scale, which also began with Henry VIII and was gradually stepped up until it involved large numbers and massive expenditure by the English government. The sequel was conquest, followed by colonisation, and a new Ireland began to emerge.

The removal of Kildare, then, can be seen as part of a pattern of events which were to change Ireland. The manner of his removal —his arrest, the rumour of his execution, the sudden rebellion of his son, his death in sorrow, and the execution of his son and five brothers in a vicious act of revenge—left bitter memories. Religious change also introduced a new element which was further to exacerbate relations with the Anglo-Irish. Already the Tudor monarchy was following a road in Ireland from which there was to be no turning back. It was committed to a policy which was to be costly, demanding military skills which had been beyond the capacity of governments in the past. All of this was supplied in phasing out medieval Ireland. It is significant that in the Dublin parliament of 1541, which proclaimed Henry VIII to be king of Ireland and which thus brought to an end the medieval lordship, Gaelic lords for the first time sat with their Anglo-Irish peers, an event which would have been inconceivable in the days of the medieval lordship. But then, these Gaelic lords were themselves a sign of the new times, bearing English titles and pointing the way to a degree of Anglicisation which was eventually to bring to an end the Gaelic order which had for so long ruled in Ireland. A fitting comment came from a northern Gaelic poet: 'These new-fashioned Gaels of the bright field of Niall, it were more fitting to call them Galls: they agree not with the sages of the schools. If they are Gaels, I know it not'.

X The Heritage

THE middle ages made their own distinctive contribution to the shaping of modern Ireland. This can be seen most obviously in the Irish landscape. The clearance of the primeval woods which once covered part of the island was first seriously undertaken in medieval times, so that by the end of the sixteenth century the way was really clear for the great onslaught which was made by the charcoal burners in the following century. Enclosure, too, had already begun to produce the field pattern which has lasted in many places down to the present day. More striking as a feature of the landscape are the cities, boroughs and towns which were first founded as part of the medieval settlement. To this day the central street plan of many an Irish town is medieval, as are some of the buildings (a church, a friary or a castle) which are prominent features, although most of them today are in ruins. Villages and rural boroughs, often deserted now, are commonly a medieval addition to the countryside. The navigable channels of many rivers, the bridges which span them and the roads they carry are often medieval in origin. All over the country the remains of mottes, castles, tower houses, friaries and monasteries are physical reminders of the middle ages.

But even more important, if immediately less obvious, is the rich legacy of law, institutions and ideas which has helped to shape the way of life which we enjoy. Some of these we take for granted now, like the principle of representation which underlies our parliamentary institutions (themselves medieval), forgetting that they had to be worked out in the middle ages to meet the needs of the times. Our literature and languages were enriched by the contributions of many people who settled here during the medieval centuries. One of the most remarkable examples is the persistence of the Flemish tradition in Wexford, where the people of the baronies of Bargy and Forth retained not only customs which were peculiar to themselves, but a dialect which was Germanic in origin and which marked them off to the end of the eighteenth century. Here the newcomers seem to have virtually blotted out the native population and to have succeeded in retaining their distinctive identity for many centuries. They were never assimilated to the Gaelic tradition which existed before they came, unlike many other settlers who succumbed in greater or lesser degree. Some were completely assimilated, others only partially so. As a result, two cultures were to survive in Ireland, quite distinct and yet part of the same Irish tradition which we today have inherited. The Gaelic and the Anglo-Irish worlds overlapped, the one impinged upon the other, and through the ages many Anglo-Irish were swallowed up so as to become quite indistinguishable (except in name— and even that is dangerous evidence since so many Gaelic Irish at one time assumed Anglo-Irish names in order to enjoy the benefits of English law without purchasing a charter of denizenship) from Gaelic neighbours. The one culture greatly enriched the other, even though they were sharply distinguished wherever they met. The mark of distinction was linguistic rather than racial, though antagonism based upon race did exist continuously throughout the middle ages and has played its part in helping to perpetuate animosities, fortified by religious bigotry, ignorance, persecution and the deliberate falsification of history by unscrupulous politicians throughout the succeeding ages. Even today many of the tensions which are just below the surface of life in Ireland and which manifest themselves occasionally in explosive fashion, are ultimately derived from the two culture situation which we inherited from the medieval lordship.

For many people, then, the middle ages represents the beginning of nearly eight hundred years of English rule. The 'good' Gaels were persecuted by the 'bad' Normans, which was the start of all Ireland's woes. Most people naturally identify themselves with, say, the O Connors against the de Burghs, or the O Briens against the de Clares. This partisan approach is so rooted that it often comes as a shock to a Barry or Burke to be told that he is not 'Irish' (by which is meant, of course, Gaelic Irish). Worst, it is hard to swallow that the man closest to canonisation in the catholic Church is a scion of one of the great families of the Pale, namely Blessed Oliver Plunkett; or that another, who is the subject of the greatest popular cult, Matt Talbot, is a descendant of an even greater Pale family. Even at a more sophisticated level the same inbred prejudice manifests itself, as with the use of 'pale' as a derogatory adjective. It is important, therefore, to understand why it is possible to view the medieval lordship in such an absurd way—to discover what kind of division, cultural and racial, was established then and which was passed on to the more modern generations.

An obvious fact which was probably the root cause of all the trouble was the failure of the Anglo-Normans to conquer the whole of Ireland and to impose their own culture on the Gaelic lordships. They themselves were impossible to absorb and so they created the two-culture situation which has survived ever since. The early invaders were French speaking and imposed the French language and institutions as the standard of civilisation wherever they founded their manors in Ireland. Hence it was that in 1228 the Cistercian Abbot, Stephen of Lexington, during his visitation of the Cistercian houses in Ireland, insisted that the Rule should be explained in each house in French, the language of civilised people. It was only gradually with the arrival of settlers who were English speaking that the English language became the norm as French disappeared. By then the settlers were no longer pure English, but rather Anglo-Irish (or 'English Irish', as they were called by John Dymmok in the sixteenth century). So the two cultures which survived were Gaelic and Anglo-Irish.

The failure of the conquest is therefore of crucial importance. There was probably a simple military reason for it. so that the Anglo-Normans, who had no difficulty in winning and occupying much of the open ground of Ireland, failed to secure either the high ground or the woods and bogs which remained in Gaelic hands. Giraldus Cambrensis takes a very simple view when he says that the failure was the result of Henry II's premature departure before he had completed his work in Ireland. The truth is a great deal more complicated. But whatever the reason, failure had the one result. For as Richard Stanyhurst so well expressed it in the sixteenth century, 'where the country is subdued, there the inhabitants ought to be ruled by the same law that the conqueror is governed by, to wear the same fashion of attire wherewith the victor is vested, and speak the same language that the vanquisher parleth. And if any of these three lack, doubtless the conquest limpeth'.

19

What emerged in Ireland in the middle ages, then, was a divided land, with a racial and linquistic barrier separating one culture from the other. When Richard II told his ambassadors in 1381 to ask the pope to instruct all the prelates of Ireland to make sure that all their subjects should learn English, he added the observation that 'experience teaches that of the diversity of tongues in that land wars and divers tribulations have arisen'. Such 'wars and tribulations', which were endemic in medieval Ireland, are a reminder that the failure of the conquest meant the creation of a permanent frontier in the lordship which was to last until the island was finally conquered in later times. The existence of this frontier prevented the complete assimilation of the two worlds, Gaelic and Anglo-Irish, tribal and feudal. No real fusion of the two cultures ever really took place, such as eventually happened in England after the Norman conquest. Not that the two worlds kept rigidily apart, or that there was no mingling of the races. After all, many of the early settlers married the daughters of Gaelic lords and a mixed race quickly resulted. In many Anglo-Irish lordships during the later middle ages there was such a medley of Gaelic and English, expressed in customs, institutions, languages and manners, that they were hardly distinguishable from the Gaelic lordships upon which they bordered. We have already seen many examples of changes of nomenclature and the adoption of Gaelic ways, which show how hibernicised many of the settlers became. Indeed as early as the beginning of King John's reign, Giraldus Cambrensis reported a rumour that many of the new settlers were already taking to themselves the rights of Gaelic lords; 'For, if report speaks true, their folly is risen to such a pitch of arrogance and presumption, that they even aspire to usurp in their own persons the rights of dominion belonging to the princes of that kingdom'. There were Berminghams, de Lacys, Verduns, Burkes, Powers and Barrys in plenty who denied the laws of their ancestors and turned to Gaelic ways. But if there were, the great majority never became wholly assimilated, but always remained conscious of their Englishness. This is brought out very well in the reply of the great lords to Sir Richard Edgecomb in 1488, when he tried to get the assembled lords to accept certain conditions which they found impossible: 'whereat they declared,' we are told in the account of Edgecomb's voyage, 'with one voice they would sooner turn Irish every one'.

That was the ultimate threat, to turn Irish, and it shows that however far the process of assimilation had gone, however 'degenerate' many of the settlers had become they were still a race apart from the Gaelic Irish. So that when, in the fourteenth and fifteenth centuries, we find poems being addressed to the great magnates almost as if they were Gaelic chieftains, we must not jump to the conclusion that they had been wholly assimilated. That a Burke was urged to conquer Ulster, the lordship of which rightfully belonged to him and not to O Neill, is the court poet's way of saying (albeit in the most orthodox Gaelic fashion) that he comes from non-Gaelic stock.

Partial assimilation, then, or partial hibernicisation, was the norm. To go any further was to degenerate because everything Gaelic was supposed to be inferior. This attitude of superiority is a typical result of conquest. Naturally the conqueror despises as inferior that which he has conquered and seeks to impose his own language, law, customs and manners. The native way of life was strange to the Anglo-Normans and therefore barbarous and uncivilised. Giraldus Cambrensis never minced his words when writing of the 'barbarous people', who are 'so barbarous that they cannot be said to have any culture'. He is being perfectly honest when he writes that they are 'a most filthy people, utterly enveloped in vices, most untutored of all peoples in the rudiments of faith . . . practising always treachery beyond all other races: they keep their plighted faith to no man'. This was how he had to see Gaelic Ireland and he naturally believed all of it, as did all who came to conquer and to civilise the barbarous land. Abbot Stephen of Lexington, as we saw, thought that the Irish were a 'bestial people', because they were ruled by emotion rather than by reason. They had an outlandish language and preposterous customs. They were altogether uncivilised. Any who wished to become Cistercians, he thought, should go to some famous school like Oxford or Paris and be educated. Much the same kind of phraseology was used by visitors to Ireland in the later middle ages, who wrote vivid and no doubt highly coloured accounts of what they witnessed during pilgrimages to Lough Derg. Official records consistently employed the phrase 'wild Irish', using the adjective 'wild' to mean uncivilised, and sometimes using 'savage' in the same way (as Richard II did in his famous tripartite division of the peoples of Ireland—*irrois savages, nos enemis,* 'savage Irish, our enemies'). These same adjectives, 'wild' and 'savage', were also used in contemporary Scotland to describe the people of the highlands and the isles: John of Fordun used them in the late fourteenth century, contrasting those people with the more domesticated, and Anglicised, inhabitants of the lowlands. Even in the fifteenth century the term 'wild' was still applied to Gaelic Irish. For example, the commons in the English parliament of 1422 petitioned the king that all *wilde Irisshmen* should be excluded from the realm and three years later they demanded that sureties should be required of all who were then living in England. It wasn't the first time that 'wild Irish' had been ordered out and the story of what happened to Nicholas Hogonana (Hogan?) of Ireland shows well how hardship could result. He went on a pilgrimage to Rome in 1401 and on his way through England he stopped for a time at Oxford. There he fell in with an Augustinian friar to whom he lent money. They came together to London and there Nicholas unsuccessfully tried to get back his money. In a petition to the king he later explained how the friar 'went to certain people of London and made an untrue suggestion, submitting that he was *un wilde Irisshman* and an enemy of our lord the king'. This simple charge was enough to land him in prison, where he languished until his petition to the king effected his release. 'Wild Irish' were, by definition, dangerous.

A certain reserve was necessary, therefore, in dealing with Gaelic Irish, even if in the course of time expediency might demand the marriage of a son (not usually the eldest) with the daughter of a Gaelic lord. But even at that level some kept their distance. When Geoffrey de Geneville, lord of Trim, petitioned the pope for a dispensation so that his son could marry his cousin, he offered as justification the fact that it would not be possible to find a wife among the natives of the country, but only among the 'great folk' of the land.[20]

The official attitude was that too close a contact with Gaelic

[20]Geoffrey was making a case, but nevertheless his attitude was clear: before Henry II 'reduced the land and its inhabitants to obedience', the Irish, 'as if unbridled, strayed over the plain of licence'. Henry appointed 'men of another nation to continue there the same obedience' and Geoffrey has always tried to 'keep the peace and retain the inhabitants in obedience'. He is engagingly frank in admitting that 'to that end he requires many kinsmen and friends by marriages, who cannot be easily obtained'.

Irish led to the adoption of Gaelic language and customs and thus degeneracy. It must therefore be checked and from the thirteenth century onwards parliamentary statutes and royal ordinances tried to keep the two cultures apart. At the same time the government tried to foster the English language and way of life and to depress, at least in those parts of the island amenable to English law, Gaelic culture at every level. Thus began the official policy of repression which was to last until the end of the middle ages, reflected most notably in the Statutes of Kilkenny, which represent a whole body of similar legislation spanning the centuries of the medieval lordship. Gaelic Ireland naturally retaliated and a war of culture resulted.

This cultural war can be seen most vividly within the Church, where it had a most damaging effect. It was natural that a division along cultural lines should take place, so that many dioceses were split into two cultural regions. This in itself created an impossible situation for some bishops and contributed to the decline in standards which is such a marked feature of the late medieval Church. But more pernicious was the attempt to keep certain offices or areas or monastic houses and friaries racially exclusive. One of the famous Statutes of Kilkenny had ordained that 'no Irish of the nations of the Irish be admitted to any cathedral or collegiate church by provision, collation, or presentation of any person whatsoever, or to any benefice of Holy Church amongst the English of that land' and this was confirmed by an English statute of 1416. It was subsequently rigorously enforced, even though licences of exemption were occasionally issued. This resulted in a lack of clergy in some areas, a fact which was frequently a cause of complaint. An Irish statute of 1485 brings out vividly how the care of souls was being neglected:

As divers benefices of the diocese of Dublin are situated among Irish enemies, of which the advowsons belong to the archbishop of Dublin, in right of his see; and as no Englishman can inhabit the said benefices, and divers English clerks, who are enabled to have care of souls, are inexpert in the Irish language, and such of them who are expert disdain to inhabit among the Irish people and others dare not inhabit among them, by which means divine service is diminished and care of souls neglected.

Such exclusiveness was by no means one-sided. In 1250 Pope

Innocent IV ordered the 'archbishops, bishops and chapter of Ireland' to revoke their statute which said that no Englishman should be admitted to a canonry in Ireland, and in 1297 the archbishop of Armagh and the bishop of Down were accused of refusing to admit English clerks into religious houses in Ireland. An early instance occurred in 1217 when the king ordered that only 'honest Englishmen' should in future be promoted in any cathedral. By then the Cistercian order in Ireland was torn asunder by racial strife, with the monks in Gaelic abbeys resorting to violence in their efforts to resist the attempts to impose a foreign culture on them. Racial exclusiveness naturally followed and persisted despite all attempts by the pope to prevent it. It went so far that the abbot of Maigue in county Limerick alienated much of the property of the monastery 'in hatred of the English race' and to prevent English monks from living in the monastery. Pope John XXII was informed in 1325 that in Ireland 'discords are fostered and wars promoted because monks in very many places, and canons regular having the most abundant possessions in the midst of the English, and also other religious of the orders of mendicants in divers places, admit no others to the order in their monasteries except pure Irish'.

The Irish Franciscans showed an early tendency to split along racial lines and to become involved in the politics of the Gaelic revival. The famous report on the state of Ireland of c. 1285, which advocates that no Irishman should ever be a bishop 'because they always preach against the king', noted that 'the Dominicans and Franciscans made much of that language (i.e. Irish)'. Around the same time Bishop Nicholas Cusack of Kildare, himself a Franciscan, wrote to Edward I about the seditious activities of certain religious in Ireland: 'the peace of the land is frequently disturbed by the secret councels and suspect and poisonous colloquies which certain insolent religious of the Irish tongue, belonging to divers orders, hold with the Irish and their kings', when they instigate rebellion and tell those lords that 'lawfully according to human and divine law the same kings and their subjects of the Irish nation . . . may fight for their native land (*patrie*) . . . and war on the English conquerors (*conquisitores*) of Ireland and attack their movable goods and canonically appropriate them wholly to themsevles'. There is no doubt that some Franciscans did preach rebellion, so that attempts were made to dilute the Gaelic friaries with 'good and chosen English'. The papal legate to Ireland ordered just such a dilution in 1324 in certain houses, because the communities there 'are gravely suspect and a danger to the king's peace and the state of the realm'. One of those communities was that of the friary in Cork, where in 1291 during a general chapter racial antagonism had exploded into violence, resulting in the deaths of sixteen friars. Eventually the only solution seemed to be to keep the two races apart and this is what was done in the fourteenth century when the province was virtually split in two. But the government continued to try to insure, not always successfully, that the Provincial Minister should always be non-Gaelic. Henry VI wrote to Richard duke of York, when he was lieutenant of Ireland, about William O Reilly 'that is our enemy born and of Irish blood, name and nation' who had managed to become Provincial contrary to the law. He is therefore to be arrested.

The other mendicant orders were also subject to the same official attempt to keep the races separated, though this did not always succeed. In 1455, for example, the superiors of the four mendicant orders were summoned before the mayor of Dublin and his council and compelled to enter into recognisances binding them to expel immediately from their friaries those with Gaelic names. Unlike the Franciscans, the other three orders never succeeded in establishing an independent Irish province during the middle ages and had to be content to remain as vicariates of the English province.

At all levels, then, within the Church the principle of racial exclusiveness was practiced and even if it was not always successful, it was a constant source of friction. Nowadays there is a tendency to play down the importance of this racial/cultural division within the Church. And that is proper, because it was all too easy in the past to seize on this fact in a one-sided way and to use it to demonstrate the injustices which the unfortunate Irish suffered at the hands of the oppressor in the middle ages. Nevertheless in emphasising that both races could and did co-operate harmoniously, especially in defending ecclesiastical liberties, that a prelate was a bishop first and Gaelic Irish, or Anglo-Irish or English second, we should be careful not to underestimate the pernicious effects of the racial division which undoubtedly existed. Many evils did result from cultural partition and there were many who spoke out against them in the middle ages. Primate Swayne ordered each of his bishops in the province of Armagh 'to labour to reform, hold and preserve peace between the English and Irish of Armagh province according to his power. . . . Any sower of discord between said English and Irish to be not only suspended from pontificals, but by that very fact excommunicated'. An earlier archbishop, the great fitz Ralph, had preached a sermon on the same theme at Dundalk, and earlier still another archbishop, the German Albrecht Suerbeer, praised the community of the priory of Llanthony in county Meath for the good work they did in the 1240s, 'situated as you are on the borders of Ulster and Leinster, between two nations which persecute each other, you stretch forth your hands in charity, being generous to the stranger, merciful to the poor, compassionate to the sick and weak, so that you seem to embrace all your neighbours and foster them by your charity'. But Llanthony was not typical and racialism was rampant throughout most of the religious orders.

It was to be observed in the secular world, too, in the attempt to keep urban communities English, to exclude the Gaelic Irish from the guilds, to give the English a monopoly of all governmental posts and so on. In 1279, for example, the mayor and community of Cork wrote to the king complaining that the Lombard merchants, the customers of the king in that city, had chosen a certain Irishman, by name Stephen Brendan, as a customer with them, giving him custody of the coket seal and also of the money collected. They object, they say, 'because the Irish race (*lingua*) is an enemy to you and yours and your aforesaid city is situated in the marches of the Irish' and so the king is to ask Percival of Luca, master of the Lombards in Ireland, to assign the office to someone in place of Stephen. 'Nor do we care of what people or race he is, either Lombard or English, as long as no Irishman is assigned to the said office'.

This attempt to suppress Gaelic culture and to promote English culture was the result, as we have seen, of the natural feeling of superiority which the conqueror had for the conquered. It was reflected in the belief that all who spoke Irish were inferior. To be *merus Hibernicus* ('pure Irish') meant that one could never be the equal of an Englishman, whether one born in England or in Ireland. It was easy, therefore, to discriminate against the Irish merely because of their Irishness. This occasionally happened. In July 1252 Innocent IV condemned as 'a pernicious corruption of good morals' the 'detestably vicious custom' which, he had been informed, prevailed in Munster:

> that if an Englishman there residing loses any of his property, he makes oath that it was stolen by some Irishman, whereupon six other Englishmen swear that they regard the sworn declaration of the former as true. . . . The Irish, however, though they may be innocent, and of good repute and blameless life, and though they may be in a position to prove their innocence of the alleged crime by thirty sworn witnesses or more, yet are they compelled to make restitution as though they were thieves. On the other hand, if the Irish lose any of their property, even though they know for certain that it has been stolen by an Englishman, and are ready to substantiate the charge by sworn testimony, yet are their sworn declarations summarily rejected by the English. And thus, in each case alike, justice is trodden underfoot, and grievous wrong is often done to our churches and tenants.

The most famous instance of discrimination against natives on grounds of race occurs in the remonstrance of 1317 addressed to Pope John XXII, where it is stated:

> For not only their laymen and secular clergy but some also of their regular clergy dogmatically assert the heresy that it is no more sin to kill an Irishman than a dog or any other brute. And in maintaining this heretical position some monks of theirs affirm boldly that if it should happen to them, as it does often happen, to kill an Irishman, they would not on that account refrain from saying mass, not even for a day.

The document instances the Cistercian monks of Granard and Inch as examplees and also quotes a Franciscan friar Simon as evidence. It is interesting that in the report sent to the pope by Edward II not long after, which was clearly a reply to the charges levied in the remonstrance, the same 'heresy' is quoted, but with this important twist that the Irish 'say that it is not a sin to kill any Englishman'. We don't know if that was the case, since no evidence is produced. But no less a person than Richard fitz Ralph condemned the other. In one of his Dundalk sermons he complained that men stole, raped and burnt because their ancestors had always done so and because they had been told by learned men that the custom of the march (or march law) allowed it. We have already quoted what Piers Bermingham is supposed to have said, according to the *Annals of Inisfallen*, when he was reproached with the murder of the O Connors: 'he said that he was not aware that there was a foreigner in Ireland who had not undertaken to slay his Gaelic neighbour, and he knew that they would slay, as he had slain'—an attitude which is reflected in the contemporary Anglo-Irish eulogy of Piers, written on his death, where he is praised for hunting out the Irish everywhere, 'as hunter doth the hare'.

One result of all this was to embitter the Gaelic Irish and to encourage the hostilities which are of such frequent occurrence. The bitterness which colours so much of the 1317 remonstrance to the pope is undoubted, whatever may be the truth of many of the statements made. Such bitterness was natural, specially among a people as proud and class-conscious as were the Gaelic lords. We sometimes forget that in the early period of settlement the Gaelic kings were very conscious of their royal dignity. When, for example, Innocent III wrote to Cathal O Connor of Connacht in 1200, he used the highest form of address reserved for kings (as distinct from princes, dukes or the inferior nobility). To be treated as inferior, then, was all the more shocking and promoted a violent reaction. Out of this was to come an awareness of nationality which was to further alienate Gaelic Ireland from the mass of the Anglo-Irish. This awareness is well reflected in the literature of the later middle ages, so that all the Anglo-Irish, however Gaelic they may have become, are always called *Gaill* or 'foreigners'. It emerges with startling clarity in phrases used and sentiments expressed in the 1317 remonstrance:

and in order to shake off the hard and intolerable yoke of their slavery and to recover our ancient liberty, which for a time through them we lost, we are compelled to wage deadly war with them, preferring under stress of necessity to put outselves like men to the trial of war in defence of our rights, rather than to bear like women their atrocious outrages.

What pride of ancestry there is in the final sentence: 'for know, our reverend father, that besides the kings of lesser Scotia who drew all the source of their blood from our greater Scotia, retaining to some extent our language and habits, one hundred and ninety-seven kings of our blood have reigned over the whole island of Ireland'.

On the other side, the Anglo-Irish, too, developed a sense of nationality which was no less important for the future history of the island. The frontier conditions which existed in Ireland, the constant need to fend for themselves and to be self-reliant, naturally made them independent and individual in a way that is always typical of frontier areas. If their feeling of cultural superiority was necessary for survival in the endless battle against Gaelic Ireland, independence was no less necessary. They arrived in Ireland with a belief in their own destiny—witness the grand speeches which Giraldus Cambrensis puts into the mouths of his Geraldine heroes during moments of crisis—and they were determined to win glory, renown and fortune in Ireland. They knew, too, that by throwing in their lot with Ireland, where their future lay, they would quickly be alienated from their homeland (as not infrequently happens with colonists). It is startling to find just such a sentiment expressed by Giraldus in a speech which he gives to Maurice fitz Gerald: 'Such in our lot that what the Irish are to the English we, too, being now considered as Irish are the same. The one island does not hold us in greater detestation than the other'. They quickly became a 'middle nation', which is what the remonstrance of 1317 says they called themselves. They were a group apart, neither English nor Irish, but Anglo-Irish and conscious of it. The remonstrance clearly recognises them as a separate 'nation', as when it talks of the '50,000 human beings of each nation' who have been killed by the wars, or when it emphasises how they are so 'different in character from the English of England and from other nations'. The phraseology employed by government records also recognises the same separateness. When the English government made a special 'ordinance concerning the state of Ireland' in 1357, it referred to the problem of the 'divers dissensions' between the Anglo-Irish and the English and in describing how these differences arose, it used the very significant phrase 'by reason of race'—as if they were two races indeed.

Even if they never renounced their Englishness, then, the colonists quickly developed a consciousness of being separate from England and the pure English. Occasionally this manifested itself sharply in bitter clashes with Englishmen, when their Irishness came through. This can be seen very clearly at Oxford, where the Anglo-Irish were significantly classed as 'Irishmen' (*Hibernienses*) in the nations which made up the university. They were frequently involved in riots which arose from national feelings. These were common enough at Oxford, where young men speaking different languages often came to blows because of apparent insult to a national saint during a celebration of the saint's feast. These disturbances became so bad that the university banned all such national festivals. In 1252, however, the Irish and the northerners were involved in a bloody feud which was ended only with great difficulty. As a result they were compelled to enter into an agreement, subscribed to by twenty-one representatives of the north and twenty-eight of Ireland (four masters and twenty-four scholars), that they would not disturb the peace in future, would not shield offenders and would secretly denounce rioters to the chancellor. Of the twenty-eight 'Irishmen' who took the oath, twenty-five, and possibly twenty-six, were Anglo-Irish. The northerners and the Irish came to blows again, and in 1273 several of the Irish were killed.

At home in Ireland, the sensational accusation by John fitz Thomas against William de Vescy, lord of Kildare, before the Irish council in 1293, that he said that 'the people of Ireland . . . would be, if they willed anything, great lords, and would well maintain the lands and franchises of Ireland, notwithstanding the king', may not be true; but at least it shows that such treasonable sentiments existed. An even better example comes from 1341, a time of great crisis in Ireland. John Morice, deputy to the justiciar, introduced an act of resumption of all grants which threatened many of the titles, offices, lands and revenues enjoyed by many of the Anglo-Irish. It naturally produced a fierce reaction, which an Anglo-Irish chronicler reported: 'on account of the resumption of which a great dispute arose in the land, and the land of Ireland was on the point of separation from the hands of the king of England'. Here was separatism with a vengeance. Matters came to a head during the parliament in October, 'before which time', the same chronicler wrote, 'there never was such a notable and manifest division between the English born in England and the English born in Ireland'.

An interesting example of Anglo-Irish resentment of English interference is provided by the Hospitellers during the period of the great schism. In the mid-fourteenth century the highest office of the order in Ireland, hitherto held by Anglo-Irish, was taken

over by a succession of English born knights, a development
which was naturally resented by the Anglo-Irish. Their chance to
force a change came when the schism split the order. When the
English knights followed Clement VII, the Anglo-Irish switched
to Urban VI and secured the continuance of one of themselves in
office. The subsequent events showed a continuing stuggle, but
in 1399 the Anglo-Irish knights again recognised a Roman pope,
Boniface IX, who confirmed an Anglo-Irish prior in office.
Eventually in 1410 the Anglo-Irish won their point when the
general chapter of the order at Aix made a unique provision
which allowed them always to elect one of themselves as prior.

The Dominicans, too, showed the same bitter resentment of
control from England and on more than one occasion they tried
to break away. One Saturday in August, 1380, John of Leicester,
who had been sent from England on a visitation of the Irish
houses, turned up at the Dublin convent, which was Anglo-Irish
through and through. He was met by the brothers with swords
and spears at the door of the church. Not satisfied with that, the
brothers called on Dubliners for help, which they got, and drove
off John and his English entourage.

Such a state of tension between Anglo-Irish and English was no
unusual thing in medieval Ireland. We have seen how in 1357 the
king referred to it in his special ordinance for Ireland. A letter
from Edward III in June 1364 contains a similar reference and
again emphasises that 'in times past hurt and peril has happened
in Ireland' because of it. The Statutes of Kilkenny supposedly
dealt with the problem in a famous act, which laid down that 'no
difference of allegiance shall henceforth be made between the
English born in Ireland, and the English born in England, by
calling them *Englishhobbe* (or 'English clowns') or *Irishdogg*, but
that all be called by one name, the English lieges of our lord the
king'. But as late as 1441, as we saw, the Irish council was asking
the king that 'Englishmen born in Ireland' should have the same
rights as Englishmen born in England. The mutual dislike of one
for the other was to outlast the middle ages.

It was their identification with Ireland which made the Anglo-
Irish self-conscious and resentful of any interference from England
In the Dublin parliament of 1324, which investigated the charges
of witchcraft against Alice Kyteler of Kilkenny, the seneschal of
Kilkenny, Arnold Power, made a speech in which he attempted to

turn the parliament against Bishop Ledrede of Ossory. What is interesting is that Arnold cleverly played upon the anti-English feelings of his listeners, by denouncing the bishop as an Englishman who calumniated the Irish:

> You well know that in the land of Ireland no heretics were ever found, but it was wont to be called the island of saints. Now, if you please, comes some foreigner from England and says that we are all heretics and excommunicate, and to prove it brings up some papal constitutions that none of us have ever heard of before now; and because the disgrace of this country touches every one of us it is the duty of all of you to take part against him.

This pride in the *patria*, so that its disgrace is their disgrace, comes out again in the great debate over the so-called Pilkington case in the fifteenth century. Parliament was debating the plea made in London by Pilkington, a former escheator, that no justiciar had the right to summon a parliament and that 'parliament is only a convocation called a parliament, made amongst the men in Ireland to oust the power of our lord the king and to annihilate in substance all letters patent made to men born in England'. The course of the debate showed that the Anglo-Irish regarded this not only as 'slanderous words' touching themselves and parliament, but treason to the 'justiciar, lords and commons of the said land'.

The separatist tradition was strong, therefore, among the Anglo-Irish and it voiced itself most strongly in the famous 1460 declaration of the independence of the Irish parliament and in the independent line subsequently taken to the end of the middle ages. If it was to some extent restricted by the operation of Poynings' law, it never really died and was to reappear in stronger form long afterwards.

We have seen, then, that as a result of the Anglo-Norman invasion and failure to conquer the whole of Ireland, two races and two very different cultures were left confronting each other. Neither was able to blot out or to be assimilated to the other. There was another race, the Scandinavian population of the pre-Norman towns—the *Ostmanni* ('Ostmen')—but they were pushed aside by the newcomers into ghettoes of their own, like the *villa Ostmannorum* of Dublin (the 'town of the Ostmen', the modern Oxmantown), where they soon drop from sight.

Racialism and a cultural war became permanent features of the medieval Irish scene. The descendants of the original settlers, and the new ones who arrived later, developed a self-consciousness, an awareness of being apart, which marked them off as Anglo-Irish, different from the Gaelic Irish on the one hand, but hardly any less different from the pure English on the other. On the other side, this same situation bred among the Gaelic Irish a no less acute self-consciousness which was eventually to ripen into a sense of nationality. On the whole it probably made Gaelic society more reactionary, tending to make it conserve archaic features and to slow up that development of new political and social concepts which had been a feature of the period before the invasion—to preserve what the late Frank O'Connor so aptly called 'the backward look'.

Worst of all, perhaps, the medieval lordship left a legacy of mutual distrust, born of generations of war, outrage, betrayal and personal hardship, which left its mark on later ages. The author of the famous report of 1515 on the state of Ireland tells an old story of how St Brigid asked her good angel in what Christian lands were most souls damned? She was shown a land in the west and the angel told her that there the Christian folk died most out of charity, 'for there is most continual war, root of hate and envy, and of vices contrary to charity: and without charity the souls cannot be saved. And the angel did show her the lapse of the souls of the Christian folk of that land, how they fell down into hell as thick as any hail shower'. The author says that there is no doubt that Ireland was the land shown by the angel: 'for there is no land in the world of so long continual war within himself, nor of so great shedding of Christian blood, nor of so great robbing, spoiling, preying and burning, nor of so great wrongful extortion continually as Ireland'. Perhaps Giraldus Cambrensis had the right of it when he wrote, early in the thirteenth century, that the island was not conquered because it was not God's will that it should be. The Irish, he wrote, 'had not so strictly offended God that it was his will that they should be entirely subjugated; nor were the deserts of the English such as to entitle them to the sovereignty over and possible obedience of the people they had partly conquered and reduced to obedience. Therefore, perhaps, it was the will of God that both nations would be long engaged in mutual conflicts'.